AF531783

MICROBIAL APPLICATIONS AND ENVIRONMENT

MICROBIAL APPLICATIONS AND ENVIRONMENT

Editor-in-Chief

Dr. Pawan Kumar 'Bharti'

Centre for Agro-Rural Technologies (CART-India)
20, Jamaalpur Maan, Raja Ka Tajpur
Bijnore (UP)-246 735 (India)
E-mail: gurupawanbharti@rediffmail.com

Associate Editors

Dr. Narendra A. Kulkarni

Department of Botany
Raje Ramrao College
Jat (Dist: Sangli) (M.S.) (India)

Dr. Avnish Chauhan

Department of Applied Science
Phonics Group of Institutions
Roorkee, Haridwar (Uttarakhand) (India)

DISCOVERY PUBLISHING HOUSE PVT. LTD.

NEW DELHI-110 002

Published by:
Tilak Wasan
DISCOVERY PUBLISHING HOUSE PVT. LTD.
4383/4B, Ansari Road, Darya Ganj
New Delhi-110 002 (India)
Phone : +91-11-23279245, 43596064-65
Fax : +91-11-23253475
E-mail : discoverypublishinghouse@gmail.com
sales@discoverypublishinggroup.com
parul.wasan@gmail.com
web : www.discoverypublishinggroup.com

***First Edition:* 2014**

ISBN: 978-93-5056-515-5

Microbial Applications and Environment

Printed at:
Aditi Fine Art Press
Delhi

Preface

Environmental microbiology is the study of the composition and physiology of microbial communities in the environment. The environment in this case means the soil, water, air and sediments covering the planet and can also include the animals and plants that inhabit these areas. Environmental microbiology also includes the study of microorganisms that exist in artificial environments such as bioreactors.

Microorganisms are cost effective agents for in-situ remediation of domestic, agricultural and industrial wastes and subsurface pollution in soils, sediments and marine environments. The ability of each microorganism to degrade toxic waste depends on the nature of each contaminant. Since most sites are typically comprised of multiple pollutant types, the most effective approach to microbial biodegradation is to use a mixture of bacterial species/ strains, each specific to the degradation of one or more types of contaminants. It is vital to monitor the composition of the indigenous and added bacterial consortium in order to evaluate the activity level of the bacteria, and to permit modifications of the nutrients and other conditions for optimizing the bioremediation process.

Biotechnology may be used alongside microbial ecology to address a number of environmental and economic challenges. For example, molecular techniques such as community fingerprinting can be used to track changes in microbial communities over time or assess their biodiversity. Managing the carbon cycle to sequester carbon dioxide and prevent excess methanogenesis is important in mitigating global warming, and the prospects of bioenergy are being expanded by the development of microbial fuel cells. Microbial resource management advocates a more progressive attitude towards disease, whereby biological control agents are favoured over attempts at eradication. Fluxes in microbial communities have to be better characterized for this field's potential to be realised. In addition, there are also clinical implications, as marine microbial symbioses are a valuable source of existing and novel antimicrobial agents, and thus offer another line of inquiry in the evolutionary arms race of antibiotic resistance, a pressing concern for researchers.

This book provides comprehensive coverage of the fundamental principles and current practices and trends in the field of microbial applications & ecology, environmental pollution, conservation, agriculture, environmental biotechnology and environmental microbiology. This book updates the subject matter, illustrations and problems to incorporate new concepts and issues related to microbial applications & ecology, environmental pollution, agriculture ecology, environmental microbiology and biotechnology.

Particularly thanks are due to all contributors from Egypt, India; and publisher also for their contribution and assistance. I hope this book will be of benefit to both present and future colleagues, who teach, study and working in the field of microbial applications & ecology, aquatic ecology, environmental pollution, agriculture ecology, forest conservation, environmental microbiology and biotechnology.

Dr. Pawan Kumar 'Bharti'

gurupawanbharti@rediffmail.com

Contents

Ecological Studies on the Mangroves Along the Coast of Maharashtra State With Respect to Their Conservation

Narendra A.Kulkarni* and **Leela J.Bhosale****

* Department of Botany, Raje Ramrao College, Jat (Dist : Sangli) (M.S.), India.

** Department of Botany, Shivaji University, Kolhapur (M.S.), India.

ABSTRACT

Mangroves are typical group of plants which are adopted for survival in sheltered brackish water habitats along coasts of tropical and sub-tropical regions. Mangroves play a key role in maintaining the quality and productivity of coastal waters. Mangroves are known as primary producers, shoreline protectors, nursery grounds and habitat for variety of animals, bridging components and unique biological resources. They provide erosion control and shoreline stabilization, they are also involved in complex detritus food webs. The Tsunami occurred on 26th Dec. 2004 along the East west of south India created a massive destruction in these areas and killed over thousands of people. It is also found that Tsunami has created greater destruction where there are no mangroves. On the other hand it is found that the areas with thick mangrove forests have received least impact of Tsunami. It is the need of time that the present mangrove ecosystem are to be protected first and rehabilitation of destructed mangrove areas is to be undertaken.

Keywords: Mangroves, Status, Diversity, Threats, Maharashtra.

INTRODUCTION

Mangroves are typical group of plants which are adopted for survival in sheltered brackish water habitats along coasts of tropical and sub-tropical regions. Mangroves play a key role in maintaining the quality and productivity of coastal waters. Mangroves are known as primary producers, shoreline protectors, nursery grounds and habitat for variety of animals, bridging components and unique biological resources. They provide erosion control and shoreline stabilization, they are also involved in complex detritus food webs (Odum and Heald, 1972).

The Tsunami occurred on 26th Dec. 2004 along the East west of south India created a massive destruction in these areas and killed over thousands of people. It is also found that Tsunami has created greater destruction where there are no mangroves. On the other hand it is found that the areas with thick mangrove forests have received least impact of Tsunami. Shekhawat and Dixit (2005) have suggested that mangroves can save us from natural disasters like Tsunami.

It is the need of time that the present mangrove ecosystem are to be protected first and rehabilitation of distructed mangrove areas is to be undertaken.

Mangrove Food Chain (after Bhosale, 2005)

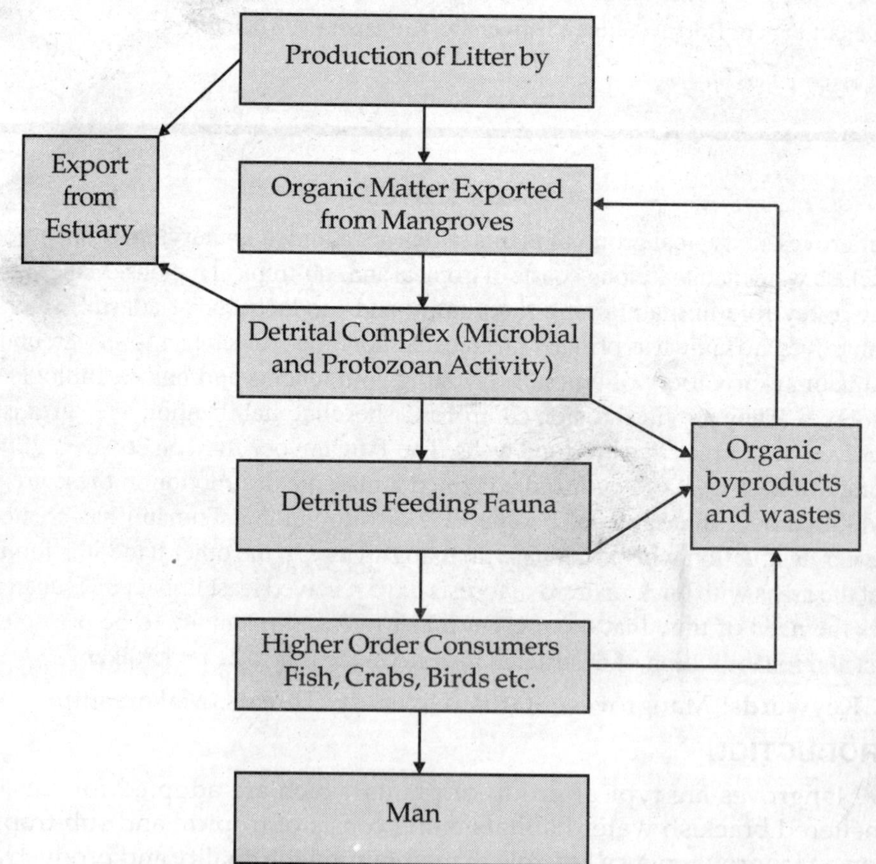

MATERIAL AND METHODS

Present study involves collection of plant samples, i.e. twigs (as far as possible flowering twigs) from the study area. These samples were pressed and herbarium sheets were prepared.

For the preparation of herbarium freshly collected twigs were brought to the laboratory. The twigs were first carefully washed with water to remove the dirt and dust. Then the twigs were soaked in 4% formaldehyde for about two hours. This helps to keep the plant parts intact. After two hours the twigs were washed with water and blotted dry carefully with blotting paper. The twigs were placed in paper cover and pressed under weight. The paper was changed from time to time till the twig complete dries. Then the twigs were mounted on the herbarium sheets. The herbaria were then maintained by the method suggested by Rao and Sharma (1990). All the herbaria have been deposited in the Department of Botany. These sheets are used for the identification of the species.

Survey, Mapping and Remote Sensing

Survey of all estuaries in the two districts was undertaken by several field visits. A record of species occurring at each site was prepared. The field survey is based on maps of the area. The maps of all the estuaries were obtained from various sources, such as Survey Of India (SOI) toposheet maps from the department of Geography, Shivaji University. The local maps were obtained from the Government Departments like Land development, Maritime board, Forest departments of the concerned area. These maps were used as base maps for understanding the preliminary information about the location, villages in and around the site, approach roads etc. The latitude and longitude of the estuaries were obatined from the toposheet maps of SOI and also compared with the computer software named 'ENCARTE' 2002 version.

Mapping meant, making a chart of vegetation as per the chart quadrat method. However, in the present study area selected was not one unit area but was entire pocket of the vegetation. Some of the estuaries were mapped for all the details such as direction, outline of the bank of the estuaries and distribution of mangrove vegetation with exact location of the species. The boundary of the vegetation, all along was marked with the help of 'Bearing' (USA make), a combination of degree and north south direction on mariner's compass. The caliberated steps and measuring tape were used to record the distance between any two points of observation. This kind of mapping presents exact copy of vegetation with contributing species.

Remote sensing is a technique recently followed for vegetation study. In the present study this technique is also taken into consideration. The maps were studied and interpreted.

For learning the techniques of the remote sensing studies the National Remote Sensing Agency (NRSA) Hyderabad, was visited and training was obtained.

The remote sensing (RS) data used in the present study is IRS-1 B Liss-II data. The imageries in the form of paper prints on 1 : 50000 scale were procured from National Remote Sensing Agency, Hyderabad. The imageries were analysed using a magnifying hand lens and a light table (Nayak, 1993). The data was analysed with respect to total estuarine area, mangrove cover (sparse and dense) along an estuary. The area of each category was calculated on the area meter. An image interpretation key was prepared with respect to the ground objects . The survey of India topo-sheet maps were used as base maps. Attempts were also made to collect classified maps prepared earlier by Maharashtra Remote Sensing Agency (MRSAC) Nagpur in 1994.

Analysis of Vegetation

Floristic Composition

During the field surveys the vegetation was critically observed for its Floristic Composition. Detailed field notes were prepared. The flowering twigs were brought to the laboratory and were identified with the help of published literature on identification keys. It was further extended to record quantitative aspects of number of individuals of each species. The field data was used to determine diversity indices, as given below.

The Simpon's index of species diversity is calculated as described by Williams (1987) for all the estuaries in the study area, by using formula:

Simpson's index of species Diversity (Di)

$$Di = \frac{N\,(N-1)}{\sum n\,(n-1)}$$

Where, Di = Diversity index

N = Total number of plants

n = Numbr of individuals per species

Simpson's index of Diversity (D) is calculated by the formula

$$D = 1 - \sum_{i=1}^{S} (p1)^2$$

Where, pi = is the proportion of total number of individuals in the ith species.

S = Number of species.

Alpha-Beta Diversity

Alpha diversity, defined as species packing within a demarcated area, was measured as an absolute number of species (Whittaker, 1972), whereas the change or replacement of the taxon composition from one plot to another (beta-diversity) was calculated as 1-Jaccard's index of similarity (Magurran, 1988). The Jaccard's Index of similarity between two plots/estuaries was calculated using following formula:

$$J x y = \frac{C}{(A + B) - C}$$

Where, C is the number of species found in both the plots and A is the number of species in plot x and B the number of species in plot y (here x and y represent estuary). The index has been designed to equal 1 in case of complete similarity and 0 if the plots of no species in common.

The change in the species composition (assemblage of species) across the estuary, district, macrohabitat appear to reflect the characteristics of the macrohabitat in which they occur. Negi (2001) has analyzed the liverworts of Garhwal Himalaya region using the similar technique.

During the present study similar method is used to analyze the alpha and beta diversity of mangrove in the study area.

Distribution and Zonation Pattern of the Species

Mangroves show a distinct zonation/distribution pattern. It was studied for almost all the estuaries/creeks in the study area. For this purpose study was conducted along the length of estuary from mouth to upstream region. All the observations were recorded in the form of a distribution diagram for each estuary as per Bunt (1999). The observations are presented in the form of distribution diagrams.

Comparison with Other Districts

Comparison of the floristic composition, distribution and zonation pattern of the species in the study area is made between the other districts like Raigad and Mumbai and present area.

Flowering Phenology

The flowering calender in mangroves is of importance. Some of the mangrove species were observed for the period of Budding, Flowering, Fruiting and Mature propagules. A few sites were selected on the basis of presence of the species concerned, viz. Kolamb, Kalavali and Tarkarli.

Height and Girth Analysis

During the field visits some species, viz., *A. officinalis*, *A. marina* var. *acutissima*, *A. marina* (dwarf), *R. mucronata*, *S. alba*, *A. corniculatum*, *K. candel* were chosen for measurement of height of the tree and girth or circumference. The sampling was random and atleast 50 records were made.

Mangrove Soil

The type and/ or nature of soil playrole in species occurrence at any site. So as to know the soil supporting the mangroves, analysis was carried out.

Physical Parameters

Soil texture (granulometry) was determined from 100 gms air dry soil. It was passed through seives having pore size ranging from 25 mm to 2057 mm.

Chemical Parameters

Aqueous solution (1:5) of air dried soil was used to study chemical parameters (A.O.A.C, 1973).

Electrical Conductivity (EC) was determined using conductivity meter (Elico PE-133) and expressed as mS/cm.

The pH was recorded with digital pH meter (Global DPN-501, ELICO LI-10T).

Chlorides were estimated from (1:5) aqueous solution by titration with $AgNO_3$ using potassium dichromate indicator.

Na, K, Ca were analysed by standard acid digestion method and using flame photometer (Jackson, 1958).

IUCN Categorization

International Union for Conservation of Nature and Natural resources (IUCN) has given Red list criteria (IUCN, 1994, 1999, 2000). A special BCPP workshop was organized by IUCN Office based at Coimbature on mangroves, July 1997. The same method is followed in present study. The 2000 updating also confirms the method. These criteria were used for assessing the status of mangroves of the study area. The categorization process requires following data.

Taxon Data Sheet

It is an important document of IUCN categorization process entitled 'Biological Information Sheet'. The data sheet is the overall appearance of the species in an ecosystem. The parameters used to prepare the data sheet are useful in deciding the status of a species. The details of the Taxon Data Sheet are given in following pages.

Population density/Mature individuals

This data is needed to decide the range of population of a species. For the density, the number of mature individuals were counted individually for a small area by quadrat method of required size usually (10 × 10 m or 20 m × 20 m). Number of quadrats were placed and averaged for the site.

Area Under Each Species

This data is required to decide the area of accupancy of the species. The canopy area of each species is calculated from the canopy circumference of the species by the formula:

Area = πr^2

Threats

The threats to the mangroves in the study area were recorded on the basis of threat categories given by IUCN such as habitat loss, fragmentation, human interference, Trade etc.

Status of the Species (Classification)

IUCN red list categories and criteria are used for assessing status of the species for conservation. These are presented in the following pages.

IUCN Red List Categories (Classes)

CR - Critically endangered - a taxon is Critically Endangered when it is facing an extremely high risk of extinction in the wild in the immediate future as defined by the criteria.

EN - Endangered - a taxon is Endangered when it is not Critically Endangered but is facing a very high risk of extinction in the wild in the near future as defined by the criteria.

VU - Vulnerable - a taxon is Vulnerable when it is not Critically Endnagered or Endangered but is facing a high risk of extinction in the wild in the medium term future as defined by the criteria.

LR - Lower risk - a taxon is Lower Risk when it has been evaluated and does not qualify for any of the threatened categories. Critically endangered, Endangered, Vulnerable or Data Deficient (LR-nt- near threatened, LR-ic-Least concern, LR-cd-conservation dependent).

DD - Data Deficient - A taxon is Data Deficient when there is inadequate information to make a direct or indirect assessment of its risk of extinction based on its distribution and/or population status.

NE - Not Evaluated - A taxon is not evaluated when it has not yet been assessed against the criteria.

IUCN Red List Criteria

(A) Population reduction

1. Observed, infered, suspected or estimated reduction, or
2. Projected or predicted reduction of at least 20% (VU), or 50% (EN) or 80% (CR) in 10 years or 3 generations whichever is longer based on
   (a) Direct observation

(b) Index of abundance appropriate for the taxon

(c) Decline in areas of accupancy, extent of occurrence and/or quality of habitat

(d) Actual or potential levels of exploitation,

(e) Effects of introduced taxa, hybridization, pathogens, pollutants, competitors, or parasites.

(B) Restricted distributions

Extent of occurrence estimated to be less than 20,000 sq. km. (VU), or 5000 sq. km. (EN) or 100 sq. km. (CR) and/or area of occupancy estimated to be less than 2000 sq. km. (VU), or 500 sq. km. (EN), or 10 sq. km. (CR), and qualifying for any two of the following:

1. Severly fragmented, or known to exist in not more than 10 locations (VU), or 5 locations (EN) or single location (CR).
2. Continuing decline observed, inferred or projected in any of the following:
   (a) Extent of occurrence
   (b) Area of occupancy
   (c) Area, extent and/or quality of habitat
   (d) Number of locations or sub-populations
   (e) Number of mature individuals
3. Extreme fluctuations in any of the following:
   (a) Area of accurrence
   (b) Area of occupancy
   (c) Number of populations or sub-populations
   (d) Number of mature individuals.

(C) Population estimates

Population estimated to number less than 10,000 (VU), or 2500 (EN), or 250 (CR) mature individuals.

1. Estimated, continuing decline of at least 10% in 10 years or 3 generations or whichever is longer (VU), or 32% in 5 years or 2 generations whichever is longer (EN), or 25% in 3 years or 1 generation whichever is longer (CR).
2. Continuing decline, observed, projected inferred number of mature individuals and population structure in the form of either.
   (a) Severely fragmented (no sub-population estimated to contain more than 1000 (VU), or 250 (EN), or 50 (CR) mature individuals)
   (b) All individuals are in a single sub-population.

(D) Restricted populations

1. Population estimated to number less than 1000 (VU), or 250 (EN), or 50 (CR) mature individuals.
2. Population restricted in area of occupancy of less than 100 sq. km. or less than 5 locations (VU).

(E) Probability of extinction

Quantitative analysis showing the probability of extinction in the wild is at least 10% in 100 years (UV), or 20% in 20 years or 5 generations, whichever is longer (EN) or 50% in 10 years or 3 generations, whichever is longer (CR).

No. of Locations : F = Fragmented

Range A =<100 sq.km.; B =<5000 sq.km.; C =<20000 sq.km.; D =>20000 sq.km.

Area; A = < 10 sq.km.; B =<500 sq.km.; C=<2000 sq.km.; D = > 2000 sq.km.

Data Quality

1 = Reliable census or population monitoring
2 = General field studies
3 = Informal field sightings
4 = Indirect information
5 = Museum/herbarium/collection/records
6 = Hearsay/popular belief

Threat

Al =	Artificial lighting,	L =	Loss of habitat,
Lf =	Loss of habitat due to fragmentation	D =	Diseases
E =	Edaphic factors (changes in);	H =	Harvest
Hf =	Harvest for food;	I =	Human interference
P =	Predation;	Ps =	Pesticides
Pu =	Pollution	R =	Road kills
Sf =	Fire as catastrophic event	Sn =	Situation
T =	Trade	Tp =	Trade of parts

Research Recommendations

G =	Genetic management	H =	Husbandry research
Hm =	Habitat management	Lh =	Life history studies
Lm =	Limiting factor management	Lr =	Limiting factor research

M = Monitoring
O = Other (specific to the species)
P = PHVA pending further work
S = Survey search and find
T = Taxonomic and morphological genetic studies
Tl = Translocations.

Cultivation Recommendations

1. = Captive breeding for conservation either only *in situ* and *ex situ* or both with the population maintaining 90% genetic diversity for 100 years.
2. = Same as '1' but periodic reinforcement of captive stock with genetic materials from the wild.
3. = Captive breeding only for research education or husbandary but not of conservation.
4. = Captive breeding for commerce.
5. = Restructive breeding, P = Pending.

Level of Difficulty

1. = Least difficult
2. = Moderately difficult
3. = Highly difficult, Unk = Unknown

STUDY AREA

The study area is the coastal Maharashtra which lies between 15°44′ N to 20°08′ N and 72°44′ E to 73°39′ E. The Ratnagiri district lies between 16°13′ N to 18°04′ N and 73°02′ E to 73°52′ E and Sindhudurg district lies between 15°37′ N to 16°40′ N and 73°13′ E to 73°19′E. The study area has tropical climatic conditions. Three distinct seasons are observed as Monsoon (June to Sept.), Winter (Oct. to Jan.) and Summer (Feb. to May). The maximum annual rainfall that occurs along the coast is 2500 mm. The relative humidity ranges between 60 to 80%. The temperature varies from 20°C to 35° C.

The Estuaries of Study Area

Almost all the streams flowing in the study area are marked by drowned estuaries. The estuaries in the study area are disposing amount of fresh water received from the catchment area to the Arabian sea. The rivers are rushing, short coarse and are almost empty during summer. The silt carried by surface runoff is trapped by the complex network of roots of mangroves on the bank of estuary. Study of toposheet maps published by survey of India (SOI) shows that there are 29 estuaries in Ratnagiri and Sindhudurg districts. Out of these, sixteen estuaries are from Sindhudurg district and thirteen from Ratnagiri district. These estuaries are mentioned in Table 1.2.

Table 1.1: Image Interpretation Key for IRS 1B LISS-II Photographic imagery

Category	Tone	Shape	Texture	Location	Association	Remarks
Agricultural Land	Red/Pinkish Red/Maroon	Irregular	Rough/ Smooth	On the main land	—	Agriculture near the coast is paddy, cashew area having geometrical shape.
Forest	Deep red	Irregular	Smooth	On the land	—	Forest comprises of various species and densities of trees.
Plantation	Dark brownish red/dark brown/ pale brown	Linear Irregular	Smooth	Along the coast	Sandy beach/ dunes	Plantation usually consists of *Casurna.*
Mangrove	Bright to dull orange red/ Bluish brown pale brown	Irregular	Smooth	In the intertidal area/along the creeks and low lying flats.	Low energy coasts/quiet depositional area. Networks of creeks present.	Grows on substrate mud/ mud-sand composition. A single patch has 2-3 shades of orange red, may be due to different species, height or densities. Bluish brown are species of mangroves.
Mud/tidal	Brown/gray/ grayish blue	Irregular	Smooth	Intertidal area	Low energy coast	Composition is fine grained mud-sand flats
Sandy beach	White	Linear crescent	Smooth	Adjacent to coast, on the land water boundary.	Open coast	Made up of fine sand particles, broken molluscan shell etc.
Other vegetation	Brownish red/bright pinkish red	Irregular	Smooth/fluffy	In the intertidal/ supratidal area.	Patches in between mangroves/along creek etc. where tidal influc is not daily	Also present in brackish water.

(Contd...)

Category	Tone	Shape	Texture	Location	Association	Remarks
Creeks	Blue	Meandering	Smooth	Intertidal/ supratidal area	Mudflat	Intricate network of narrow inlets of sea water in tidalflats.
Waterbodies	Blue	Varying	Smooth	—	—	Water present after monsoon. Manmade/natural.
Aquaculture	Blue/black	Rectangular/square	Smooth	Intertidal/ supratidal area	Near coast where tidal influx is present. Substrate mud	Cluster of ponds together for culturing prawns, shrimps etc. with bunds and is dykes. At places paddy fields converted to ponds after harvest.

Table 1.2: Estuaries Present in Ratnagiri and Sindhudurg Districts

Sindhudurg District		Ratnagiri District	
Location	Geo. Position	Location	Geo. Position
Terekhol	15°42′ N 73°40′ E	Rajapur	16°36′ N 73°19′ E
Shiroda	15°45′ N 73°37′ E	Vetye	16°38′ N 73°19′ E
Mochemad	15°47′ N 73°38′ E	Purnagad	16°48′ N 73°18′ E
Vengurla	15°51′ N 73°36′ E	Pavas	16°53′ N 73°17′ E
Vaingani	15°54′ N 73°35′ E	Bhatye	16°58′ N 73°17′ E
Kalvi	15°56′ N 73°32′ E	Kalbadevi	17°01′ N 73°16′ E
Khavane	15°58′ N 73°33′ E	Are	17°04′ N 73°17′ E
Nivti	15°59′ N 73°29′ E	Kelye	17°05′ N 73°17′ E
Tarkarli	16°00′ N 73°28′ E	Malgund	17°06′ N 73°15′ E
Kolamb	16°02′ N 73°27′ E	Jaigad	17°18′ N 73°12′ E
Kalavali	16°05′ N 73°27′ E	Dabhol	17°34′ N 73°09′ E
Achara	16°11′ N 73°25′ E	Harnai	17°50′ N 73°05′ E
Mithbav	16°16′ N 73°24′ E	Savitri	17°59′ N 73°01′ E
Mumbra	16°21′ N 73°22′ E		
Deogad	16°23′ N 73°21′ E		
Vijaydurg	16°33′ N 73°20′ E		

RESULTS AND DISCUSSIONS

Survey, Mapping and Remote Sensing

Ground Surveys

Synecological methods are involved in vegetation studies. For the analysis of the vegetation several techniques are used. The most authentic method is ground survey, which provides the factual data without any imagination. The field studies are usually undertaken from various angles like charting, photography, population dynamics, phytosociology etc. In the present study vegetation analysis was carried out for knowing the Biodiversity, which covers charting, photography and population studies.

The survey of India toposheets, Remote sensing imageries from NRSA, Hyderabad and the classified maps prepared by MRSAC, Nagpur are found helpful during the ground surveys.

The mangroves in the study area were analysed according to system given by Raunkiaer (1934) (in Misra, 1968). This projects the nature of dominance seen in the ecosystem. According to Raunkier's frequency distribution pattern the value of dominants is low, whereas species belonging to class A with less than 20% frequency are more in number.

The mangroves in the study area are considered on the basis of their percent occurrence . The individual frequency of occurrence is given in Table 1.3 whereas Table 1.4 records frequency classes.(Tables 1.3 to 1.5)

This form indicates the homogenous nature of community. It indicates that floristic uniformity is variable directly with the values of frequency of Class-A and Class-E. The number of species in Class-A are greater including *B. cylindrica, A.alba, S. caseolaris, X. granatum, C. iripa, C. manghas* and *T. indica* than other classes including *K. candel, S. apetala, B. gymnorrhiza, L. racemosa.* The class-E includes species like *A. marina* var. *acutissima, A. officinalis, R. mucronata, S. alba, A. corniculatum* and *E. agallocha*.

The presence of the mangroves has also been explained by Braun-Blanquet (1932) as recorded. The system indicates that greater number of species are rare and less number of species are dominant or sub-dominant. It is found that the species like *B. cylindrica, A. alba, A. marina* var, *resinifera, S. caseolaris, X. granatum, C. iripa, Tamarix, Cerbera* are rare in their occurrence while the species like *A. marina* var. *acutissima, A. officinalis, R. mucronata, S. alba, C. tagal* and *A. corniculatum* dominate the vegetation.

The mangroves from all the 29 estuaries in the study area are considered for the analysis of percent occurrence. The table indicates that the mangroves are variably distributed at various sites. Some of the species are occur at all the sites whereas other species show limited occurrence. The distribution of mangrove is governed by various factors. Some of the species like *E. agallocha* and *A. ilicifolius, R. mucronata, A. corniculatum* are present at all the sites indicating their wider ecological amplitude. Species like *B. cylindrica, S. caseolaris, X. granatum, C. iripa, C. manghas* and *T. indica (gallica)* show restricted distribution and occur at few sites with limited number of individuals. Species like *C. tagal, R. apiculata, B. gymnorrhiza, L. racemosa, K. candel* and *S. apetala* are moderately distributed.

During the ground surveys the mangroves are also studied for their area under vegetation. The area covered by the mangroves is also an important part of the present study as a ground survey confirmation for R.S. The present study used number of individuals of a species and its average area, to calculate the total area occupied by the speices. It is found that some of the species have larger number of individuals but the area occupied is comparartively smaller e.g. *A. corniculatum, L. racemosa* as compared to the species like *S. apetala, X. granatum, A. alba* which are limited in number with greater area cover. The average area occupied by an indidvidual is recorded. The area occupied by the species is useful to estimate the total mangrove cover of the concerned site. The mangrove so obtained area, is helpful in knowing the increase or decrease in the mangrove cover, which helps to undertake the conservation programme.

During the analysis of ground survey data, attempts were made to compare it with remote sensing data. The data for few sites has been recorded. The comparison of the data for Kalavali estuary, Kalbadevi estuary, Rajapur and Achara estuaries shows marked differences.

It is found for Kalavali estuary that some of the sites show considerable mangrove area during the ground visits, which are not demarketed on RS imageries. The table shows that there are ten sites on the ground survey record having sizable mangrove area. But there are only 3 pockets seen on the RS imagery.

The comparison for the Kalbadevi estuary show that the site-2 near the south bank of Sakhartar bridge has thick mangrove pockets with *S. alba* and *R. mucronata* dominating and site-5 at the south of the Mamurwadi village towards the upstream also has mangrove pockets. The mangroves from both these sites are not found on RS imagery. It is evident that the mangrove area analysed by RS data and the data collected during the ground visits show considerable variations.

For the Rajapur estuary the comparison indicates that the site-11 near the Jaitapur village, site-12 near the village Padave and site-13 near the Govalwadi are with considerable mangrove area which could not be located on RS imagery. The mangove cover recorded during the Ground Survey and that analysed by using RS imageries at sites of Achara estuary has been recorded in Tables 1.6 to 1.9.

The differences in the values are due to many reasons. The RS data and aerial photographs give only the aerial extent of the vegetation and can not explain the understorey or overlapping in vegetation. Secondly, the demarcation between the mangroves and the adjoining vegetation is very difficult. These values will give the area covered by all species including non-mangroves. The data collected during ground surveys is more factual and it is analysed for each species and by considering all the ground details.

The scattered individuals which could not be marked by any aerial device were considered during the ground surveys. This may be the reason of showing higher values during the ground surveys. Some of sites with good mangrove pockets also were not mapped by aerial device. The aerial surveys/data collection depends upon, amongst several other factors, climatic conditions, angle of photography, resolution of the device as well as tidal status (Low or High).

Such type of studies were made by Nayak *et al.* (1993) to generate the use of RS data and the ground truths. Bahuguna *et al.* (1994c) has used similar methodology for the sunderban mangroves and mangroves of Bhitarkanika. Bahuguna *et al.* (1995) has analysed the mangroves of Andaman and Nicobar islands. Several studies by Jagtap *et al.* (1994), Bahuguna and Nayak (1994),

Ramchandran *et al.* (1998) are made by using the similar techniques. The 'ground truths' method was employed in these surveys but detailed surveys are not given.

Murthy *et al.* (1998) suggested the RS data and GIS techniques followed by the ground surveys is the efficient tool for the forest management. The present study projects the essentiality of ground survey. Some of the estuaries like Achara, Kalbadevi and Are are studied for vegetation surveys in detail.

Table 1.3: Per cent Occurrence of the Species in the Study Area

Name of Species	Per cent Occurrence
E. agallocha	100
A. ilicifolius	100
R. mucronata	96.55
A. officinalis	96.55
A. marina var. *acutissima*	96.55
S. alba	93
A. corniculatum	93
C. tagal	72.4
R. apiculata	55.2
A. marina (dwarf)	51.7
B. gymnorrhiza	47.9
L. racemosa	41.4
K. candel	34.5
S. apetala	27.6
A. aureum	27.6
C. iripa	13.8
X. granatum	13.8
A. alba	10.3
S. caseolaris	10.3
A. officinalis (dwarf)	6.89
A. marina var. *resinifera*	3.4
B. cylindrica	3.4
C. odollum (manghas)	3.4
T. gallica	3.4

Table 1.4: Scaling System for Dominant Mangroves in the Study Area Based on Presence Along Different Estuaries

Sl. No.	Frequency Class	Species
1.	A (1-20%)	*A. marina resinifera, A. alba, A. officinalis* (dwarf), *B. cylindrica, S. caseolaris, X. granatum, C. iripa, C. manghus, T. gallica.* (9)
2.	B (21-40%)	*K. candel, S. apetula, A. aureum* (3)
3.	C (41-60%)	*A. marina* (d), *R. apiculata, B. gymnorrhiza,L. racemosa* (4)
4.	D (61-80%)	*C. tagal* (1)
5.	E (81-100%)	*A. marina acutissinma, A. officinalis, R. mucronata, E. agallocha, A. ilicifolius, A. corniculatum, S. alba.* (7)

Braun-Blanquet (1932).

1-20 : Rare
21-40 : Less common
41-60 : Common
61-80 : Sub-dominant
81-100 : Dominants

Table 1.5: Average Area Occupied (m^2) per Indiviudual of the Species

Name of the Species	Average Area of Occupany
E. agallocha	2.95
R. mucronata	4.52
A. officinalis	9.85
A. marina var. *acutissima*	6.91
S. alba	6.68
A. corniculatum	0.64
C. tagal	1.12
R. apiculata	2.16
A. marina (dwarf)	0.5
B. gymnorrhiza	3.05
L. racemosa	0.96
K. candel	1.49
S. apetala	2.45
C. iripa	10.8
X. granatum	7.33
A. alba	10.95
S. caseolaris	3.1
A. officinalis (dwarf)	1.37
A. marina var. *resinifera*	5.6
B. cylindrica	2.92
C. odollum (*manghas*)	1.46

Table 1.6: Mangrove Cover Recorded during the Ground Surveys and the Data Analysed by using RS Imageries at Kalavali Estuary

Site No.	Name of Site	Mangrove Cover (m²)	
		Ground Surveys	RS Data (2000)
1.	Near mouth	3087	–
2.	Talashil	11437	–
3.	Bridge (Hadi)	6689	–
4.	Aquaculture (tondwali)	25132	–
5.	Trimbak	2941	–
6.	Kawawadi	37334	1,62,500
7.	Magavane		
8.	Chanderwadi	412638*	7,35,000
9.	Kandalgaon		
10.	Juwa	1,44,405	1,40,000
	Total	643663	1037500

* Values combined to Sr. No. 7, 8 and 9.

Table 1.7: Mangrove Cover Recorded during the Ground Surveys and the Data Analysed by using RS Imageries at Sites of Kalbadevi Estuary

Site No.	Name of Site	Mangrove Cover (m²)	
		Ground Survey	RS Data
1.	Bridge North	6149	15700
2.	Bridge south	18993	–
3.	Mamurwadi-I	19231	82500
4.	Mamurwadi-II	171042	87500
5.	Mamurwadi (south)	4273	–
6.	Adi	4398	50000
7.	Kelye	2751	57500
	Total	222564	293200

Studies on Data from Remote Sensing

In recent years the advanced technique of Remote Sensing (R.S.) is commonly used for various large scale planning by the Government and Non-Government organisations. It is found that the RS data is reliable data and available in multispectral and repetitive forms. It is commonly used in the coastal studies to collect the information in various forms for forcasting.

Table 1.8: Mangrove Cover Recorded during the Ground Surveys and the Data Analysed by using RS Imageries at sites of Rajapur Estuary

Site No.	Name of Site	Mangrove Cover (m^2)	
		Ground Survey	RS data
1.	Jaitapur	7142	125000
2.	Jawalewadi	26447.7	192500
3.	Marveli	483645.8	50000
4.	Devachigothane	3287247	302500
5.	Sagamwadi	515023.4	407500
6.	Shindewadi	238883	55000
7.	Sonarwadi	216264	37500
8.	Chavanwadi	251022.3	255000
9.	Devachi (south)	423969.6	162500
10.	Marveli Island	199521	690000
11.	Jaitapur-II	75716.3	–
12.	Padve	135409.5	–
13.	Govalwadi	206656.5	–
	Total	60669481	2277500

Table 1.9: Mangrove Cover Recorded during the Ground Surveys and the Data Analysed by using RS Imageries at Sites of Achara Estuary

Site No.	Name of Site	Mangrove Cover (m^2)	
		Ground Survey	RS Data
1	Island-I	62442	62500
7	Island-7	27555	85000
10	Island-10	25603	122500
14, 15	Gaudwadi and Kaziwada	67169	47500
16, 17, 18	Baudhwadi, Bhandarwadi and Dongarewadi	510564	172500
19	Dongarewadi-II	298306.8	122500
20	Parwadi	581.38	37500
22	Canal	519.9	67500
	Total	992741.08	717500

Table 1.10: Comparison of the Mangrove Cover Analysed from Classified Maps of MRSAC, Nagpur, RS Imageries from NRSA, Hyderabad and Data Collected during Field Surveys at Achara Estuary

Name of Estuary	Mangrove Area by MRSAC, Nagpur (1993-94) (ha)	Mangrove Area by NRSA, Data (2000) (ha)	Mangrove Area by Ground Surveys (1999) (ha)
Achara	94.3	94.5	150.96*

* Bhosale (2002)

However RS data has also some limitations in the study of mangrove vegetation due to various reasons. Some of these are the demarcation of the mangrove vegetation from adjoining vegetation. Secondly, it only give aerial extent and can not analyse ground storey. This can be minimized using high resolution data. By using the Liss-II data, the centres like the Maharashtra Remote Sensing Application Centre (MRSAC), Nagpur have analysed the mangrove cover for all the sites in Maharashtra State. The centre has prepared classified maps by denoting various numbers for various components as (3.1) for estuary, (3.10) for mangroves, (3.11) for marshy vegetation, (3.12) for other vegetation, (3.8) for coral reefs, (3.7) for sand-bar etc. The area given as mangroves (3.10) was analyzed for some estuaries during the present study. Attempts were made to compare the data available from NRSA, Hyderabad, MRSAC, Nagpur and the actual data collected during the ground survey. It is found that the data shows considerable variations.

Several workers have used this technique using RS data for the study of wetlands, oceanic activities, aquaculture ponds, forest, urban planning, railways etc. Nayak *et al*. (1993) has generated information about aerial extent of Indian mangroves and its conditions using IRS Liss-II, Landsat-TM and spot data.

The forest survey of India (FSI) has used similar technique to analyse the forest cover including mangroves in India and estimated 108 km^2 mangrove area for India. However the Status of Forest Report (1997) shows 0.48 million ha mangrove area.

Bahuguna *et al*. (1994c) has studied the mangroves of Sunderbans, West Bengal and Bhitarkanika sanctuary of Orrisa coast using RS data. They have separated these mangroves into five zones using IRS-1C Liss-II high resolution data, as *Avicennia* zone, mixed *Rhizophora* forest, *S. apetala* zone, mixed *Avicennia* with *Phoenix paludosa* and mangrove scrub. Bahuguna *et al*. (1995) have studied the small tidal estuaries, neritic inlets and lagoons of Andaman and Nicobar Islands using RS data.

Jagtap *et al*. (1994) have reported studies on the mangrove environment of Maharashtra coast using RS data and aerial photographs of 1973, and recorded 210 km^2 as mangrove area along Maharashtra coast.

Department of space (Government of India) has mapped the area under mangroves using RS data with 83 to 90% accuracy. Singh *et al.* (1986), Rajgopalan (1987), Dagar (1987) have given extent of mangroves on Andaman and Nicobar islands. Rangnath *et al.* (1989) used RS data for coastal studies. Nayak (1993) have analysed the mangrove cover in India.

Bahuguna and Nayak (1994) have studied the Orrisa coast for mapping for the aquaculture sites using Liss-II data of 1:50, 000 scale and showed broad land use pattern, mangroves, mudflat, sandy areas etc. Ramchandran *et al.* (1998) have studied the coastal wetland ecology of Tamil Nadu and Andaman and Nicobar islands with special reference to mangroves. They suggested that IRS Liss-II and TM data is useful in the study of mangrove ecosystem and to prepare GIS maps. Murthy *et al.* (1998) suggested the use of RS and GIS data for efficient forest resource management including the mangrove forests. They reported that the status of Indian mangrove forest cover has considerably increased from 1972 to 1995.

Clark *et al.* (1998) analysed the florida mangroves using high resolution multispectral RS data. Green (1998) also has suggested RS techniques for mangrove mapping at Eastern Carribean islands. Blasco *et al.* (1998) suggested RS techniques for mangrove studies.

In the present study IRS-1B Liss-II data of 1:50,000 scale for the year 2000 and classified wetland maps produced by Remote sensing application centre (MRSAC), Nagpur are used. The survey of India (SOI) toposheet maps are used as base maps. It is found that Liss-II data is helpful in determining the extent of mangoves.

The satellite data of IRS-1B Liss-II of the year 1993-94 in the form of classified wetland maps were procured as has been stated earlier. The data interpreted from these maps is presented in Table 1.11. From the data it is found that there are many estuaries which have large mangrove areas like, Mithbav, Mumbra, Deogad and Tarkarli with some of the important and uncommon species not recorded on these maps.

For the further analysis IRS-1B Liss-II RS data of 1:50,000 has been used. The imageries are in the form of paper prints which are analysed using hand lens and light table. The classification system along with image interpretation keys are developed to distinguish various categories like, length of estuary, estuarine area, sand, mangroves (sparse and dense), aquaculture ponds etc. The key has been prepared on the basis of category, tone, shape, texture, location, association on FCC print and confirmed along with ground truths. Mangroves show bright to dull orange red, bluish brown, and pale brown colours. The texture with smooth bright orange red colour indicates dense mangroves and bluish or pale brown colours indicate sparse mangroves. The location of mangroves is unique on FCC as in the intertidal area along the creeks, low lying flats in the estuaries, quiet depositional areas, and network of water channels.

Table 1.11: Data Interpreted from Classified Wetlands Maps of IRS-1B L-II Data (1993-94). MRSAC, Nagpur

Sl. No.	Name of Estuary	Area (ha)
1.	Aronda	114.4
2.	Kolamb	18.36
3.	Kalavali	57.2
4.	Achara	94.3
5.	Vijaydurg	164.35
6.	Purnagad	119.1
7.	Pavas	28.05
8.	Bhatye	101
9.	Kalbadevi	33
10.	Are	36.7
11.	Jaigad	633
12.	Dabhol	633
13.	Harnai	75
14.	Savitri	1016

Source: MRSAC, Nagpur.

A single mangrove patch shows variable tones due to the different species, height and densities which cannot analyse at Liss-II data. The imageries are analysed for Pavas, Deogad, Are, Kalbadevi, Kelye, Rajapur, Vijaydurg and Bhatye estuaries. The mangroves are analysed as dense and sparse categories. The data interpreted is presented in the Table 1.12. Deogad estuary is also analysed for the aquaculture pond constructed at the upstream region. The area of pond is 5 ha. The ground surveys found that this pond is constructed by cutting mangroves from this area. The area is dominated by the presence of *B. gymnorrhiza* which is a rare species.

Various investigators have studied mangrove areas by RS data. According to RS data total mangrove cover is reported as 4,474 sq. km but earlier report is 6,740 sq km. by Ministry of Environment and Forest Report by Krishnamurthy *et al.* (1987).

The low values of mangrove areas shown by satellite data may be due to:

1. reduction in mangrove area
2. mangrove area smaller than 2 ha were not mapped on imageries.
3. mixing of mangrove vegetation with adjoining forest
4. insufficient ground surveys. RSAM (1992).

From the present study it is found that:

1. RS data is useful in understanding the mangrove locations.
2. IRS-1B Liss-II data is useful for study of mangrove cover and areas of other categories.
3. As the resolution of IRS-1B is less it can not map the smaller areas less than 2 ha and can not be applicable upto species level.
4. Higher resolution data in digital form is required to different mangroves, even in small pockets
5. The mangroves in the study area are estuarine and distributed along the banks forming narrow strips all along the banks of estuary these strips are not visible in Liss-II data.

Table 1.12: Mangrove Cover Analysed from IRS-1B L-II Data of Year 2000

Estuary	Length of Estuary (km)	Estuarine Area (km²)	Sparse Mangrove (ha)	Dense Mangrove (ha)	Total Mangrove (ha)	Aqua Ponds (ha)
Pavas	2.75	2.25	16.5	–	16.5	–
Deogad	16	18.70	12.5	28	40.5	6
Are	2.85	0.94	7.25	32	39.25	–
Kalbadevi	7.25	5.67	21.5	57.8	79.3	–
Kelye	1.25	0.33	6.25	–	6.25	–
Rajapur	22.5	15.73	119.3	231.7	351	–
Vijaydurg	23	37.88	264.75	374.75	639.5	–
Bhatye	11	9.73	22.75	59	81.75	–
Kalavali	16	7.6	30.25	73.5	103.75	8
Achara	4.5	3.55	18.6	75.9	94.5	30
Tarkarli	12	65	30	23	53	–

Floristic Composition

The physiognomy of any ecosystem depends almost entirely upon the Floristic composition. The appearance, structure and function of any ecosystem is in response to Floristic composition. The floristic composition is a reflection of environmental conditions and genetic flexibility of species (ecological amplitude). The occurrence of a species itself indicates the set of environmental conditions. For example the species requiring low salinity represents the character. Therefore species composition of a given place is of prime importance. The seral stages like *Porteresia coarctata* also play significant role in development of climax vegetation.

The floristic composition of mangroves is governed by various factors like the geographical position of the region, soil and water temperatures, tides, various chemical and physical parameters of soil and water. Saenger (1998) emphasized that evolutionary processes are also responsible for the global distribution of the mangroves. He also explained that there are several other factors like latitudinal limits, temperature, aridity, endemism, hybridizations, human-induced factors which also influence the Floristic setup of the mangroves.

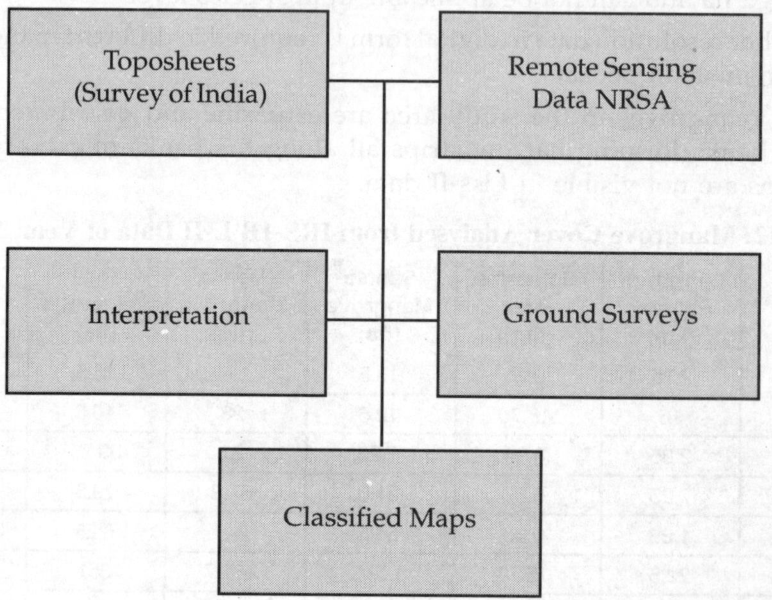

Fig. 1.1: Classification System used during Remote Sensing Studies

The Floristic composition or the diversity of world mangrove has been reported by Chapman (1974), SCOR/COE working group (1981), Tomlinson (1986), Bunt (1992), Farnsworth and Ellison (1997) and Kathiresen (2005).

As stated earlier the diversity of Floristic composition of Indian mangroves has been reported by Chatterjee (1958), Sidhu (1963), Dwiwedi (1975), Bhosale (1978), Rao *et al*. (1998) and Kathiresen (2002).

The Floristic composition of Indian Mangroves has been described by Blasco (1975). Kathiawar peninsula of western India supported 11 mangroves and associate species (Blasco, 1975, 1977). Kerala coast possesses 12 mangrove species (Chatterjee, 1958; Dwiwedi, 1975 and Blasco, 1975 and 1977). They have also reported mangroves from East-coast and Andaman-Nicobar Islands. Blasco (1975, 1977) have reported 17 species from Cauvery delta; 19 species from Krishna and Godavari deltas; 21 and 31 mangroves from Mahanadi and Ganges delta respectively. Untawale (1985) has given distribution of mangroves along the west coast of India, recording 34 species from the west coast and 29 species from coast of Maharashtra.

Bhosale (1987) has compared the species composition of west coast with that of the East coast. She has listed 24 species of mangroves and associates occurring along west coast of Maharashtra.

Kotmire and Bhosale (1985) have given Floristic composition of Deogad estuary. More recently Bhosale (2005) has reported 24 typical mangroves, 11 halophytes and 9 mangrove associates from Maharashtra.

A. Ratnagiri District

Ratnagiri district is the central district of coastal Maharashtra. It is important from mangrove diversity point of view. The district has wide network of rivers, estuaries, creeks and backwaters. The estuaries, namely from south to north are, Rajapur, Vetye, Purnagad, Pavas, Bhatye, Kalbadevi, Are, Kelye, Malgund, Jaigad, Dabhol, Harnai (Anjarle) and Savitri. The Savitri river forms boundary between Ratnagiri and Raigad districts and is the largest of all. The dominant genera in the district are *Avicennia, Rhizopora* and *Sonneratia*.

Typical Mangrove Species

Ratnagiri district harbours typical mangrove species as well as associates. These species are distributed all along the banks of various estuaries, creeks and backwaters. Rajapur, Kalbadevi, Purnagad, Are, Bhatye and Dabhol have greater diversity. Some species commonly distributed are, *Avicennia marina* var. *acutissima, A. officinalis, Rhizophora mucronata, Ceriops tagal, Sonneratia alba, Aegiceras corniculatum, Excoecaria agallocha* and *Acanthus ilicifolius*. The species like *Rhizophora apiculata, Lumnitzera racemosa* and *Avicennia marina* (dwarf) have a limited distribution in few estuaries. The uncommon species are *Bruguiera gymnorrhiza* and *Sonneratia apetala* recorded from Five estuaries, viz. Rajapur, Purnagad, Malgund, Jaigad and Dabhol. *S. apetala* is recorded from Vetye, Purnagad, Kelye, Dabhol and Savitri.

Bhosale (2002) has reported the most unique species *Xylocarpus granatum* from two estuaries, namely, Purnagad and Jaigad from the district. *X. granatum* has been observed during the present study with few number of individuals. Another uncommon species *Kandelia candel* has been recorded from three estuaries namely, Rajapur, Bhatye and Dabhol. It is also recorded with few individuals.

A. marina var. *acutissima* is the most adaptive species recorded from all the sites in the district. It has a wide range of salinity tolerance. It can tolerate salinity upto 90 parts per thousand (Macnae, 1968). The species has shown different growth performances in the district. At the estuaries like Bhatye, Dabhol, Savitri the species has grown upto 8 to 10 m with bole size of 1 to 2 metres. But at other places like Kalbadevi, Are, Malgund, the *A. marina* has shown considerable reduction in its height. This reduction in height of *A. marina* has been observed during the field visits. It can be attributes to human pressures on the ecosystem. Vanucci (1989) has stated that *A. marina* has received maximum insults. Sathe and Bhosale (1991) stated that *Avicennia* species are in general more tolerant to salt and organic pollution than other species of mangroves in Ratnagiri. Tare (1993) has studied some aspects of dwarfism from the district about *A. marina*. Dwarfism in *A. marina* has been observed considerably and it has occupied larger area along with regular sized *A. marina,* hence the species *A. marina* (dwarf) considered separately.

The species *Avicennia officinalis* has also shown wide range of distribution all over the district. It shows adaptibility for various conditions except shelter *A. officinalis* show variable performance from site to site. At the estuaries like Bhatye, Malgund and Dabhol *A. officinalis* has developed boles upto 2 to 3 meter. Like *A. marina,* there is dwarf life from of *A. officinalis* observed at a single site Pavas.

Avicennia alba has a restricted distribution in the district. It has been recorded from Rajapur and Pavas estuaries. The species is very much typical about the leaf shape and beaked fruits.

The species *A. corniculatum, C. tagal, E. agallocha, R. mucronata, R. apiculata, S. alba* and *A. ilicifolius* are distributed at all the estuaries in the district.

A. ilicifolius grows luxuriently along with *A. marina*. As these two species are more tolerant to water pollution (Bhosale and Mulik, 1991) perhaps, have occupied all the polluted areas. *A. ilicifolius* and *A. aureum* are commonly found. According to Joshi and Jamale (1975) *A. ilicifolius* is accompanied by *Acrostichum aureum* in Maharashtra.

The presence of *Lumnitzera racemosa* is frequent with an exception of three estuaries viz. Dabhol, Harnai an Savitri.

Halophytic Species

The halophytic species are recorded during the present study. The species like *Halophila beccarii, Aleuropus lagopoides, Acrostichum aureum, Ipomea pes-caprae, Porteresia coarctata, Sesuvium portulacastrum, Stenophyllus barbatus, Sporobolus virginicus* and species of *Cyperus javanicus* and *Najas* species are distributed unevenly in estuaries of the district. Among all the species *Ipomea pes-caprae* is more or less commonly occurring.

Halophytes play important role in the succession and productivity of the estuarine ecosystems, species like *P. coarctata* plays significant role as the seral stage in the development of mangrove ecosystem.

Joshi and Bhosale (1982) reported *Derris heterophylla, A. lagopoides, H. beccarii, S. portulacastrum, Salvadora persica, Clerodendrum inerme, Premna integrifolia, Thespesia populnea, S. barbatus, Cyperus* and *Ipomea pes-caprae* from Ratnagiri, Ganapatipule (Malgund), Deogad, Mumbra and Bhatye estuaries. These species are also collected from various sites of Ratnagiri district in present study.

Blasco (1975), Tomlinson (1986), Naskar and Bakshi (1987), Singh (1993), Bannerjee and Rao (1990) and Kurlapkar (1993) have given the list of halophytes occurring in different parts of India and the world. The species recorded during the present study, like *A. aureum, A. lagopoides, H. beccarii, I. Pes-caprae, S. portulacastrum* are also recorded in the above reports.

These halophytes grow along with the mangroves and add to the productivity of the ecosystem.

The halophytic species like *H. beccarii* shares a major contribution to the input of primary production into the bays and estuaries. The halophytes also adds the organic matter that leads to the estuarine detritus based food webs, that form the energy base to many commercial species of fish. Halophytes like *H. beccarii* due to their dense root systems stabilize the bottom to some extent. Halophytic vegetation also offers good substrate for epiphytic small algae, diatoms and sessile Fauna and plays the role of sediment trap. *Halophila* along with the other monocot in the submerged marine environment are commonly termed as seagrasses. Seagrass productivity ranges from 5 to 15 g c/m^2 per day (McRoy and Helfferich, 1977).

Bhosale (1990) has recorded the biomass production of *H. beccarii* as 42.67 g.Fwt/m^2 and 56.28 g.Fwt/m^2 from Kalbadevi and Are estuaries respectively.

Bhosale (1974), Ghewade and Joshi (1980) have reported *H. beccarii* from Ratnagiri.

In the present study *H. beccarii* has been recorded from three estuaries namely Bhatye, Kalbhadevi and Are.

Tomlinson (1986) and Lakshminarasimhan (1996) have reported *Cyperus javanicus* as a halophytic species occurring along with the mangroves. Lakshminarasimhan (1996) has reported it from Raigad, Ratnagiri and Sindhudurg district. During the present study it has been collected from few estuaries of the district.

Borderline Mangroves

Different mangrove species occupy different places in an estuary, creek or lagoon. Different terminologies are used to explain or to record the plants other than the typical mangroves. Saenger *et al.* (1983) used the term 'non-exclusive mangroves' for such plants. Tomlinson (1986) has used the term 'mangrove associated plants' or 'mangrove associates'.

Depending upon the position in the estuary these plants are separated as borderline mangroves (bordering the vegetation) and mangrove associates (occasional occurrence in mangroves, but common as glycophyte) in the present study.

The borderline mangrove plants recorded from Ratnagiri district. The species recorded are *Barringtonia racemosa, Caesalpinia nuga, Clerodendrum inerme, Derris heterophylla, Dolicandron spathecae, Premna coriaceae, Premna integrifolia, Pongamia pinnata, Salvadora persica*. Boer and Gliddon (1998) considered Tamarix as a halophye. *Tamarix gallica, Thespesia populnea* and *Vitis palida*.

These species play important role in deciding the structure and appearance of the mangrove ecosystem. They are usually found along the borderline of the estuaries and creeks. Occasionally these species are intermingled with the typical mangrove species.

It is observed that the species like *Caesalpinia nuga, Derris heterophylla, Clerodendrum inerme* are more or less commonly occurring along with *Acanthus ilicifolius* and *Aegiceras corniculatum*.

From the table it is also clear that the species like *C. nuga, C. inerme, D. heterophylla, S. persica* and *T. populnea* are commonly found in estuaries of Ratnagiri district.

The species *Tamarix gallica* has been reported for the first time in the present study. It has been recorded from the upstream region at Purnagad estuary.

The species usually prefers sandy, sheltered places with low salinity. Naskar and Guhabukshi (1987) has reported it from Sunderbans area. They noted *T. gallica* from sandy areas impregnated with salt.

Banerjee and Rao (1990) reported it from Mahanadi and Dhamra delta, on the areas prevalent within the zone of fresh and brackish water mixture frequent along the sea-shore.

Banerjee, Ghosh and Sastry (1998) reported it from Coringa river mouth in the Godavari delta.

Cooke (1901) have reported the *T. gallica* on the banks of Indus and throughout Sindh.

At many sites like Pavas it is found that *C. inerme, D. heterophylla* are close to the *L. racemosa, A. corniculatum* and *A. officinalis*. At Malgund, Bhatye and Kalbadevi estuaries it is found that *S. persica, P. coriaceae, C. inerme* are distributed at the banks with drier soils and near to the species like *E. agallocha* and *A. corniculatum*.

The species like *B. racemosa, D. spathecae, V. palida* are found as uncommon species and found on the drier and gravelly borders of the vegetation. These borderline species also add the detritus in the mangrove ecosystems.

The species like *C. inerme* are also occurring frequently with certain succulent halophytes like *S. portulacastrum*.

Banerjee and Rao (1990) reported *T. populnea, C. inermae, S. persica, T. gallica* and *A. aureum* as a borderline or transition zone species between supra-tidal region and mid-tidal flat of the Orrisa coast.

Singh and Garge (1993) reported *B. racemosa, C. nuga, D. spathecae, P. pinnata* popular as borderline species from the mangrove swamps of Andaman Islands. The present study also reports these species from Ratnagiri district.

Mangrove Associates

The mangrove forest in general does not have understorey of hearts except their own seedlings. But some times the forest floor is colonized by other plants from adjacent fresh water species or saline marsh species (Tomlinson, 1986). Thus the mangrove associates are mostly introduced into the mangrove forests by natural dispersal mechanisms through the water currents or ways.

The mangrove associated plant species also contribute to the functioning of mangrove ecosystem. They may grow along with the mangroves in intertidal regions or they may establish in close vicinity. The associate species play key role in the succession process and also as the indicators of ecological changes.

In India, the mangrove ecosystems have 809 species of associated flora (Kathiresen and Quasim, 2005) including 12 species of salt marsh vegetation, 11 species of seagrasses, 55 species of algae, 69 species of bacteria, 102 species of fungi.

In Malaysia, 57 mangrove associate species are present besides 9 species of bryophytes and pteridophytes (Japar, 1994).

East Africa coast has 8 salt-marsh and other halophytes, 2 lichens, 1 seagrass species and about 17 algal species (Diops *et al.*, 2000 and Julius, 1997).

Tomlinson (1986), Singh (1993), Naskar and Bakshi (1987), Bannerjee (1998), Blasco (1985) and IUCN (1983) have given the account of various parts of the world.

The mangrove associate species recorded during the present study are *Acampae premorsa, Bauhinia racemosa, Calophyllum inophyllum, Fimbristylis ferrugenia, Flacourtia montane, Holiogarna antidysentrica, Hygrophila auriculata, Lindernia antipoda, Mimusops elengi, Nymphea nauchali, Paspalum vaginatum, Ruppia maritima, Scirpus littoralis, Vitex nigundo.*

The presence of species like *Acampae premorsa* on the mangroves like *S. alba* indicates the evergreen type of vegetation which is a characteristic feature of mangroves with some exceptions like *Excoecaria agallocha*.

In Thailand (Santisuk, 1983) 18 species of epiphytes that include 13 species of Orchidaceae are found. These are belonging to *Dendrobium, Bulbophyllum* and *Eria*.

IUCN (1983) and Santisuk (1983) have reported several genera of Orchidaceae from the world and Thailand respectively. They have reported the genera like *Dendrobium, Cymbidium, Myrmecodia, Polypodium, Bulbophyllum* and *Eria*. But they have not reported *Acampae premorsa* which is recorded during the present study from Purnagad and Kalbadevi on *Sonneratia alba*.

Some of the species like *Stenophyllus, Sporobolus, Scirpus* and *Najas* indicate the encroachment through reclaimation or aquaculture ponds.

Naskar and Bakshi (1987) reported *Fimbrystylis halophilae* and *F. subbispicata* and *Scirpus triquetta* as associates for Sunderban mangroves. During the present study *Fimbrystylis Ferrugenia* and *Scirpus littoralis* from the similar genera are recorded. These species are also reported by Bannerjee and Rao (1990) from Orrisa coast. During the present study these species are recorded from Vetye, Bhatye, Kalbadevi, Malgund and Jaigad estuaries.

Tomlinson (1986) has reported *Calophyllum inophyllum* as a commonly encounted as a mangrove associate, which is also recorded from six estuaries in the district.

Significant Observations

The mangroves of Ratnagiri district are described by many workers Untawale (1985), Radhakrishnan (1985), Navalkar (1956), Joshi and Shinde (1978), Bhosale (1990) and Kurlapkar (1993). These reports do not report presence of important species *Xylocarpus granatum* in Ratnagiri district. During the present study this species has been recorded from Purnagad and Jaigad estuaries. The seeds of *X. granatum* have medicinal property and used locally against stomach disorders and fever. The local people collect the mature seeds during the fruiting season and store in houses to use for the whole year. The number of fruits per plant are less and due to collection of seeds for medicinal purpose the regeneration has greatly hampered. Secondly, the immature seeds are much favoured by the monkeys which also decreases the available mature seeds for regeneration.

Tamarix gallica is another species recorded during the present study which has not been reported earlier from Ratnagiri district. It is recorded from upstream region with few individuals from Purnagad estuary.

The limited distribution of *K. candel* is to be noted. *S. apetala* is another interesting species distributed over five estuaries in the district. The species has almost disappeared from Vetye and Purnagad. The better performance of *S. apetala* has been observed at Dabhol and Savitri estuaries, where huge trees of *S. apetala* are observed with height of 10 to 13 metres (better growth amongst other estuaries).

B. gymnorrhiza is fast disappearing from estuaries like Malgund and Purnagad. The best grown monotypic stands of *S. alba* is the unique feature of Narayanmali site of Bhatye estuary. The site also has few full grown trees of *R. apiculata*.

Some of the unique halophytic species recorded from three estuaries in the district is *H. beccarii.*

B. Sindhudurg District

It is the southernmost district of state of Maharashtra having a common border with state of Goa. Terekhol estuary is the boundary between two states, the north bank is in Maharashtra and the south bank is in Goa. On the northern side the district has a common boundary with Ratnagiri district, which is marked by the Vijaydurga estuary. The estuaries lying towards the north of Terekhol estuary in Sindhudurg districts are Shiroda, Vengurla, Mochemad, Khavane, Kalvi (Kelus), Vaingani, Nivti, Tarkarli, Kolamb, Kalavali, Achara, Mithbav, Mumbra, Deogad and Vijaydurg. Vijaydurg estuary is largest of all and has north boundary is in Ratnagiri district. The important feature of the district is Achara estuary having mouth region with estuarine delta. It is the unique estuary with greater species diversity which comes under protected forest. The estuary harbours one of the best mangrove stands of the west coast of Maharashtra. The tall mangroves and large mangrove islands, are the unique features of the estuary.

Typical Mangrove Species

Sindhudurg district harbours some of the uncommon mangrove species of the district. Some species are recorded with few individuals which need immediate conservation attempts. It is also observed that the mangroves in the district are under severe threats. The species like *A. alba, C. iripa, L. racemosa* and *S. apetala* are uncommon and recorded from a few estuaries.

The unique and rare species recorded from the district are *A. marina* var. *resinifera, B. cylindrica* and *X. granatum.* Sathe and Bhosale (1991) has reported *A. marina* var. *resinifera* from the same locality which is observed during the present study.

Bhosale (2002) have reported the presence of *X. granatum* from few sites in the district after Cooke (1901).

B. cylindrica is another unique species reported from Vengurla (Manasi) estuary in the district. During the present study *X. granatum* has been recorded from Achara and Vijaydurg estuaries.

C. iripa is another species reported by Bhosale (2002) from the district which is observed from Achara, Kalavali and Mithbav estuaries.

A. marina var. *acutissima* is the dominant species recorded from almost all the estuaries in a larger extent except at Deogad estuary. It is interesting to note that another estuary, namely, Mumbra which is separated by a hill from Deogad has the presence of *A. marina* var. *acutissima*. The dwarf life of the species is found at many estuaries like Terekhol, Vengurla, Mochemad, Vaingani, Nivti, Kolamb, Kalavali, Achara, Mumbra and Vijaydurg. These dwarf *A. marina* plants are considered as *Avicennia marina* (dwarf).

A. officinalis is another principal mangrove species recorded from all the 16 estuaries in the district. It is observed that the species perform better when the sheltered conditions are available. At many estuaries like Kolamb, Kalavali and Achara the full grown trees with large boles are recorded. One of the unique observation on *A. officinalis* is from Kalavali estuary. Several sites in Kalavali estuary have sheltered areas where the water rises and receds very slowly. In such areas *A. officinalis* has developed pure pockets of tall trees with larger area coverage.

At Achara and Kalavali *A. officinalis* has shown a considerable dwarfism in its habit and these dwarf *A. officinalis* plants have occupied a sizable area with large number of individuals. Due to this, these plants are separated from *A. officinalis* and considered as *A. officinalis* (dwarf).

Avicennia alba has a limited distribution and recorded from Vengurla, Mochemad, Vaingani, Nivti and Kolamb.

A. corniculatum is recorded as a wide spread species and recorded from almost all the estuaries except Vaingani.

Distribution of *Sonneratia* species in Sindhudurg district is also unique with respect to species. *S. alba* is distributed at all the estuaries except at Kalvi (Kelus) estuary. From the field study it is observed that the species might have vanished due to the reclamation of huge mangrove area.

S. apetala is the another uncommon species recorded from Terekhol, Achara and Mumbra estuaries. The species has been found with countable number of individuals. Severe cutting of *S. apetala* is observed at Mumbra for fuel and timber. The bole size is pretty large (about 2-3 m) but stump is about 5-6 feet in height. It was a dense pocket of *S. apetala* about a decade or two ago.

S. caseolaris is a very uncommon species found in Sindhudurg district but not recorded in Ratnagiri district. The species is recorded from Terekhol, Tarkarli and Khavane. At tarkarli huge trees of *S. caseolaris* are recorded with a height of 10 to 12 metres. The typical tall pneumatophores of more than 5 feet height are observed at this site. It is also observed that the riped fruits of *S. caseolaris* give sweet sour taste, these fruits are much favoured by local peoples.

S. caseolaris was recorded from Achara by Radhakrishnan (1985) but she has not recorded *Sonneratia apetala* from the same locality which was observed during present study in comparatively large number. The occurrence of *S. caseolaris* in Maharashtra was doubted by Untawale (1985) when only locality of Achara was reported for it. However, it has been recorded from said places of Sindhudurg district in present work and identified correctly. Its report from Achara can not be supported in present situation.

L. racemosa is another typical mangrove recorded from Khavane, Mithbav, Mumbra and Vijaydurg estuaries. The better trees of *L. racemosa* is observed at Khavane with height up to 5 m. It is found in association with *C. manghas, S. caseolaris, R. apiculata* and *A. aureum*. It is found only at the distal zones.

Kandelia candel prefers open canopy and sheltered areas. It has recorded from Terekhol, Tarkarli, Kalavali, Achara, Mithbav, Mumbra and Vijaydurg. *K. candel* is distributed more frequently as compared to Ratnagiri district. The full grown trees with buttresses upto 60 cm are observed at Tarkarli and Kalavali estuaries.

R. apiculata is distributed along the eight estuaries in the district. The salinity tolerance of *R. apiculata* is low as compared to *R. mucronata*. It prefers places of lower salinity (Walter, 1977). *R. apiculata* has been found along with *A. officinalis* at many places.

C. tagal has been recorded from ten estuaries in the district. It is observed growing along the landward side luxuriently, where there is possibility of getting freshwater supply. Such sites are found at Achara, Mithbav, Mumbra and Vijaydurg. *A. corniculatum* and *Cerips tagal* are also distributed at distal and middle zones of mangrove vegetation. These species can be distributed near the mouth regions of the estuary if the area is sheltered. *C. tagal* is also recorded along with *S. alba, A. officinalis* and *E. agallocha*.

The best populations of *A. corniculatum* has been observed at Achara and Kalavali estuaries. At Achara (Dongrewadi site) and at Kalavali (Kandalgaon site) large stands of *A. corniculatum* are observed. At Kalavali it is found along with *K. candel*.

E. agallocha, A. ilicifolius and *A. corniculatum* are more or less commonly found all along the estuaries in the district. These species rarely found near the mouth region but found commonly in distal and middle zones in the upstream and middle part of the estuary.

The species like *K. candel, B. gymnorrhiza, S. apetala* and *S. caseolaris* are not common in their occurrence along the estuaries. *K. candel, B. gymnorrhiza* and *S. caseolaris* are preferring the sites beyond the middle part of the estuaries towards the upstream region. *S. caseolaris* prefers upstream region with good fresh water supply. *S. apetala* is better growing in the Mumbra estuary.

Untawale *et al*. (1982) have stated that *K. candel* (*K. rheedi*) and *S. caseolaris* are common along Goa coast, however in present study area these species are less common.

Blasco (1977) reported *K. rheedi* (Synonym *K. candel*) is on the verge of extinction from Maharashtra, but the present study reveals that, at the places like Tarkarli and Kalavali the species is growing luxuriently, but needs protection.

Halophytic Species

Sindhudurg district harbours major halophytic species occurring along with the mangroves. The study reveals the presence of halophytic species like *H. beccarii, A. lagopoides, A. aureum, C. javanicus, I. Pes-caprae, Najas* Spp., *P. coarctata, S. portulacastrum, S. barbatus* and *S. virginicus*.

The mangrove fern *A. aureum* has been recorded from Terekhol, Khavane, Kalavali, Mumbra, Deogad and Vijaydurg estuaries. *A. aureum* has recorded on the drier and reclaimed areas, in upstream region or in organicaly polluted areas. The tidal water, except of equinoxial tides, will never rise beyond the *A. aureum*. In all the estuaries considered for the study, the *A. aureum* is the limit of vegetation. At some places it is with *A. officinalis, A. ilicifolius* or *A. corniculatum*, but beyond this towards the upstream or landward side no species of mangroves or associates is observed. At places like Khavane it is found along with *C. manghas, S. caseolaris* and *L. racemosa.*

The distribution of halophytic members of family Poaceae in the district is also important. The species like *A. lagopoides* and *P. coarctata* are distributed at some estuaries. *A. lagopoides* is found at Terekhol, Khavane, Kalavali, Mumbra, Deogad and Vijaydurg. *P. coarctata* is found at Terekhol, Nivti, Tarkarli and Kolamb and Bhosale (1985) have reported *A. lagopoides* from Mumbra and Deogad estuaries. Kurlapkar (1993) has gives the occurrence of *A. lagopoides* and *P. coarctata* along the various estuaries of Maharashtra coast.

P. coarctata is the unique species and indicates the course of succession. At many sites at Kolamb and Tarkarli *P. coarctata* has found as a pioneer species on newly formed islands.

The halophytic members of family *Cyperaceae* also contribute in the productivity of mangrove ecosystem. During the present study the members like *C. javanicus, S. barbatus* and *S. vigiricus* are recorded from various localities in the district.

C. javanicus is reported from Kalavali, Mumbra and Deogad. It is found along with *A. officinalis, E. agallocha, A. corniculatum* and *A. ilicifolius*. It is regularly found along with *A. aureum*. The members of family Cyperaceae colonise rapidly after the rainy season when the salinity is low.

H. beccarii usually referred as marine angiosperrm and a halophytic species is recorded from Terekhol and Achara estuaries. As described earlier the species adds to the productivity of the mangrove ecosystem.

I. pes-caprae is recorded from Terekhol, Vaingani, Kolamb, Achara, Mithbav, Mumbra and Vijaydurg. It is also called as sand-binder. At many sites it is observed that *I. Pes-caprae* migrates on both the slopes of soil bunds constructed through the mangroves, as at Kolamb, Achara, Dogad, Mithbav and Mumbra.

Banerjee, Ghosh and Sastry (1998) reported *I. Pes-caprae* along the seashores and open sandy places near the river banks and estuarine islands of Godavari and Krishna delta.

Tomlinson (1986) included *I. pes-caprae* in the tropical beach community which are dispersed by sea currents and are characteristic of open coastal communities in the tropics.

Distribution of *S. portulacastrum* is uncommon in the district. It is recorded from Achara estuary only.

Species of *Najas* has been recorded from Kolamb and Kalavali estuaries.

The occurrence of *S. portulacastrum* is peculiar (Chapman, 1977). He has explained its occurrence in the transition region between the mangroves and the fresh water land plants. *S. portulacastrum* is also denoted as salt marsh plant. However, in the present study, it is recorded from mouth and mid regions also. Macnae (1968) reported the presence of *S. portulacastrum* along with the dwarf *A. marina* and *L. racemosa* towards the landward fringes. Puri and Jam (1958) observed *S. portulacastrum* at the adjacent saline areas to the mangroves. Bannerjee and Rao (1990) reported it as a salt loving plant occurring along the pioneer zones of sandy or muddy sea-beaches with high salinity. Naskar and Bakshi (1987) have reported *S. portulacastrum* from muddy river banks of the Sunderban area.

Borderline Mangroves

The distribution of border line mangroves in the Sindhudurg district is represented. It indicate that some of the species are distributed along the mangrove areas and frequently observed along the borders or on the banks.

The borderline mangroves recorded in the district are *B. racemosa, C. nuga, C. manghas, C. inerme, Derris heterophylla, D. spathecae, P. coriaceae, P. integrifolia, P. pinnata, S. persica, T. gallica, T. populnea* and *V. palida*.

These species are distributed unevenly along the estuaries and playing important role in the structure and function of the mangrove ecosystem.

B. racemosa is recorded as borderline species at the estuaries like Tarkarli, Kalavali and Achara. At Tarkarli *B. racemosa* is found very close to the *S. caseolaris* towards the landward side on drier soils. The species prefers soil with low salinity. At Kalavali the species has found in association with *A. officinalis, B. gymnorrhiza* and *A. corniculatum*.

Tomlinson (1986) have reported *B. racemosa* as abundant along tidal rivers subjected to tide and salinity. Macnae (1968) has the opinion that *B. racemosa* requires rather better drained soil than typical mangroves. In the present study *B. racemosa* has also been found in association with *E. agallocha, T. Populnea* and *C. javanicus*. Naskar and Bakshi (1987) has reported *B. racemosa* from Andaman and Nicobar Islands and Sunderbans area.

The species like *C. nuga, C. inermae, D. heterophylla, P. pinnata* and *S. persica* are commonly found along the banks in association with *A. corniculatum, B. gymnorrhiza, E. agallocha, X. granatum* and *C. iripa*.

C. manghas (*C. odollum*) is another borderline mangrove species recorded from Khavane estuary only. The species has been recorded on the landward side along with *R. apiculata, S. caseolaris, L. racemosa* and *A. aureum*. The species has been recorded with few individuals scattered on the drier soils.

Chapman (1974) has recorded *C. manghas* from the intermediate regions between the highest low water mark and lowest high water mark. He also reported it with *Rhizophora, S. acida, X. granatum* and *E. agallocha*. In India *C. manghas* has been reported from Sunderbans by Naskar and Bakshi (1987). The species is medicinally important as a purgative, narcotic and poisonous. Bannerjee and Rao (1990) reported it from Mahanadi delta and Bhittarkanika forest.

C. inerme is reported from almost all the estuaries from the district. The species is commonly occurring along the landward fringes in association with *B. gymnorrhiza, E. agallocha, A. corniculatum, S. caseolaris* and *A. ilicifolius*.

Banerjee, Ghosh and Sastry (1998) has reported on banks of creeks and channels towards brackish water zones of Krishna and Godavari delta. They have reported *C. inerme* along with *A. ilicifolius*. With the increasing level of the land and flooding. *C. inerme* found in association with *E. agallocha* and *A. ilicifolius* (Puri and Jam, 1958). *C. inerme* has also reported along the intertidal zones of creeks and channels towards back mangroves (Banerjee and Rao, 1990). Chapman (1974) stated *C. inerme* as least salinity tolerant species and can form dense thicket along edges of creeks where the water is brackish.

Dolicandron spathecae is reported from Kolamb estuary as a unique borderline species.

D. heterophylla is reported from almost all the estuaries except Khavane. The species is found as a dense colony along with *C. inerme, C. nuga* and *V. nigundo*. It is frequently found along the banks of creeks and channels in the mangrove forests. Joshi and Bhosale (1982) found it as common along the estuaries of Ratnagiri, Ganapatipule (Malgund), Deogad, Mumbra and Bhaṭye. In the present study the species has been found all along the estuaries. The species has recorded along with *R. apiculata, A. officinalis, S. alba, A. ilicifolius, E. agallocha* and *S. persia, P. coriaceae* and *P. integrifolia* are recorded from seven and three estuaries respectively on the drier soils along with *S. persica, C. inerme* and *I. pes-caprae*.

Though *T. populnea, P. pinnata* and *V. palida* are occasionally found commonly along the various estuaries in the district. Kotmire (1983) has reported the distribution of *T. populnea* at various sites along Mumbra and Deogad estuaries.

Mangrove Associates

As described earlier the mangrove associates are the other plants which have migrated from adjacent fresh water on saline habitats (Tomlinson, 1986). The species found are *A. premorsa, B. racemosa, C. inophyllum, F. ferrugenia, Flacourtia montana, Holiogarna antidysentrica, H. auriculata, Lindernia antipoda, M. elengi, N. nauchali, P. vaginatum, R. maritima, S. littoralis* and *V. nigundo.*

A. premorsa has been recorded from Nivti and Tarkarli. It is recorded as an epiphyte on *S. alba*. This is the only species of family *Orchidaceae* reported by IUCN (1983) found in the study area.

Fimbrystylis ferrugenia and *Scirpus littoralis* are the members of family *Cyperaceae* which are recorded from eight and six estuaries respectively from the district. These associates colonise rapidly after the rainy season.

The associates like *F. montana, H. antidysentrica, H. auriculata, L. antipoda, M. elengi, N. nauchali, P. vaginatum, R. marittima* are recorded from few estuaries as uncommon species.

V. nigundo has been recorded as a common associate from ten estuaries in the district.

F. montana is the uncommon associate recorded at Vijaydurg estuary in association with *C. tagal, L. racemosa, R. mucronata* and *A. ilicifolius.*

M. elengi is the typical fresh water species but at Kolamb and Kalavali estuaries it is found along the bank and can receive the tidal water at high tide. From the field observation it can tolerate low salinity.

N. nauchali is the member of family *Nypheaceae,* which is at Kalavali. It is found at the upstream region in association with *A. officinalis, K. candel* and *A. aureum.* It prefers low salinity and colonise rapidly after the rainy season. Ceratopteris is found where there is increase in fresh water inflow. It is observed at Kolamb.

Significant Observations

The mangroves of Sindhudurg district are unique in their appearance and add to the diversity of Maharashtra coast. The district harbours some of the best mangrove stands of the west coast. It also has greater diversity in borderline, halophytic and associate species.

Vijaydurg estuary is largest one, so far as water course is concerned whereas Achara is largest for diversity and area cover of the species. The total mangrove area of Achara is 153 ha (Bhosale 2002). Achara estuary has many mangrove islands with tall trees of *Rhizophora* and *Sonenratia*. The estuary harbours great diversity along with *Xylocarpus granatum* and *Cynometra iripa* (Bhosale, 2002). Monotypic stands of *Aegiceras corniculatum* and *Acanthus ilicifolius* are observed at Achara.

The presence of *B. cylindrica* is unique in the district. Sathe and Bhosale (1987) have reported *Avicennia marina* var. *resinifera* from the district, which is also confirmed during the present study.

Sonneratia caseolaris is uncommon species recorded from three estuaries of the district.

Sonneratia apetala is struggling for its survival in the district. One of the important borderline mangrove is *Cerbera manghas* which has been recorded only from Khavane estuary in the district.

The luxuriant patches of *Kandelia candel* at Tarkarli and Kalvali is also one of the unique features of mangroves in the district.

Table 1.13: Biodiversity Components of Mangroves in Relation to World

No.	Family	Genus	Number of Species/Varieties				
			World*	India	Maha	Ratn	Sind
1.	*Avicenniaceae*	*Avicennia*	8	3	2	1	2
2.	*Combretaceae*	*Lumnitzera*	2	2	1	1	1
3.	*Rhizophoraceae*	*Bruguiera* *Ceriops* *Kandelia* *Rhizophora*	6 2 1 9	4 2 1 5	2 1 1 2	1 1 1 2	2 1 1 2
4.	*Sonneratiaceae*	*Sonneratia*	5	4	3	2	3
5.	*Euphorbiaceae*	*Excoecaria*	1	1	1	1	1
6.	*Meliaceae*	*Xylocarpus*	3	3	1	1	1
7.	*Myrsinaceae*	*Aegiceras*	2	1	1	1	1
8.	*Acanthaceae*	*Acanthus*	2	2	1	1	1
9.	*Pteridaceae*	*Acrosticum*	1	1	1	1	1
10.	*Tamaricaceae*	*Tamarix*	4	4	1	1	1
11.	*Leguminoceae*	*Cynometra*	2	2	1	1	1
12.	*Apocynaceae*	*Cerbera*	2	2	1	1	1
13.	*Palmae*	*Nypa*	1	1	–	–	–
14.	*Combretaceae*	*Languncularia*	1	NR	–	–	–
15.	*Bombacaeae*	*Camptostemon*	2	NR	–	–	–
16.	*Lythraceae*	*Pemphis*	1	1	–	–	–
17.	*Myrtaceae*	*Osbornia*	1	NR	–	–	–
18.	*Pellicireaceae*	*Pelliciera*	1	NR	–	–	–
19.	*Plumbaginaceae*	*Aegialitis*	2	1	–	–	–
20.	*Rubiaceae*	*Scyphiphora*	1	1	–	–	–
21.	*Sterculiaceae*	*Heritiera*	4	3	–	–	–

* Tomlinson (1986)

Maha – Maharashtra, Ratn – Ratnagiri, Sind - Sindhudurg

C. Species Diversity Index

During the field visits the data was collected required for Diversity indices. The Simpson's Index of Species Diversity (Di) and Simpson's Index of Diversity (D) have been calculated. (Table 1.14)

Table 1.14: Simpson's Index of Species Diversity (Di) for Estuaries in the Study Area

Estuary	Index	Estuary	Index
Terekhol	7.02	Rajapur	7.24
Shiroda	5.11	Vetye	6.4
Mochemad	5.21	Purnagad	9.47
Vengurla	5.52	Pavas	5.57
Vaingani	3.34	Bhatye	9.1
Kalvi	5.72	Kalbadevi	5.62
Khavane	10.65	Are	6.58
Nivti	3.88	Kelye	5.1
Tarkarli	7.15	Malgund	5.31
Kolamb	6.64	Jaigad	5.9
Kalavali	4.99	Dabhol	9.13
Achara	10.85	Harhai	6.16
Mithbav	7.44	Savitri	10.91
Mumbra	7.22		
Deogad	5.51		
Vijaydurg	7.39		

The word diversity means variety. So the species diversity means variety of species. In a community usually relatively small number of species are abundant and a large number of species are uncommon. It is the large number of rare species that largely determine species diversity taken into consideration along with number of individuals. During the present study the number of species and number of their individuals are considered for measuring diversity of the estuary and the mangrove stands.

Simpsons Index of species Diversity (Di) for estuaries in the study area.Earlier Kurlapkar (1993) has analyzed various indices for some estuaries on the west coast of Maharashtra.

Lugo and Snedaker (1973) have given 0.4979 index of diversity for Florida mangroves. For mangroves of Chantburi and Trad in southeast Thialand the diversity index is 0.8790 (Aksornkoae, 1976) and 0.7806 (Patanaponppaiboon, 1979), respectively. The diversity for other mangroves at Thialand, like Phananga and Ranong, southern Thialand are 0.4103 to 0.7576 and 0.4330, respectively (Aksornkoae 1980, 1982).

The maximum diversity (Di) is shown by Savitri, Achara and Khavane (more than 10.0) followed by Dabhol, Bhatye and Purngad (more than 9.0), lowest being Vaingani. Table records stand diversity of species. It is helpful to know the maximum diversity spot along the estuary in question. The value near to one indicates maximum diversity and vice-versa. For instance, Achara estuary has maximum diversity index (D) as 0.923 at site No. 13 which is a mid-stream location.

Alpha and Beta diversity of the species can be analyzed by using Jaccards index of similarity (Magurran, 1988). The index has been designed to equal 1 in case of complete similarity and '0' if the plots/estuaries have no species (genera, families) in common, i.e. total dissimilarity.

The change in the species composition or assemblage of species across the area (estuary, district or macrohabitat) appear to reflect the characteristics of the macrohabitats in which they occur.

Mangroves are very sensitive to the micro and macro habitat conditions. The common occurrence of some species along the estuaries is due to similar habitat conditions and the adaptability of the species to changed conditions. The dissimilarity in the composition of large number of species is due to changing habitat conditions or their narrow range of adaptability (ecological amplitude).

It is observed in the present study that the species like *A. marina* var. *acutissima, A. officinalis, A. corniculatum, E. agallocha, R. mucronata, S. alba* and *A. ilicifolius* are more or less commonly occurring in estuaries as compared to the species like *A. marina* var. *resinifera, B. cylindrica, K. candel, S. apetala, S. caseolaris, X. granatum* and *C. iripa* which are uncommon in their occurrence and are mainly responsible to decide the alpha and beta diversity status.

Distribution and Zonation Pattern

Mangroves grow in the intertidal and sheltered places of the tropical and sub-tropical countries. Mangroves exhibit unique behavioural and ecological characters. Majority of mangroves belong to the families Rhizophoraceae, Avicenniaceae, Sonneratiaceae, Acanthaceae and Meliaceae. The species of these families are distributed at various geographically different locations as estuaries, creeks, lagoons and deltas (Kjerfve 1990).

Rao and Sastry (1974) used ecological basis for classification of mangroves. According to them the mangroves are divided into two broad groups, viz. Estuarine and proestuarine. The estuarine group is found on muddy relief under constant influence of tides and fresh water. The proestuarine group comprises of different zones like high and low salinity zones.

Certain species of mangroves dominate specific zones. This characteristic zonation in mangroves can be found all along the gradient from mean sea level to above the high water lines, along and across the bank of the estuary.

Watson (1928) has classified the mangrove vegetation of west Malaysia into five zones with respect to tidal inundations and dominant species association. According to him *Rhizophora mucronata* is dominant in class-1 which is inundated by all tides. *Sonneratia alba, Avicennia* and *R. mucronata* are prominent in class-2 which is inundated by medium high tides. *R. mucronata, Ceriops tagal, Xylocarpus, Sonneratia, Bruguiera* dominate class-3 which is inundated by normal high tides. In addition with the above species *Lumnitzera, Excoecaria* dominate class-4 which is inundated by spring tides only. In class-5 all these species are present with *Heritiera* which is inundated by equinoctial or other exceptional tides only.

Walter (1936 a, b) has stated that zonation is related to the capacity of mangroves to complete and survive in saline soils.

Macnae (1968) in his general description of mangrove vegetation differentiated six zones as Landward zone, *Ceriops* zone, *Bruguiera* zone, *Rhizophora* zone, *Avicennia* zone and *Sonneratia* zone.

Aksornkoae (1976) has observed similar zonation pattern in mangroves of southern Thialand. He found that the mangrove vegetation varies from river edge to inland sites. He also found that *Rhizophora apiculata* and *R. mucronata* are dominant along river and channel edges, whereas *Avicennia* and *Bruguiera* are found associated with *Rhizophora* to form more distinct zone. In further inland on more dry soil he found the species like *Xylocarpus, Excoecaria, Ceriops* and *Lumnitzera*. According to him *Acrostichum* is found from the defforested and degraded areas. He concluded that the zonation in mangroves is based on the amount of light or shade, degree of inundation, sediment accretion and erosion.

Percival and Womersley (1975) precisely explained zonation in mangroves of Papua New Guinea. According to them different species occupy different areas in the swamps. They stated that zonation and distribution of mangroves is controlled by interaction of tidal flooding, soil salinity and drainage of the soil. They divided mangrove swamps into six zones based on dominant tree species and tidal status. These zones are *Sonneratia* zone, *Avicennia* zone, *Rhizophora* zone, *Bruguiera* zone, *Ceriops* thickets and landward fringe. They found landward fringe is the most diverse zone with more species.

Champion and Seth (1936) and Champion and Puri (1968), on the basis of their studies in the Sunderbans divided Indian tidal forests into five types depending upon frequency of inundations, soil types, physical features and nature of vegetation.

Walter and Steiner (1936) named the zones in East African mangroves after each dominant tree, and this was further developed by Macnae (1966) to cover in general all mangrove areas.

In the present study area the mangroves are found in the prominent zones, in addition various species are also found on landward fringes. At many places like

Deogad, Mumbra, Achara and Vijaydurg the typical mangrove species are found mixed with borderline or non-exclusive species.

Plant communities and soil properties of mangrove stands along Madras coast are studied by Selvam *et al.* (1991). According to them salinity is the major factor responsible for zonation and stunted growth of *Avicennia marina*. Sathe and Bhosale (1987) concluded that *Avicennia* species are in general more tolerant to salt and organic pollution than other mangrove species.

Bunt (1996) provided definitive evidence of variety in zonation notably in the complex riverine mangroves of north eastern Australia. Bunt and Thomas (1999) extended studies to more detailed analysis. They noted that *Avicennia marina* and *Bruguiera gymnorrhiza* are two species extending over the full distance from the river mouth to its tidal limits. *A. marina* is most common in the down stream and *B. gymnorrhiza* in upstream and others at variable limits neither near mouth nor upstream.

Bunt (1999) found considerable variety in zonal expression within the mangroves of estuaries in tropical north eastern Australia. He mentioned that clarity and pattern of zonation may also be affected by overlap in species distribution.

Bunt and Bunt (1999) in their detailed analysis numerically and graphically explained that there are differences in species sequencing with the study area and to the complexities associated with overlap in species distribution. According to them the species centres of distribution across the intertidal zone are variable.

Tomlinson (1986) also elaborated that zonation in mangroves is often species specific which can be modified by local topography, tide, sediment composition and stability, and mangroves can grow along river banks or front steep shores.

Satyanarayan *et al.* (2002) have studied the zonation pattern of Coringa, Kakinada bay, East coast of India and found *Excoecaria agallocha* on landward side.

In the present study the zonation and distribution in mangroves of Ratnagiri and Sindhudurg districts is attempted.

Earlier zonation in mangroves has been attempted by many investigators (Watson, 1928; Tansley 1935; Chapman, 1944; Macnae, 1968; Warick, 1960; Joshi, 1976; Kotmire, 1983; Kotmire and Bhosale, 1985).

During the present study it is found that the species are specific to their zonation and distribution in the estuary. It is also found that species like

Avicennia, Excoecaria, Ceriops and *Acanthus* have greater ecological amplitude and found all along the banks. It is also observed that the species like *Kandelia* and *S. caeolaris* are restricted to specific zones and found at places with lot of mixing of fresh water.

The present study attempts to represent the distribution in the mangroves of study area in the form of chart diagrams as described by Bunt and Thomas (1999).

Both the districts viz. Ratnagiri and Sindhudurg, harbour some of the unique species hence district wise explanation is necessary to understand the distribution pattern.

A. Ratnagiri District

The district has thirteen estuaries and the mangrove distribution in these sites is discussed here.

Avicennia marina var *acutissima* is recorded from all the estuaries in the district. The species has greater ecological amplitude with wide range of salinity tolerance (Macnae, 1968).

The species is distributed on the banks of estuaries and channels. It is found near to the mouth where the salinity is more with tidal impact, upto the upstream and distal zones as at Bhatye Purnagad Are and Malgund estuaries. The species is surviving also on the degraded or reclaimed soils. If the protected conditions are available dense and continuous patches of *A. marina* var. *acutissima* are observed as at Kalbadevi and Rajapur. At Rajapur it is found that *Avicennia* has grown densely to form single species Island, indicating its capacity of tidal resistance. The species forms pure patches or can be found along with *Rhizophora, Sonneratia* and *Ceriops*.

Bunt and Thomas (1999) considered *Avicennia* as an indicator of zonation with wide ecological amplitude, similar observations are made during the present study.

A. marina seedlings respond variously to wave action during their plantation (Kurlapkar, 1993). He quoted that if *A. marina* seedlings planted exposed to the waves and wind, they show dwarf and slow growth. Comparatively seedlings which are planted in more elevated and sheltered areas show better growth. From these observations it is clear that the sheltered banks play an important role in establishment and growth of the mangrove though, *A. marina* is capable of tolerating the high energy tides and strong winds.

At many places the transition in the habit of *A. marina* var. *acutissima* has been observed. This habit is characteristically different than tall *A. marina* var. *acutissima* trees. Such dwarf *A. marina* are found at five sites, namely, Malgund, Bhatye, Kalbadevi, Rajapur and Pavas in large number and occupied a considerable area.

Sathe and Bhosale (1991) and Selvam *et al.* (1991) stated that the salinity is the major factor in transition of habit in *A. marina*. These dwarf *A. marina* may grow in association with *R. mucronata, S. alba* and *Acanthus* as at Bhatye, Kalbadevi, Rajapur and Pavas and can form understorey of it.

Avicennia officinalis has shown a wide range of distribution all over the estuaries in the district. It shows 100 percent distribution, indicating its broad adaptibility to various conditions. It is found at various positions in the estuary from mouth region to the upstream. It is less tolerant to tidal waves, wind and salinity. It is usually found at the proximal zone with low water salinity and tidal impact. Characteristically *A. officinalis* develops large sized boles at sheltered conditions and also show the large crab monds underneath. The species is distributed in the distal zones of the Rajiwade Karla islands of Bhatye estuary, middle and distal zones in the Chinchkheri, Narayanmali and Vechurlewadi of Bhatye estuary and Dhamdewadi of Are estuary. It is distributed along the streams in upstream region of Bhatye estuary at Nachane, Pomendipur and at Sadye village and extreme upstream of Are estuary. *A. officinalis* has been reported luxuriantly growing near the disturbed zones (Joshi and Shinde, 1978). It is stated that *A. officinalis* is distinctly more numerous near the inhabited zones where biotic and anthropogenic interference's are frequent, as seen at Vasishthi and Terekhol estuaries.

At many places *A. officinalis* shows considerable dwarf and bushy form than its normal tall life form. The dwarfism in *A. officinalis* has been found at places like Pavas and Malgund. The bushy form of *A. officinalis* is considered separately. The species is recorded from upstream region with minimal tidal impact. It is found along with *S. alba, Ceriops* etc.

Rhizophora mucronata is a wide spread species having hundred per cent occurrence in the estuaries of the district. The species is distributed prominently near mouth and middle zone of the estuary. Its frequency of occurrence decrease from mouth to upstream.

Navalkar (1956) has shown distribution of *R. mucronata* on the soil near by the sea water. Its distribution in proximal zones facing the sea are also marked by Singh *et al.* (1986) in Andaman and Nicobar mangroves. During the present study no species is found in the regions with direct exposure to high energy tidal waves. The presence of *R. mucronata* reveals some characteristics as it prominently grows along the streams, channels and on islands, where the tidal water has low waves. Some of the best stands of *R. mucronata* are recorded at Kalbadevi Bhatye and Purnagad estuaries. These stands have 6 to 8 metre tall trees with thick vegetation. After the rainy season the species forms the understorey of its own seedlings. The species is sensitive to anthropogenic interference's.

Rhizophora apiculata is less widely spread species as compared to *R. mucronata*. It has been recorded from nine estuaries. It is found in the middle part of the estuary. During the present study *R. apiculata* is found as isolated patches. The best performance of the species is recorded at Chinchkheri region in Bhatye estuary. The stand is very old and with luxurient trees of *R. apiculata*. The isolated individuals of the species along with *R. mucronata* are recorded from Purnagad, Rajapur and Jaigad estuaries.

A. corniculatum and *C. tagal* are distributed at distal and middle zones of mangrove vegetation like the *E. agallocha* these are also distributed near the mouth region if the area is sheltered and not flooded daily. Both the species with higher densities are recorded at Rajapur, Bhatye, Kalbadevi and Jaigad estuaries. The dominant patches of *C. tagal* are recorded at Adi region of Kalbadevi estuary. It is also remarkably distributed on the Islands of upstream region of Are estuary, along with *A. corniculatum*. At some sites it is also found along with *R. mucronata, K. candel* and *S. alba*.

K. candel is uncommon in the district and recorded from three estuaries as Bhatye Rajapur, Purnagad and Dabhol. *Kandelia* prefers the site beyond the middle part of the estuaries towards the upstream region. It is found along the banks of small channels with soft and muddy substratum, along with *R. mucronata* and *C. tagal*. It is found very sensitive to anthropogenic pressures.

Bruguiera gymnorrhiza is another rare species in the district and recorded from five estuaries, as Rajapur, Purnagad, Malgund, Jaigad and Dabhol. It is found as the landward fringe or proximal zones on drier soils which are inundated by normal tides. Macnae (1968) described its presence in inland region with drier soils along with *Avicennia, Xylocarpus* and *Excoecaria*. Percival and Womersely (1975) has made similar observations. In the present study it is found along with *Xylocarpus, Avicennia* and *Cynometra*. Bunt and Thomas (1999) has described its presence from mouth to tidal limits, which is not observed in the present study.

S. alba is the common species recorded from all the estuaries in the district. Present study has recorded many favourbale localities for *S. alba* from many estuaries. The species prefers protected areas. The most favourable sites for this species are shallow basins where water enters and receds slowly. This calm water encourages the accumulation, spreading and resting of *S. alba* seeds on such areas. These sites are also rich in the litter content and have high capacity of nutrient cycling. The monogenic stands of *S. alba* are found at different locations.

S. apetala is less common species recorded from five localities. It prefers zones flooded by normal high tides. The species with few individuals is recorded at Purnagad, Malgund and Vetye where it is disappearing fast.

Interestingly another unique *Sonneratia* species *S. caseolaris* has not been found in the district.

A. corniculatum is the another common species recorded from all the estuaries present in the district. It is distributed at the distal and middle zones. Well grown patches are found at Bhatye and Purnagad. The species has wide range of association as with *Ceriops, Acanthus, Lumnitzera* and *Avicennia*.

L. racemosa is another second order dominant species recorded from ten estuaries. It is found distributed in the middle and distal zones. It prefers elevated areas along the banks with drier soils where the substratum is sandy with less gravel content. It is found in association with *Ceriops* and *Aegiceras*. Some of the well grown isolated patches of *Lumnitzera* are found at Pavas, Are and Kalbadevi estuaries. At estuaries like Vetye and Purnagad the full grown stands of *Lumnitzera* are disappearing due to land reclaimation.

Xylocarpus granatum is another uncommon and unique species recorded from two estuaries namely Purnagad and Jaigad in Ratnagiri district. It prefers middle and distal zones with drier soils, It is in association with *Bruguiera, R. apiculata, E. agallocha, A. corniculatum, K. candel* and *P. pinnata*.

Bannerjee and Rao (1990) found it as a member along the intertidal zones of Orissa coast. Singh and Garge (1993) recorded it form Andaman Islands on muddy habitat at middle and landward shore. Naskar and Bakshi (1987) found it on the river banks and on the sides of the creeks at Sunderbans.

Tamarix gallica is a non-exclusive (trans grass) species recorded only from Purnagad estuary. The species is recorded from the upstream distal zones where the salinity is slow with less tidal impact. The species has been recorded almost 15 kms from mouth region as the pioneering on newly formed Island. It is found associated with some *Cyperaceae* members.

Excoecaria agallocha is recorded from all the estuaries in the district as a common species. *A. aureum* is the brackish water Fern recorded from three estuaries as Are, Dabhol and Savitri. It is found at the upstream region on drier soil. Its association with *Acanthus* is more common.

Acanthus ilicifolius is common species recorded from all the sites. It is growing on variety of soil conditions. It has wide ecological amplitude and grows in association with almost all the other mangroves.

B. Sindhudurg District

The distribution pattern in the mangroves of Sindhudurg district has been explained here.

A. marina var. *acutissima* is the most widely spread species in the district recorded from the 15 estuaries. It is the most adaptive species with a wide range of salinity tolerance (Macnae, 1968). In many sites the species is found at various locations in the estuary, indicating its greater ecological amplitude. The species exhibit a wide range of habitat tolerance. In Sindhudurg district the species is recorded from all the estuaries except Deogad. Similar observations are made by Kotmire and Bhosale (1985). Interestingly the species is recorded from Mumbra estuary which is very close to Deogad. At many sites as Tarkarli, Kolamb the species is growing as a pioneering species along with *P. coarctata* on newly formed islands. The species shows a wide association with other species. It is found in association with *A. ilifolius, R. mucronata, S. alba, A. corniculatum* and *A. aureum.*

Avicennia marina (dwarf) is recorded in 10 estuaries as at Terekhol, Vangurla, Mochemad, Vaingani, Nivti, Kolamb, Kalavali, Achara, Mumbra and Vijaydurg. The species has occupied more area as compared to Ratnagiri district.

Avicennia alba is recorded from 5 estuaries in the district as Vengurla, Mochemad, Vaingani, Nivti and Kolamb . The species found in association with *A. officinalis, A. marina, S. alba, E. agallocha,* etc. The species forms stands following *A. officinalis* and *A. marina* var. *acutissima.* Banerjee and Rao (1990) and Singh and Garge (1993).

Avicennia officinalis is recorded from all the 16 estuaries from the district. It is the widely occurring species in the district. The species is found from lower polyhaline (McLusky, 1974) zones. *A. officinalis* is found in association with *R. mucronata, R. apiculata, S. alba, A. ilicifolius, A. corniculatum, L. racemosa* and *C. tagal.* The species prefers low tidal impact with slowly rising waters. At the estuaries like Kalavali, Terekhol and Vijaydurg. The species has occupied larger areas. Kotmire and Bhosale (1985) reported 40% extent of *A. officinalis* at Deogad attaining height of 7-8 m. Similar observations are made during the present study.

Avicennia officinalis (dwarf) is recorded from Kalvali and Achara . It is found associated with *A. marina, S. alba, A. corniculatum* and *C. tagal.*

Avicennia marina var. *resinifera* is the unique *Aviceniia* species recorded during the present study. Sathe and Bhosale (1987) have reported it for the first time from (Revtale) Kolamb . The species is recorded from the upstream region.

Rhizophora mucronata is recorded from all the 16 estuaries in the district. It is the wide spread species occupying larger areas, the luxuriantly grown pockets are present at Achara, Kolamb, Vijaydurg, Mumbra and Deogad. The species is recorded as frontline mangrove facing the direct tidal currents with deep muddy soil.

R. apiculata is another species of *Rhizophora* recorded from 8 estuaries in the Sindhudurg district.

Ceriops tagal is recorded from 10 estuaries in the district. It is spread in polyhaline and Mesohaline zones. Sometimes the species is found near the mouth region. The species shows wide associations with other species such as *S. alba, R. mucronata, A. officinalis, A. marina, A. corniculatum* and *A. ilicifolius.*

Well grown plants of *C. tagal* in Sindhudurg district are observed at Tarkarli, Achara, Mumbra, Deogad and Vijaydurg estuaries. The tall plants upto 7 m are found at Danda site of Vijaydurg estuary.

K. candel is recorded from 7 estuaries in the district.

B. gymnorrhiza is another uncommon species recorded from 6 estuaries in the district. The species is found to be growing in the proximal zones in middle and upstream parts of the estuary, inundated by normal tides.

B. cylindrica is the uncommon species recorded from only one estuary Vengurla.

S. alba is the common mangrove recorded from 15 estuaries in the district. Well grown *S. alba* stands are observed at Kolamb, Achara and Vijaydurg. The species has developed into pure patches at Achara. It is commonly found associated with *R. mucronata, R. apiculata, A. officinalis, A. corniculatum* and *A. marina*.

S. apetala is a less common species recorded from 3 estuaries in the district as Terekhol, Achara and Mumbra. The species is distributed in the distal zones. It is found as countable individuals distributed along the water channels. At Mumbra there is large pocket of *S. apetala* which is presently found in the form of stumps because of cutting of trees. The boles show girth upto 3 m.

S. caseolaris is yet another uncommon species recorded from only three localities among the estuaries from study area. These are Terekhol, Tarkarli and Khavane . The species has a narrow ecological amplitude and perhaps depends on tidal amplitude (Bhosale and Mulik, 1995). The species is found in oligohaline zone along the banks toward the landward side with low salinity and less tidal action. If it is exposed to higher salinity the growth is stunted (Wells, 1982).

A. corniculatum is a common species recorded from 14 estuaries in the district. It is growing in the distal and middle zones. At the distal zones where the water receds slowly the species has developed pure patches as at Achara. Well grown *Aegiceras* stands are also found at Terekhol, Kalavali and Vijaydurg. The species shows associations with *C. tagal, L. racemosa* and *S. alba*.

L. racemosa is one of the uncommon mangroves found from 4 estuaries in the district, *Lumnitzera* has attained a height of 4 to 5 m. It is found in association with *Rhizophora, Ceriops, Sonneratia, Acanthus, Avicennia* and *Aegiceras*.

A. Ilicifolius is the most common species recorded from all the 16 estuaries in the district. A. ilicifolius *is found associated with Sonneratia, Rhizophora, Avicennia, Aegiceras, Excoecaria and Kandelia.*

E. agallocha is recorded from all the 16 estuaries in the district.

X. granatum is the unique species recorded from 2 estuaries in the district. as Achara and Vijaydurg. *X. granatum* is found distributed at different sites in the estuary. At Achara it is found in the middle as well as at the distal zone with drier soils and at Vijaydurg it is found in deep muddy soil. It prefers landward side with less tidal impact. The species is found along with other mangroves such as *Rhizophora, Bruguiera* and *Cynometra* and at Vijaydurg it is associated with *Avicennia* and *Sonneratia. Bruguiera* and *Cynometra* are common associates of the species.

C. iripa is another threatened mangrove species found from 3 estuaries in the district, as Mithbav, Achara and Kalavali . The species recorded from middle zone at Mithbav and at distal zones at Achara and Kalavali. The species prefers calm banks with little water movement. It is found associated with *Bruguiera, Ceriops, Xylocarpus* and *Rhizophora.*

A. aureum is the mangrove fern recorded from 6 estuaries. It is found in the brackish water with greater fresh water in flow. It forms as an understorey of *Avicennia,* and also found in association with *Acanthus, Ceriops* and *Aegiceras.*

C. manghas is recorded only from Khavane estuary. It is considered as non-exclusive species. It is recorded in the middle landward fringe without daily inundations. It is found along with *L. racemosa, C. tagal, S. caseolaris, A. corniculatum, R. apiculata* and *A. aureum.*

The mangroves along the coast of state of Maharashtra are distributed in five districts as Sindhudurg, Ratnagiri, Raigad, Thane and Mumbai. Mangroves all along these districts show variations in the distribution of the species. The variation is not only recorded in typical mangroves but also in their associate and halophytic species.

The species like *A. marina* var. *acutissima, A. officinalis, R. mucronata, S. alba, A. corniculatum, L. racemosa, E. agallocha and A. ilicifolius* are common to all the districts.

The species like *A. alba* and *A. marina* var. *resinifera* show restricted distribution. The later species has been recorded only from sindhudurg district. The species like *B. gymnorrhiza* and *B. cylindrica* show variable distribution *B. gymnorrhiza* is found common in the Sindhudurg and Ratnagiri district it has not been recorded from other districts. *B. cylindrica* shows its common occurrence in Raigad, Thane and Mumbai region, but is uncommon in Sindhudurg districts and not found in Ratnagiri district.

The distribution of genus *Sonneratia* is unique in the state. *S. alba* is dominant in Ratnagiri and Sindhudurg district have limited occurrence in other districts, similarly *S. apetala* is dominant in Raigad, Thane and Mumbai and restricted in Sindhudurg and Ratnagiri district. The species like *S. caseolaris* has restricted distribution in Sindhudurg district it is not found in other districts so far.

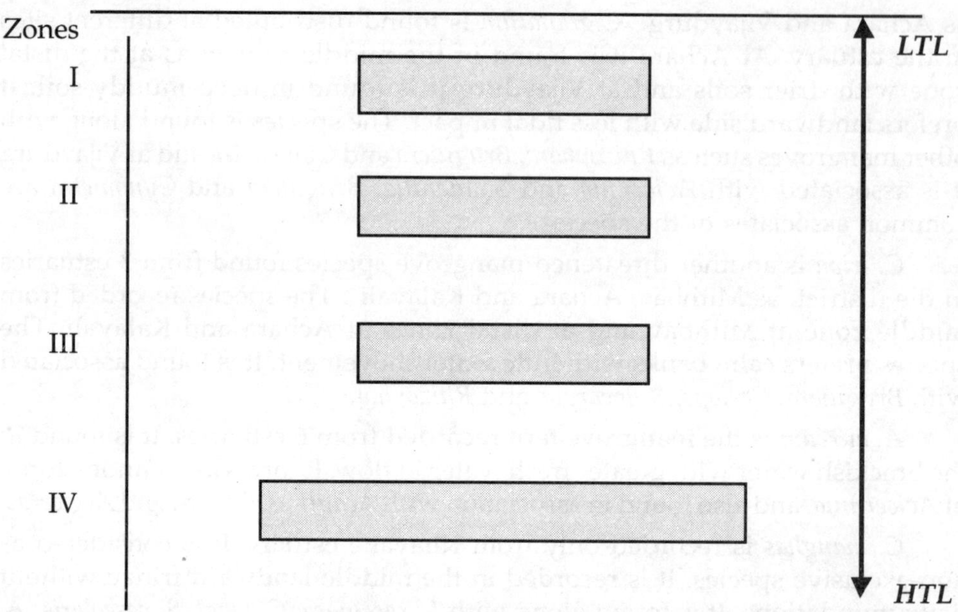

Fig. 1.2: Zonation Pattern in General, Observed in Study Area

Zones:

I - *R. mucronata/S. alba/A. marina*

II - *A. officinalis/B. cylindrica/E. agallocha/C. tagal*

III - *B. gymnorrhiza/A. officinalis/S. apetala/S. caseolaris*

IV - Borderline species like *Salvadora/C. inerme/C. nuga/D. heterophylla*

L. racemosa is comparatively common in Ratnagiri and few estuaries in Sindhudurg district found uncommon in Raigad, Thane and Mumbai regions.

The species like *X. granatum* has restricted distribution in Sindhudurg and Ratnagiri district and not reported in other districts so far. Species like *T. gallica,* is recorded from only Sindhudurg district, which is not found in other districts.

Mangrove associates are also distributed distinctly all along the coast of Maharashtra.

Species like *S. persica, C. inerme, A. lagopoides, S. portulacastrum, I. Pes-caprae, D. heterophylla, P. pinnata, T. populnea* are recorded from all the five districts. The species like *S. fruticosa* is recorded only from Thane and Mumbai region and not from remaining district. The species like *H. antidysentrica, C. spinosa, P. coarctata* and *H. beccarii* are recorded from some sites only.

Table 1.15: Comparison with Other Districts

Distribution of Mangroves in Five Districts of Maharashtra

Sl. No.	Name of Species	Sindhudurg	Ratnagiri	Raigad	Mumbai and Thane
1.	*Avicennia marina* var. *acutissima* Staf. & Mold.	+	+	+	+
2.	*Avicennia marina* var. *resinifera.* Forsk. Bakh.	+	–	–	–
3.	*Avicennia officinalis* L.	+	+	+	+
4.	*Avicennia alba* Blume.	+	+	–	–
5.	*Avicennia marina* (dwarf) Forsk. Bakh.	+	+	+	+
6.	*Avicennia officinalis* (dwarf) L.	+	+	+	+
7.	*Rhizophora mucronata* Lamk.	+	+	+	+
8.	*Rhizophora apiculata* Blume	+	+	+	+
9.	*Ceriops tagal* (Petr.) Robin.	+	+	+	+
10.	*Kandelia candel* (L) Druce.	+	+	+	+
11.	*Bruguiera gymnorrhiza* (L.) Lamk.	+	+	–	–
12.	*Bruguiera cylindrica* (L.) Blume.	+	–	+	+
13.	*Sonneratia alba* J. Sm.	+	+	+	+
14.	*Sonneratia apetala* Buch. Ham.	+	+	+	+
15.	*Sonneratia caseolaris* (L) Engl.	+	–	–	–
16.	*Aegiceras corniculatum* (L.) Blanco.	+	+	+	+
17.	*Lumnitzera racemosa* Wild.	+	+	+	+
18.	*Xylocarpus granatum* koen.	+	+	–	-
19.	*Excoecaria agallocha* Linn	+	+	+	+
20.	*Cynometra iripa* L.	+	+	-	-
21.	*Tamarix gallica* Hole	–	+	-	-
22.	*Cerbera manghas* Gaerth.	+	–	–	–
23.	*Acanthus ilicifolius*	+	+	+	+
24.	*Acrostichum aureum* L.	+	+	–	–

Table 1.16: Distribution of Mangrove Associates and Halophytes in Five Districts of Maharashtra

Sl. No.	Name of Species	Sindhudurg	Ratnagiri	Raigad	Mumbai and Thane
1.	*Salvadora persica*	+	+	+	+
2.	*Clerodendrum inerme*	+	+	+	+
3.	*Aleuropus lagopoides*	+	+	+	+
4.	*Cyperus rotundus*	+	+	+	+
5.	*Sesuvium portulacastrum*	+	+	+	+
6.	*Caesalpinia nuda*	+	+	+	+
7.	*Ipomea pes-caprae*	+	+	+	+
8.	*Derris heterophylla*	+	+	+	+
9.	*Pongamia pinnata*	+	+	+	+
10.	*Sueda fruticosa*	–	–	–	+
11.	*Thespesia populnea*	+	+	+	+
12.	*Hygrophila antidysentrica*	–	–	+	–
13.	*Cateregum spinosa*	–	+	–	–
14.	*Porteresia coarctata*	+	+	–	–
15.	*Halophila beccarii*	+	+	–	–

The study reveals that the spread of the species requires favourable habitat, there should not be any disturbance which can lead to elimination of the species or change in zonation pattern.

Flowering Phenology (Functional Diversity)

It is clear from the present study that the mangroves are threatened. They are exposed to severe anthropogenic pressure, due to which some of the species are becoming rare and extinct. To save the mangroves, regeneration is one of the ways to maintain the vegetation. It is important to know the time of flowering and fruiting or propagule development period so as to obtain seeding. This type of study is also helpful for afforestation techniques, plant management, honey analysis, floral biology and estimation of reproductive capacity. The mangroves exhibit an unique reproductive behaviour or flowering and fruiting pattern mainly governed by tidal amplitude and latitude, amongst various factors such as soil, temperature, salinity, inundations etc.

One of important environmental factor controlling the flowering is daily air temperature (Arnold, 1960, Baskerville and Emin, 1969). It may be due to an additional climatic parameters, such as solar radiation's (Caprio, 1971, 1974). The flowering initiation in mangroves is depends on the age of the plant (Bhosale and Mulik, 1991).

In the present study an attempt has been made to study the flowering and fruiting pattern in some species of mangroves (Table 1.17). The species studied from two sites, namely, Kolamb and Kalavali are discussed in following page. Repeated visits were payed to collect the data.

The flowering takes place sequentially from the phases like initiation, budding, blooming, fruiting and seed/propagule development.

It is observed that most of the species start the early stages in the early summer season. Similar, observations are made by (Jones, 1971, Graham et. al. 1975 and Saenger, 1982). The central Queensland mangroves show flowering in summer months (Saenger, 1982). Jagtap (1985) has studied the mangrove Phenology of Goa coast.

Members of family *Rhizophoraceae* show flowering throughout the year (Bhosale and Mulik, 1987, 1995)

Gill and Tomlinson, (1969) reported that in *R. mucronata* the flower primordia develop on the young plant when it is about four years old. However, Kulkarni and Bhosale (1992) reported that the propagules of *R. mucronata* planted to field can flower after completion of two years of its age. The initiation in *R. mucronata* is recorded during the month of December. The initiation is followed by budding. In the beginning the budding is slow and increases in April and May. The flowering starts from July to August and full Blooming is observed during September to November. The propagule development starts from December and continues upto March. These propagules are matured upto May to June. During this period the mature propagules show yellow separation zone at the junction of propagule and Fruit. This is the best time of collecting the propagules for plantation. The average size of the mature propagule is recorded as 55.48 cm long and 6.4 cm in girth.

C. tagal is another member of *Rhizophoraceae*. Flower initiation starts during April and continues upto August. It is followed by budding. The budding continues from early may to September. It is interesting to observe the flowering in *C. tagal* through out the year but blooming is found during September to October. Fruiting in the species starts from March. Heavy fruiting is observed from April to June. The mature propagules are recorded during June upto August. The time period from bud to mature propagule is more than twelve months. From these observations it is evident that in *Ceriops* budding, blooming and fruiting occur all around the year and the phenophases are continued in the cycle. The size of the mature propagule is recorded as 29 cm long and 2.95 cm in girth.

K. candel shows initiation from December and continues upto February. The second phase start in August, which continue upto September. The full Blooming is seen during February and March. The propagule development takes place from September upto June of next year. The propagule mature in June-July. The average size of mature propagule is 28 cm long and 4.65 cm in girth.

Table 1.17: Different Phenophases in Some Mangroves of Selected Localities

Species	Duration of the Phenophase											
	Jan.	Feb.	March	Apr.	May	June	July	Aug.	Sept.	Oct.	Nov.	Dec.
Rhizophora mucronata	I, Fr	I, Fr	I, B,P	B, D	B, P	B, P	P	P	B1	B1	B1	I, Fr
Ceriops tagal	Fr	Fr		I,	I	I, B	I,B	I,B	B,B1	B1	B1	B1
Kandelia candel	I	I, Bl	B1	B1	Fr	Fr		I	I			I
Sonneratia alba	I, B, Bl	I, B, B1	B, B1	B, B1, Fr	I, B, Fr	I, B, B1	B1	B1	B1			I
Avicennia officinalis	I	I, B	B	B	B, B1	B1, Fr	B1, Fr	Fr	Fr			
Avicennia marina var. *acutissima*	I	I, B	I, B, B1 Fr	I, B1, Fr	B1, Fr	Fr	Fr	Fr	Fr		I	I
Avicennia marina var. *Resinifera*		I	I, B	B, B1	B1	B1	Fr	Fr				
Excoecaria agallocha												
Male			I	B	B, B1	B1	Fr	Fr	Fr			
Female				I, B	B, B1	B1	Fr	Fr	Fr	I	I	
Aegiceras corniculatum	B	B, B1	B1, Fr	B1, Fr	Fr	Fr	Fr				I	B
Acanthus ilicifolius	I, B	B, B1	B, B1	B1, Fr	Fr	Fr	Fr					I
Cynometra iripa	Fr	Fr	Fr	Fr	I, Fr	I, Fr	I, B, Fr	I, B	B, B1	B1, Fr	B1,Fr	Fr

Legends – I - Initiation, B - Budding
B1 - Blooming, Fr - Fruiting
P - Viviparous propagule

S. alba shows Floral initiation in the December which continues to February and again in June and July. The budding starts from January up to August. Flowering starts from January and continues upto october. The fruits are developed in May and June, and continue upto October – November. The average size of mature Fruit is 7.68 cm in height (without style) and 15 cm of girth.

A. officinalis shows initiation From January and February. It is followed by budding which is during February and continues upto May. Flowering begins in March and extend upto July. The full blooming is during April and May. The fruit formation takes place in may to June. Maturation is in June – July. The mature fruit size is recorded as 3.7 cm long and 6.96 cm. broad (maximum breadth).

A. marina var. *resinifera* shows late initiation than *A. Officinalis* and *A. marina* var. *acutissima* . The initiation is in early February. It is followed by budding which continues upto April. Flowering starts from April. Blooming is recorded from May to June. Fruiting starts from July upto August – September. The size of mature propagule is 2.41 cm long and 1.43 broad.

E. agallocha is a diocecious tree. The budding in male plant occurs during March and blooming occurs in June–July. In female plant budding starts in April and May and blooming is recorded in May and June. Fruiting starts from July and August. The mature seeds are formed in August – September.

A. corniculatum is a much branched shrub. It shows initiation during September–October and ends in early November. Budding is seen in November which continues upto February. It starts blooming in December upto April. The propagule development starts between May to July. The mature cryptoviviparaus seedling develop in July. The mature propagule is about 5.73 cm long and 2cm in girth.

A. illicifolius shows initiation in December and January, it is followed by budding in January upto March. Blooming is found in March continues upto May.

Fruits are produced from April upto July. Matured Fruits are developed From June to end of July are released in July.

C. iripa recorded at Kalavali starts initiation from June, it is followed by budding which continues from July to September. The flowering starts in September which is heavy (blooming) in October. Fruiting starts in October and continues upto May. The mature fruits are recorded during June and July.

Such type of phenological studies are not only useful for the regeneration, but it also has impact on litterfall content. Ahmad (1999) found that the reproductive period in *A. marina* extends from April to October contributing to litter fall. He also pointed out that increase in the litterfall is recorded prior to the start of reproductive cycle and at the end of summer. Bhosale (1983) had given the adaptive strategies in mangroves. Bhosale and Mulik (1995) have reported phenology of mangroves along Ratnagiri coast. The present attempt is for the first time for Sindhudurg district.

The present report differs from that for Ratnagiri because of latitudinal differences. It is observed that flowering is delayed from lower to upper latitude. The period of delay depends upon the distance between two locations.

Height and Girth Analysis

There is scanty literature available on the relationship of girth of the tree with its height. On several occasions the girth and/or height of mangroves are recorded, however, for any specific site such records are not available. This is true also for canopy cover. Nevertheless, there is one report (Bhosale, 2002) of canopy records for mangroves in Maharashtra. In the present study the records of girth, height and canopy area were made with the view to know co-relation between either height or girth with canopy cover. The results are presented in Tables from 4.26 to 4.33. From the study area only one estuary was selected i.e. Kolamb as an example *K. candel* is available only at Kalavali.

One can expect positive co-relation between girth and canopy cover. Similarly it can be felt that girth and height are universally proportional, however the data presented in the Tables indicate that in eight species studied there is co-relation between girth and canopy cover except *Avicennia officinalus* and *Aegiceras corniculatum*. In case of *Sonneratia alba* the value of 'r' for girth and height is higher (0.61). Some of the species show distinct co-relation (*Kandelia candel*) between girth and canopy cover. In others there is narrow difference in value of 'r'.

Kurlapkar and Bhosale (1985) have given the average canopy diameter for some mangroves from Ratnagiri district. They have attempted the study in *Rhizophora apiculata*.

Ramchandran, *et al.* (1985) has given the height of some mangrove species from Kerala. He has recorded 4-6 m height for *Rhizophora mucronata*, 2-3 m height for *Kandelia candel*, 3-5 m for *Aegiceras corniculatum*, 2-4 m for *Avicennia marina*, 6-8 m for *Avicennia officinalus*, respectively. In the present study similar range of height has been recorded for these species.

The Tables 1.18 to 1.25 record values for girth, height and canopy cover as well as for correlation coefficient (r). There correlation between girth and canopy in all the species studied however in case of *A. officinalis* and *A. corniculatum* girth and height show more co-relation than girth and C. cover. The positive co-relation observed between girth and canopy is more or less 0.7 except *A. marina* (dwarf) *E. agallocha* and *A. corniculatum*. The co-relation is observed in girth and height is difficult to explain. This case is observed in *A. officinalis* and *A. corniculatum*. The only inference drawn can be, the growth is proceeding in two directions, vertical and horizontal. It is felt that mature (old) individuals may not add much to the height but can increase in the girth and produce more branches in the canopy.

Table 1.18: Height, Girth and Canopy Cover in *A. marina* var *acutissima*. (Sample size : random 50)

Value	Girth (m)	Height (m)	Canopy Cover (m²)
Lowest	0.56	5.71	2.86
Highest	2.42	18.2	49.74
Average	1.05	17.42	17.41

Correlation coefficient (r) between:

1. Girth and height = 0.5495
2. Height and canopy cover = 0.3969
3. Girth and canopy cover = **0.6731**

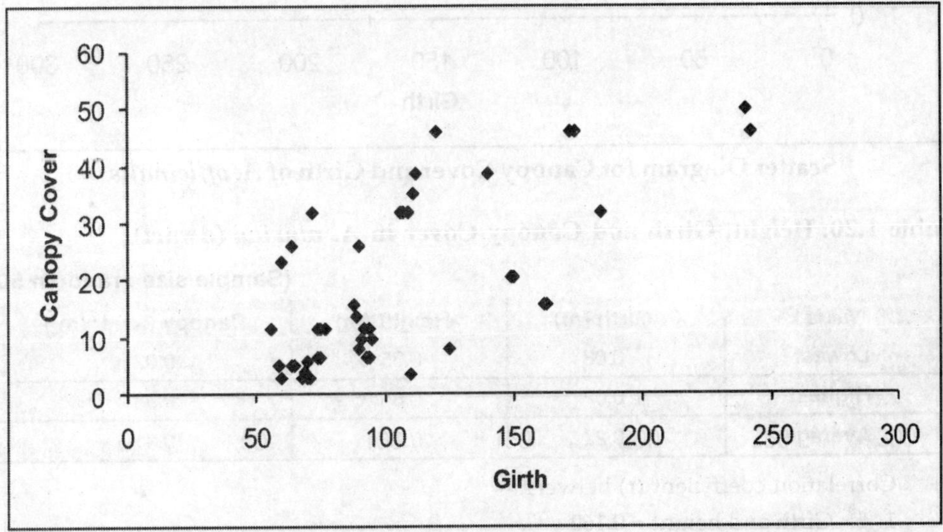

Scatter Diagram for Canopy Cover and Girth of *A. marina* var. *acutissima*

Table 1.19: Height, Girth and Canopy Cover in *A. officinalis*.

(Sample size : random 50)

Value	Girth (m)	Height (m)	Canopy Cover (m²)
Lowest	0.72	6	2.96
Highest	2.5	15.8	28.83
Average	1.24	9.02	9.85

Correlation coefficient (r) between:

1. Girth and height = **0.8279**
2. Height and canopy cover = 0.4666
3. Girth and canopy cover = **0.7335**

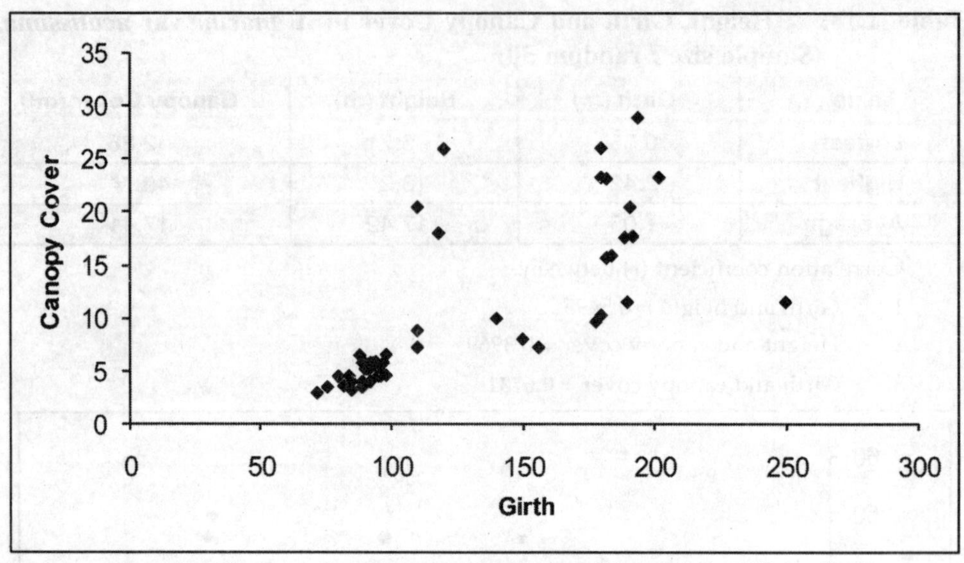

Scatter Diagram for Canopy Cover and Girth of *A. officinalis*

Table 1.20: Height, Girth and Canopy Cover in *A. marina* (dwarf)

(Sample size : random 50)

Value	Girth (m)	Height (m)	Canopy Cover (m^2)
Lowest	0.08	0.35	0.02
Highest	0.62	1.8	0.98
Average	0.22	0.72	0.31

Correlation coefficient (r) between:

1. Girth and height = 0.162
2. Height and canopy cover = 0.06
3. Girth and canopy cover = 0.57

Table 1.21: Height, Girth and Canopy cover in *Rhizophora mucronata*

(Sample size : random 50)

Value	Girth (m)	Height (m)	Canopy Cover (m^2)
Lowest	0.12	3	0.32
Highest	1.4	14.71	49.44
Average	0.38	7.63	7.53

Correlation coefficient (r) between:

1. Girth and height = 0.583
2. Height and canopy cover = 0.432
3. Girth and canopy cover = **0.723**

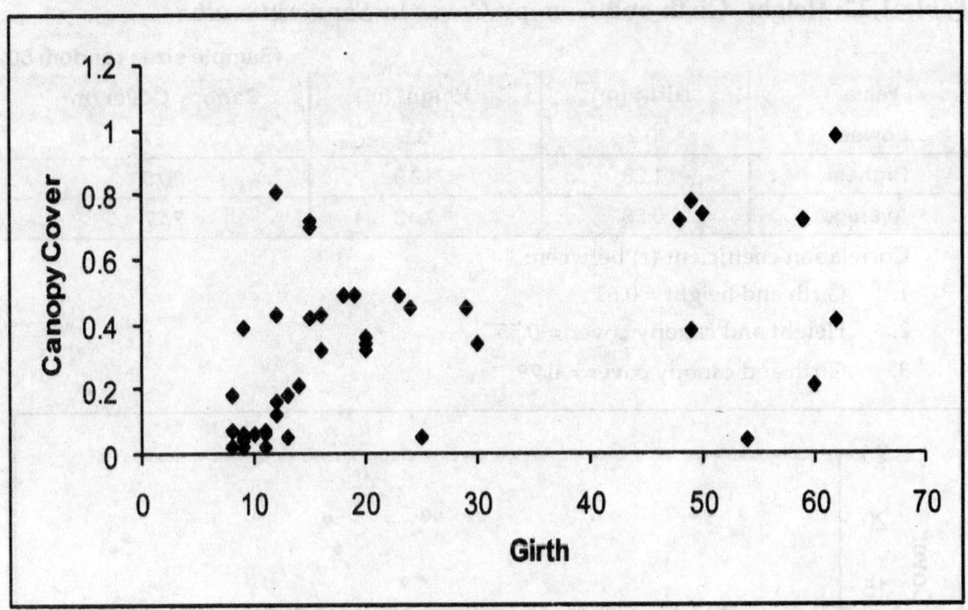

Scatter Diagram for Canopy Cover and Girth of *A. marina* (dwarf)

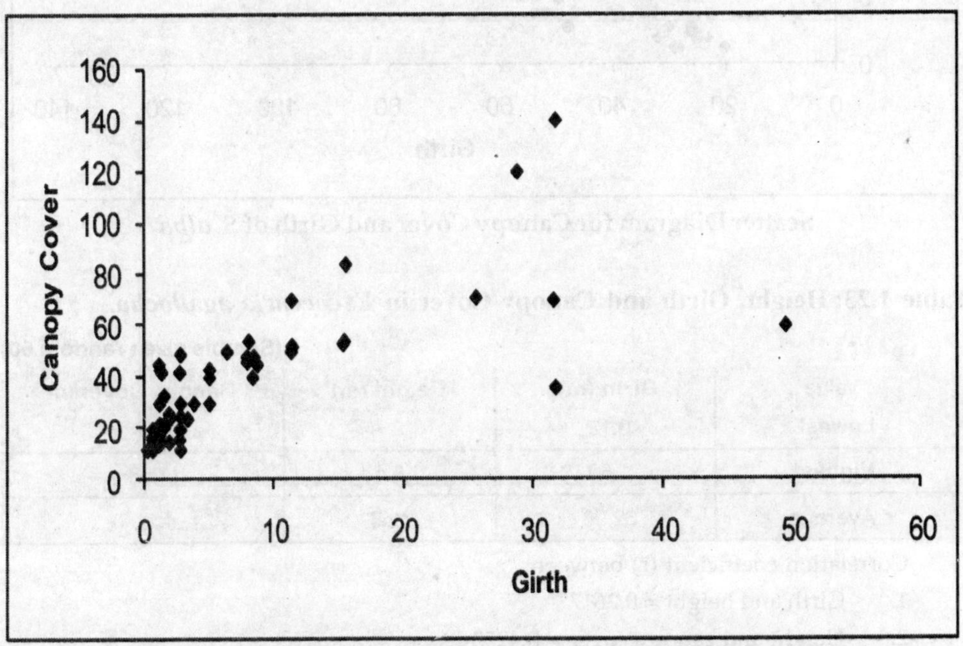

Scatter Diagram for Canopy Cover and Girth of *R. mucronata*

Table 1.22: Height, Girth and Canopy Cover in *Sonneratia alba*

(Sample size : random 50)

Value	Girth (m)	Height (m)	Canopy Cover (m^2)
Lowest	0.2	3.5	1.27
Highest	1.28	12.9	20.5
Average	0.58	7.13	7.77

Correlation coefficient (r) between:

1. Girth and height = 0.61
2. Height and canopy cover = 0.55
3. Girth and canopy cover = **0.79**

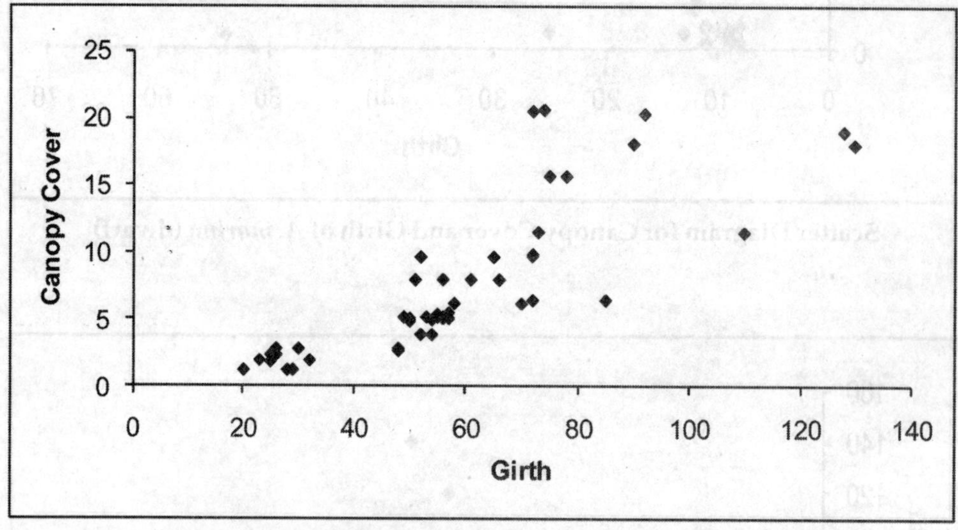

Scatter Diagram for Canopy Cover and Girth of *S. alba*

Table 1.23: Height, Girth and Canopy Cover in *Excoecaria agallocha.*

(Sample size : random 50)

Value	Girth (m)	Height (m)	Canopy Cover (m^2)
Lowest	0.12	2.7	1.27
Highest	1.60	6.4	11.58
Average	62.96	4.63	4.11

Correlation coefficient (r) between:

1. Girth and height = 0.2617
2. Height and canopy cover = 0.4253
3. Girth and canopy cover = **0.6113**

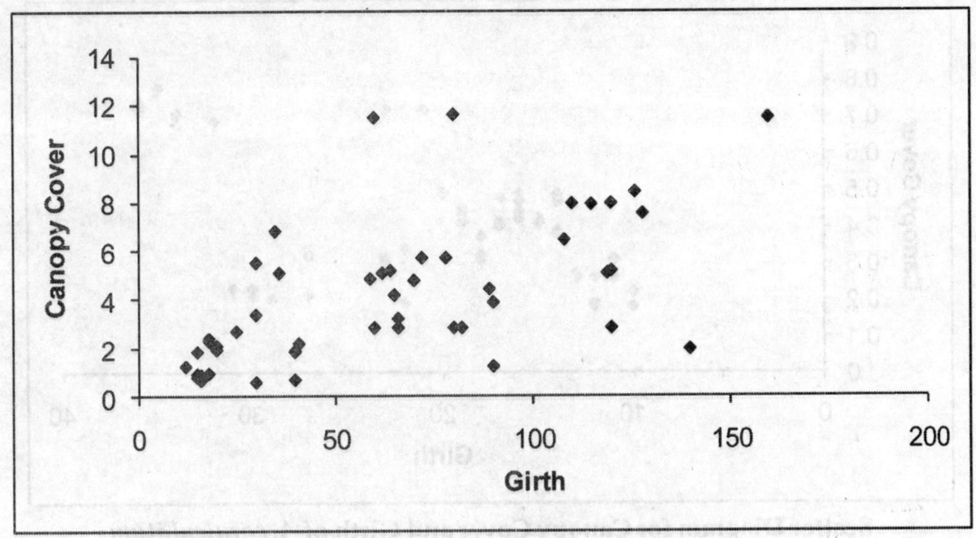

Scatter Diagram for Canopy Cover and Girth of *E. agallocha*

Table 1.24: Height, Girth and Canopy Cover in *A. corniculatum*

(Sample size : random 50)

Value	Girth (m)	Height (m)	Canopy cover (m^2)
Lowest	0.11	1.10	0.18
Highest	0.36	2.62	0.78
Average	0.21	1.71	0.41

Correlation coefficient (r) between:

1. Girth and height = 0.6113
2. Height and canopy cover = 0.5053
3. Girth and canopy cover = 0.5069

Table 1.25: Height, Girth and Canopy Cover in *Kandelia candel*

(Sample size : random 50)

Value	Girth (m)	Height (m)	Canopy Cover (m^2)
Lowest	0.2	1.05	0.28
Highest	1.32	4.8	5.85
Average	0.62	3.26	1.96

* From Kalavali estuary

Correlation coefficient (r) between:

1. Girth and height = 0.4629
2. Height and canopy cover = 0.3764
3. Girth and canopy cover = **0.7101**

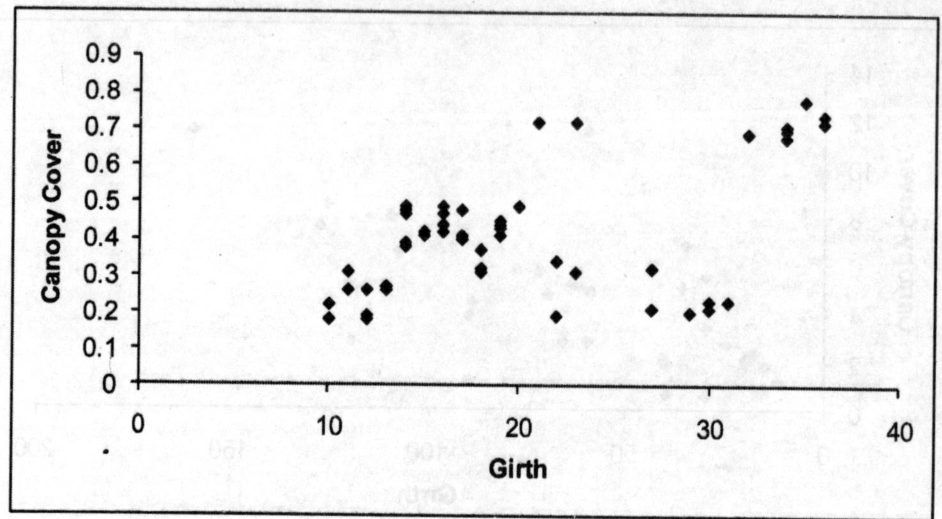

Scatter Diagram for Canopy Cover and Girth of *A. corniculatum*

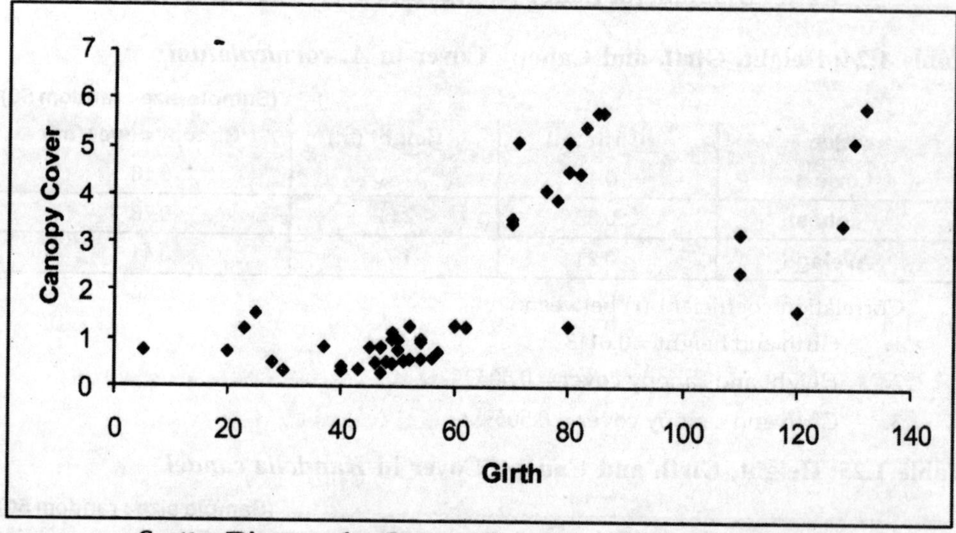

Scatter Diagram for Canopy Cover and Girth of *K. candel*

Mangrove Soil

According to Vannucci (1989) Mangrove soils, are of key importance to the functioning of the system. For the mangroves the major limiting habitat factor is the nature of substratum along with the tidal inundations. The growth of any plant is governed by two groups of habitat conditions, the above ground climatic factors and the edaphic factors. In general the loose, more aerated soil promotes profuse growth of root system whereas compact soil restricts root growth. The physico chemical properties of the soil determine the growth and development of root system which inturn reflects in shoot growth. Hence it is necessary to study the nature of mangrove soil. Broad idea of the nature of mangrove soil can be obtained from pH, Electrical conductivity, chlorides and minerals. These parameters are the result of physical and chemical activities taking place in the soil.

The preset study covers mangrove soils from 28 sites studied with respect to granulometry, pH, EC, chlorides and minerals. The occurrence, distribution, zonation and structure of the mangroves depend upon soil status. The mangrove soil is characterized by high water content, low oxygen and often high salinity and free hydrogen sulphide. Mangroves occur on wide range of substrate types including mud, sand, peat and coral soils as per Chapman (1976). The natural mangrove soil characters or activities are disturbed by human interference.

The distribution of mangroves in relation to soil for sunderbans has been studied by Naskar and Bakshi (1989). The physico – chemical characteristics of east and west Sunderbans has been given by Matilal *et. al.* (1986). Selvam *et. al.* (1991) stated that soil salinity is a major factor responsible for stunted growth of *A. marina* along Madras coast Thomas and Fernandez (1993) reported that *B. gymnorrhiza* and *A. aureum* favour low pH and salinity along kerala coast. Sediment characters of Krishna – Godavari delta are attempted by Rao ad Swamy (1991). The edaphic factors influencing mangroves of Muthupet (Tamil nadu) are studied by Gunasekaran *et. al.* (1992). Mangrove soil of Goa has been analysed by Jagtap (1987). The mangrove soils of some estuaries from Ratnagiri district have also been attempted by Mulik and Tare (1997), Kotmire (1983), Kurlapkar (1993), Sathe and Bhosale (1991), Kadam and Bhosale (1987).

Granulometry

Present study reveals the occurrence of mangroves on coarse to fine sandy and muddy substratum, but low gravely content is recorded Table 1.26 Walsh (1974) has reported occurrence of mangroves in cracks and crevices of rocky shores. The mangroves themselves may influence the sediment by promoting siltation, Davies (1977). During the field observations it is observed that the mangrove propagules can germinate in the rocky and gravely soils but it is very difficult to continue growth to adult individuals. Some of the close mangrove associate species have better capacity to withstand these conditions, while soft fine grained soil is necessary for proper mangrove development (Galloway, 1982).

Many workers have given textural classification of mangrove sediments from different localities. Ukpong (1992) has given proportion of sand, silt and clay in the mangrove soils of Nigeria, where he could not record any definite proportion. The soils analysed in the present study show lot of variations in the grain composition. The grain composition of Western Maharashtra has also been attempted by Maharashtra has been and Naidoo *et.al.* (1982) and Kurlapkar (1992). Where mangrove soil shows clay and silt contents. Sukordjo *et.al.* (1984) have recorded similar results in the mangrove soils of Bungin river Untawale (1985) has given textural composition of soils from Indian mangroves, observing variations in the soil composition.

In the present study soil samples from 28 sites of Sindhudurg district like Kolamb, Achara and from Ratnagiri district like Bhatye, Malgund and Kalbadevi are analysed for Granulometry. From the table it can be observed that most of the soils show maximum fine and coarse sand contents with very low silt and clay content. Kotmire and Bhosale (1979) have recorded lowest grain size more than 9 percent for the soils of Deogad and Mumbra estuaries.

Rao *et. al.* (1963, 1966, 1973) have shown that mangrove soils are more sandy than clayey. According to them these soils fall in the range of loamy sand to coarse sand, present study resulted on similar lines. Kulkarni (1990) studied the soils supporting *R. mucronata* and *R. apiculata,* where he has recorded 22 –24% silt and clay content which is much higher than the present study. Bhosale (1990b) also found that clay percentage of the mangrove soil in upper zone is very low. During the present study and field observations it is found that the mangrove soils are unstable due to natural factors like tidal inundations and man made factors like deforestation and reclaimation practices. This may explain lower percentage of clay/silt component.

pH

It is the measure of the degree of acidity or alkalinity of an aqueous solution. pH is governed by various factors like nature of substratum, type of parent rock, precipitation and microbial activity in the related environment. The pH of mangrove soil is depending upon the amount of organic substances mixing in the soil. According to Bhosale (1990, b) the pH values in the estuarine soil changes as per the location.

The present investigation deals with the pH of soils from different mangrove sites in the study area. The range of pH recorded during the study is from 5.15 to 7.51 in the case of Achara estuary; in the case of Kolamb it is 5.95 to 8.2. In the case of Malgund, Bhatye and Kalbadevi it is 5.84 to 7.47, 6.9 to 7.7 and 6.42 to 7.75, respectively. The pH of soil shows wide range from acidic to alkaline (Table 1.26).

The acidic values of pH for mangrove soils have also been reported by various workers. According to Choudhary *et.al* (1984), the mangrove areas of sunderbans show low pH in monsoon months. Lower pH values are reported by Sathe and Bhosale (1991) for Malvan mangroves.

During the present study lower pH values are recorded from few sites of Achara, Malgund and Kolamb estuaries as 5.15, 5.84 and 5.95, respectively, for soils surrounding *A. marina, A. officinalis, R. mucronata, C. tagal* and *S. alba*. Many workers stated that the lowering of the pH is also due to waste load and sewage inputs in the mangrove soils. (Sharma *et al.*, 1982, Nair *et al.* 1984).

Table 1.26: Granulometry of Mangrove Soils from Various Mangrove Standards of Some Estuaries

Name of the Estuary	Sites	Soil Texture > 2 mm 2.0 – 0.2 mm 0.2 to 0.02 mm < 0.02 mm					Soil Type
		Gravel %	Coarse Sand %	Fine Sand %	Silt Clay %		
Achra	1.	0.57	49.29	49.32	0.82	Sandy	**A. officinalis**
	2.	–	51.26	47.74	1.0	Sandy	*S. alba*
	3.	–	53.77	45.27	0.96	Sandy	*R. apiculata*
	4.	–	42.24	57.08	0.68	Sandy	
	5.	–	85.20	14.54	0.26	Sandy	
	6.	–	48.05	51.93	0.2	Sandy	**A. officinalis**
	7.	–	64.76	35.02	0.11	Sandy	**S. alba**
	8.	–	68.51	31.28	0.21	Sandy	**A. corni**
	9.	–	60.73	39.19	0.8	Sandy	**A. ilicifolius**
	10.	–	53.67	45.67	0.66	Sandy	*A. ilicifolius,*
	11.	–	55.40	43.73	0.87	Sandy	*K. candel*
	12.	–	78.28	20.36	0.36	Sandy	*R. mucronata*
	13.	–	60.86	38.34	0.80	Sandy	*C. tagal.*
							Mixed.
							A. marina,
							A. marina
							(dwarf) Pure
							R. mucronata.
							A. corniculatum
							S. alba
							A. corniculatum,
							A. ilicifolius

(Contd…)

Name of the Estuary	Sites	Soil Texture > 2 mm 2.0 – 0.2 mm 0.2 to 0.02 mm < 0.02 mm					Soil Type
		Gravel %	Coarse Sand %	Fine Sand %	Silt Clay %		
Malgund	1.	–	1.83	97.69	0.48	Fine sand	**S. portulacastrum**
	2.	–	7.59	92.39	0.2	Fine sand	**Fimbristylis**
							A. marina (dwarf),
							C. tagal,
							A. officinalis
Kolamb	1.	–	53.72	46.28	–	Sandy	*A. marina* (dwarf)
	2.	–	46.28	53.72	0.2	Sandy	**A. marina var.**
	3.	–	34.35	65.65	–	Sandy	**acutissima**
	4.	–	57.46	42.54	–	Sandy	*S. alba*
							A. corniculatum
Bhatye	1.	–	40.00	49.40	10.5	Sandy	*A. marina*
	2.	10.00	35.00	42.5	12.5	Loam	*A. marina,*
	3.	3.00	26.00	68.6	2.4	Sandy	*S. alba*
	4.	5.40	58.00	31.5	5.1	Loam	*A. officinalis,*
						Sandy	*C. tagal*
						Sandy	Mixed.
Kalbadevi	1.	–	15.62	70.5	13.88	Loam	*S. alba*
	2.	8.9	40.12	50.43	0.55	Sandy	*S. alba,*
	3.	10.52	56.16	32.12	1.2	Sandy	*R. mucronata*
	4.	18.70	60.12	20.18	1.00	Sandy	*A. marina,*
	5.	25.65	58.00	11.35	5.00	Loam	*L. racemosa,*
							C.tagal
							S. alba,
							A. marina
							C. tagal

The higher values of pH are recorded from Achara, Kolamb and Kalbadevi as 7.52, 8.2 and 7.75 respectively (Table 1.27).

It represents the broad pH range for mangrove soils. It also indicate that the pH changes as per the change in location. The variations in the pH values for the soil under different species may be due to differential addition of organic matter and the microbial activity, i.e. the detrital activity.

Electrical Conductivity

In estuarine habitat the electrical conductivity is usually governed by salinity, therefore, the values are parallel to salinity Bhosale (1990a).

In the present work the electrical conductivity for soils from different sites was recorded (Table 1.27).

From the table it is seen that the range of electrical conductivity for the soils from Achara is 1.29 ms/cm to 6.33 ms/cm, From Kolamb 2.13 ms/cm to 2.82 ms/cm, from Bhatye 1.73 ms/cm to 3.32 ms/cm, and From Kalbadevi 1.81 ms/cm to 3.21 ms/cm. The values for electrical conductivity change with respect to the location and surrounding vegetation in the same estuary.

Blasco (1975) has recorded electrical conductivity of Indian mangrove soils while Sah *et al.* (1986) has given the range of electrical conductivity as 2.79 to 11.47 ms/cm for the mangrove soils of Sunderbans. From the observations broadly it can be said that *S. alba, A. marina, C. tagal* have broad range of electrical conductivity as compared to *R. mucronata, L. racemosa* and *K. candel*.

Chlorides

Various chloride salts naturally occur in the soils and water. In estuarine environment these chlorides are mostly added by sea-water. The chlorides are also added by the mangrove litter. According to Gaykar (1991) mangrove litter contributes 4.94 gcl/100g of dry litter. The estuaries facing the domestic sewage pollution also get additional chlorides from such pollutants. Chlorides and salinity are positively correlated factors. The increase in the chloride level in estuarine environment increases the salinity. Therefore, the salinity can also be judged from chloride contents. Present study has recorded the variations in the chlorides from soil of different estuaries. The chloride range recorded for different locations of different estuaries is different. The range of chlorides for Achara is from 0.26% to 1.84%, for Kolamb, Bhatye and Kalbadevi it is 0.17% to 0.522%, 0.65% to 1.32% and 0.48% to 1.20% respectively, (Table 1.27). Murthy and Rao (1987) have stated that the summer evaporation plays an important role in raising the chloride levels of soils and water. Ukpong (1992) has studied the soils from different mangrove swamps in the estuaries of southern Nigeria. According to him chlorides and other elements in the soil show little to moderate variations in the values.

Table 1.27: Chemical Composition of the Soils from Various Mangrove Stands of Some Estuaries

Name of Estuary	Site No.	pH	Electrical Conductivity ms/cm	Chlorides %	Minerals (gm/100 gm)			Dominant Vegetation
					Na	K	Ca	
Achra	1.	6.53	2.10	0.39	0.45	0.28	0.15	
	2.	7.12	2.93	0.62	0.81	0.37	0.23	A. officinalis
	3.	4.95	3.02	an	0.83	0.34	0.21	*S. alba*
	4.	6.7	5.8	1.41	1.03	0.81	0.30	*R. apiculata*
	5.	7.2	3.79	0.91	0.58	0.23	0.16	
	6.	6.32	1.59	0.31	0.55	0.27	0.14	**Mixed vegetation**
	7.	5.15	2.45	0.5	1.54	0.75	0.40	*A. ilicifolius*
	8.	5.8	2.53	0.59	1.49	0.29	0.47	*K. candel*
	9.	5.15	1.48	0.3	0.47	0.22	0.14	*C. tagal, R.mucronata*
	10.	6.65	2.17	0.44	0.61	0.31	0.15	*R. mucronata*
	11.	7.2	3.43	0.86	1.15	0.83	0.21	*A. marina*
	12.	7.51	6.33	1.84	1.85	0.97	0.57	*R. mucronata*
	13.	5.35	1.29	0.26	0.27	0.18	0.07	*A. corniculatum*
								S. alba
								A. corniculatum, A.ilicifolius

(Contd…)

Name of Estuary	Site No.	pH	Electrical Conductivity ms/cm	Chlorides %	Minerals (gm/100 gm)			Dominant Vegetation
					Na	K	Ca	
Malgund	1.	7.47	2.62	0.16	0.27	0.17	0.11	
	2.	5.84	2.82	0.32	0.22	0.13	0.21	S. portulacastrum A. Marina, C. tagal, A. officinalis
Kolamb	1.	8.2	4.90	0.46	0.89	0.42	0.26	*A. marina* (dwarf)
	2.	7.5	5.76	0.41	0.56	0.28	0.15	*A. marina* var. *acutissima*
	3.	5.95	2.4	0.522	0.61	0.33	0.14	*S. alba*
	4.	6.05	2.13	0.17	1.03	0.71	0.41	*A. corniculatum*
Bhatye	1.	7.24	3.32	0.87	0.43	0.18	0.13	A. marina
	2.	7.1	2.42	0.65	0.48	0.21	0.15	*A. marina, S. alba*
	3.	7.7	3.01	1.32	0.90	0.37	0.30	*A. offici, C. tagal*
	4.	6.9	1.73	0.83	0.35	0.23	0.11	*R. apiculatla, C. tagal.*
Kalbadevi	1.	7.75	2.52	1.20	0.81	0.33	0.28	*S. alba*
	2.	6.47	1.81	0.91	0.39	0.31	0.17	*S. alba, R. mucronata*
	3.	7.2	3.21	0.56	0.22	0.17	0.13	*A. marina, L. racemosa*
	4.	6.45	2.32	0.48	0.36	0.15	0.11	*S. alba, A. marina*
	5.	6.80	2.71	0.63	0.39	0.24	0.14	*C. tagal*

Minerals

Minerals play key roles in the physiological mechanisms in the mangroves. The minerals are recycled between water, soil and plants. Various mineral constituents are required for normal functioning of the ecosystem. In the present study the soils from few sites like Achara, Kolamb, Malgund, Bhatye and Kalbadevi are analysed for the presence of minerals like Na, K and Ca. The results are depicted in Table 1.27.

The minerals of water, soil and plant material has been attempted by various workers. Kotmire and Bhosale (1983) have reported the minerals from mangrove soils of Deogad, Mumbra and Are estuaries. They got variable amounts for minerals in soils changing from location to location Warick (1960), Chirputkar (1969), Mishra (1967), Joshi (1976) have attempted the minerals from water, soil and plants.

Sodium (Na)

In the present study sodium has been analysed from the soils around the mangroves. It reveals that sodium is one of the important mineral constituent of the mangrove soil, because it is the major constituent of sea and thereby flooding water in the form of sodium chloride. The study reveals that the sodium content of soil varies from site to site. In the present study sodium in the mangrove soil of Achara is found in the range of 0.27% to 1.85%. At Malgund, Kolamb, Bhatye and Kalbadevi it is found in the range of 0.27% to 0.32%, 0.56% to 1.03%, 0.35% to 0.9% and 0.22% to 0.81% respectively. Kotmire (1983) has recorded sodium for Mumbra, Deogad and Are soil as 1.72%, 1.08% and 1.60% respectively. These values are close to the present results recorded in Table 1.27.

Potassium (K)

Besides sodium, potassium is an other important mineral in the soil. Though it is less than sodium, the proportion of K with respect to sodium varies in the soil. Kotmire (1983) has reported the similar results. In the present study the potassium at Achara is found in the range of 0.81% to 0.97% and for Malgund, Kolamb, Bhatye and Kalbadevi it is in the range of 0.13% to 0.17%, 0.28%, to 0.71%, 0.18% to 0.37% and 0.15% to 0.33% respectively (Table 1.27).

Calcium (Ca)

Calcium is another element associated with the mangrove vegetation. The soil supporting mangroves is normally rich in calcium. Calcium pectate is a constituent of middle lamellae and hence large amount of calcium is needed in the soil to ensure a good plant growth. Kotmire (1983) reported the calcium for Mumbra, Deogad and Are estuaries as 0.75%, 0.57% and 0.43% respectively. In the present study higher calcium values, from Achara,

Malgund, Kolamb, Bhatye and Kalbadevi are recorded as 0.57%, 0.21%, 0.41%, 0.30% and 0.28% (Table 1.27) respectively which are lower than those reported by Kotmire (1983).

The soil texture as well as chemical properties depend upon the total turn over in the ecosystem and exchange between the biotic and abiotic components.

IUCN Categorization

It has been realised all over the world that mangroves are to be conserved. The special feature of mangroves is that they are to be dealt with on the scale of ecosystem for conservation which is unlike other species. However, the task is difficult, for designing a action/conservation plan IUCN has developed guidelines for undertaking conservation programme where the degree of threatenment helps prioritization for conservation. It is difficult for a programme to accommodate all the threatened species, for conservation, at a time. These guidelines were made available by IUCN from time to time (1991, 1992, 1993, 1994, 1999, 2000 and 2001). The IUCN has published a data sheet specially prepared for mangrove species in the year 1997 for a BCPP workshop on mangroves. It formed the baseline for the present study.

IUCN had provided the Redlist categories to decide the status of any taxonomic species at regional, national and global level. The categories are intended to be easily understood and to implement a system for classification of a species at high risk of global extinction. The general aim of the system is to provide an explicit, objective frame work for classification of broadest range of species according to their extinction risk. The system provides the information about the species like area occupied, data quality, threats, trade etc. which helps to formulate the conservation strategy. In the present study all the above information about the mangrove species of Ratnagiri and Sindhudurg districts has been collected and the mangroves are categorized according to the system given by IUCN. The aim of the study is to decide the status of the species.

The IUCN Redlist categories and criteria are aimed at:

1. To provide a system that can be applied consistently by different people.
2. To improve objectivity by providing users assistance to evaluate different factors which affect the risk of extinction.
3. To provide a system which will facilitate comparisons across widely different taxa.
4. To help prioritization of threatened species.

Since 1994, IUCN has adopted the IUCN Red list categories, they have become widely recognized internationally and used in a range of publications, numerous government organisations and NGO's. IUCN has revised the categorization system (IUCN, 1996). Since 1991 several revisions are made in the IUCN Red list categories. Many workers have suggested their drafts, consultations and validations to these categories. It is found that these drafts and suggestions are not fit to all the species for conservation, but can be used as and when they required and ammended. To clarify the matters and to open the way for modifications as and when necessary IUCN has adopted a system for version numbering as follows:

Version 1.0: Mace and Lande (1991)

This is first version discussing a new basis for the categories, and presenting numerical criteria especially relevant for large vertebrates.

Version 2.0: Mace *et al.* (1992)

This is the major revision of version 1.0, including numerical criteria appropriate to all organisms and introducing the non-threatened categories.

Version 2.1: IUCN (1993)

In this version in consultation with species survival commission (SSC), a number of changes were made to the details of the criteria and fuller explanation of basic principles was included. A more explicit structure clarified the significance of the non-threatened categories.

Version 2.2: Mace and Stuart (1994)

Following further comments received and additional validation exercises, some minor changes to the criteria were made. In addition, the susceptible category present in version 2.0 and 2.1 was subsumed into vulnerable category. A precautionary application of the system was emphasized.

Version 2.3: IUCN (1994)

IUCN council adopted this version, which incorporated changes as a result of comments from IUCN members, in Dec, 1994. The initial version of this document was published without the necessary bibliographic details, such as date of publication and ISBN number, but these were included in the subsequent reprints in 1998 and 1989. This version was used for 1996 IUCN Red list of threatened animals (Baillie and Groombridge, 1996) and the world list of threatened trees (Oldfield *et al*. 1998).

Version 3.0: IUCN/SSC Criteria Review Working Group (1999)

In this version following several comments received and after series of workshops some changes were proposed in the criteria, definitions of some key terms and the handling of uncertainty.

Version 3.1: IUCN (2000)

The IUCN council adopted this latest version, which incorporated changes as a result of comments from IUCN and species survival commissions memberships and a final meeting of the criteria review working group in February 2000.

In the present study the recent version (3.1 : IUCN, 2000) has been used to categorize the mangroves in the study area.

Taxon Data Sheets

It is an important document of IUCN categorization process. The data sheet is the overall appearance of the species in an ecosystem. The parameters used to prepare the data sheet are useful in deciding the status of a species. The details of the Taxon Data Sheet (biological information sheet) for all species are prepared and few are presented herewith to understand its importance for conservation purpose.

Avicenia marina* var *acutissima

Name of the species	: *Avicenia marina* var *acutissima*
Family	: *Avicenniaceae*
Taxonomic status	: Species (variety)
Local Name	: Tivar
Habit	: Tree
Habitat	: Inter tidal with greater ecological amplitude.
Macrogeographic area	: West coast of Maharashtra (India)
Microgeographic area	: Ratnagiri and Sindhudurg districts
Study Duration	: 1998-2006
Extent of occurrence	: < 100 Sq. km
Area of occupancy	: A = < 10 km^2 (1.4037 Km^2)
Number of locations	: 29 Fragmented
Number of mature individuals	: 202916

D-2 population estimation in area of occupancy less than 100 Km^2.

Habitat structure:

(a) Change in the habitat	: Yes
Trade	: Unknown
More Comments	: The taxa is used by local habitants as a fodder, fuel and wood is used for house construction.
Status	: Endangered (EN)
Collection in case of plant	: Destructive
Is the trend in population	: For all sp.
If declining % over years	: For all sp.
Data Quality	: Census and field survey

Recommendations : Habitat Management
Is cultivation/captive breeding required : Yes
Does cultivation/captive breeding already exist : Yes - Plantation

Avicennia marina* var. *resinifera

Name of the species : *Avicennia marina* var. *resinifera*
Family : *Avicenniaceae*
Taxonomic status : Species (Variety)
Local Name : Tivar
Habit : Tree
Habitat : Middle Inter tidal Eumangrove
Macrogeographic area : West coast of Maharashtra
Microgeographic area : Ratnagiri and Sindhudurg districts
Study Duration : 1998-2006
Extent of occurrence : < 100 Sq. km
Area of occupancy : A = < 10 km^2 (Negligible)
Number of locations : 1 Fragmented
Number of mature individuals : 1
D-2 population estimation in area of occupancy less than 100 Km^2.
Habitat structure:
(a) Change in the habitat : Yes
Trade : Unknown
Status : Critically endangered (CR)
Collection in case of plant : Destructive
Is the trend in population : As per Table
If declining% over years : As per Table
Data Quality : Census and field survey
Recommendations : Habitat Management
Is cultivation/captive breeding required : Yes
Does cultivation/captive breeding already exist : No

Avicennia officinalis

Name of the species	: *Avicennia officinalis*
Family	: *Avicenniaceae*
Taxonomic status	: Species
Local Name	: Tivar
Habit	: Tree with aerial stilt roots
Habitat	: Inter tidal, Eumangrove
Macrogeographic area	: West coast of Maharashtra
Microgeographic area	: Ratnagiri and Sindhudurg districts
Study Duration	: 1998-2006
Extent of occurrence	: < 100 Sq. km
Area of occupancy	: A = < 10 km^2 (3.533 Km^2)
Number of locations	: 29 Fragmented
Number of mature individuals	: 358556

D-2 population estimation in area of occupancy less than 100 Km^2.

Habitat structure:

(a) Change in the habitat	: Yes
Trade	: Unknown
Status	: Endangered (EN)
Collection in case of plant	: Destructive
Is the trend in population	: As per Table
If declining % over years	: As per Table
Data Quality	: Census and field survey
Recommendations	: Habitat Management
Is cultivation/captive breeding required	: Yes
Does cultivation/captive breeding already exist	: No

Rhizophora mucronata

Name of the species	: *Rhizophora mucronata*
Family	: *Rhizophoraceae*
Taxonomic status	: Species
Local Name	: Kandal
Habit	: Tree, Tall much branched
Habitat	: Inter tidal, Eumangrove

Macrogeographic area	:	West coast of Maharashtra
Microgeographic area	:	Ratnagiri and Sindhudurg districts.
Study Duration	:	1998-2006
Extent of occurrence	:	< 100 Sq. km
Area of occupancy	:	A = < 10 km^2 (3.802 Km^2)
Number of locations	:	29 Fragmented
Number of mature individuals	:	840417

D-2 Population estimated in area of occupancy less than 100 Km^2.

Habitat structure:

(a) Change in the habitat	:	Yes
Trade	:	Not Known
More Comments	:	The taxa is used by the local habitants for fuel and the straight boles are used for construction purpose.
Status	:	Endangered (EN)
Collection in case of plant	:	Non-Destructive
Is the trend in population	:	As per Table
If declining % over years	:	As per Table
Data Quality	:	Census and field survey
Recommendations	:	Habitat Management
Is cultivation/captive breeding required	:	Yes
Does cultivation/captive breeding already exist	:	No

Kandelia candel

Name of the species	:	*Kandelia candel*
Family	:	*Rhizophoraceae*
Taxonomic status	:	Species
Local Name	:	Kandal Guria
Habit	:	Medium sized tree
Habitat	:	Inter tidal, Downstream
Macrogeographic area	:	West coast of Maharashtra
Microgeographic area	:	Ratnagiri and Sindhudurg districts
Study Duration	:	1998-2006

Extent of occurrence : < 100 Sq. km
Area of occupancy : A = < 10 km^2 (0.0239 Km^2)
Number of locations : 11 Fragmented
Number of mature individuals : 16108
D-2 population estimation in area of occupancy less than 100 Km^2.
Habitat structure:
(a) Change in the habitat : Yes
Trade : Unknown
More Comments : Sensitive to change in habitat
Status : Endangered (EN)
Collection in case of plant : Destructive
Is the trend in population : As per Table
If declining % over years : As per Table
Data Quality : Census and field survey
Recommendations : M – Monitoring
Hm – Habitat Management
Is cultivation/captive breeding required : Yes
Does cultivation/captive breeding already exist : No

Bruguiera gymnorrhiza

Name of the species : *Bruguiera gymnorrhiza*
Family : *Rhizophoraceae*
Taxonomic status : Species
Local Name : Kandal, Kankar, EK Mane
Habit : Tree, high with short buttressess, Fissured bark, knew pneumatophores.
Habitat : Inter tidal
Macrogeographic area : West coast of Maharashtra
Microgeographic area : Ratnagiri and Sindhudurg districts
Study Duration : 1998-2006
Extent of occurrence : < 100 Sq. km
Area of occupancy : A = < 10 km^2 (0.0214 Km^2)
Number of locations : 9 Fragmented

Number of mature individuals : 20445

D-2 population estimation in area of occupancy less than 100 Km^2.

Habitat structure:

(a) Change in the habitat : Yes

Trade : Unknown

More Comments : Threatened at Deogad and Achara.

Status : Endangered (EN)

Collection in case of plant : Non-destructive

Is the trend in population : As per Table

If declining% over years : As per Table

Data Quality : Census and field survey

Recommendations : M – Monitoring
HM – Habitat Management

Is cultivation/captive breeding required : Yes

Does cultivation/captive breeding already exist : No

Bruguiera cylindrica

Name of the species : *Bruguiera cylindrica*

Family : *Rhizophoraceae*

Taxonomic status : Species

Local Name : Kandal

Habit : Medium sized tree

Habitat : Inter tidal downstream.

Macrogeographic area : West coast of Maharashtra.

Microgeographic area : Ratnagiri and Sindhudurg districts

Study Duration : 1998-2006

Extent of occurrence : < 100 Sq. km

Area of occupancy : A = < 10 km^2 (Negligible)

Number of locations : 1 Fragmented

Number of mature individuals : 13

D-2 population estimation in area of occupancy less than 100 Km^2.

Habitat structure:

(a) Change in the habitat : Yes

Trade : Unknown

More Comments	: Sensitive to change in habitat.
Status	: Critically Endangered (CR)
Collection in case of plant	: Destructive
Is the trend in population	: As per Table
If declining % over years	: As per Table
Data Quality	: Census and field survey
Recommendations	: M – Monitoring HM – Habitat Management
Is cultivation/captive breeding required	: Yes
Does cultivation/captive breeding already exist	: No

Sonneratia alba

Name of the species	: *Sonneratia alba*
Family	: *Sonneratiaceae*
Taxonomic status	: Species
Local Name	: Cheep (Pandhari), Kincheepy
Habit	: Tree
Habitat	: Inter tidal.
Macrogeographic area	: West coast of Maharashtra
Microgeographic area	: Ratnagiri and Sindhudurg districts
Study Duration	: 1998-2006
Extent of occurrence	: < 100 Sq. km
Area of occupancy	: A = < 10 km^2 (3.1551 Km^2)
Number of locations	: 29 Fragmented
Number of mature individuals	: 472026

D-2 population estimation in area of occupancy less than 100 Km^2.

Habitat structure:

(a) Change in the habitat	: Yes
Trade	: Unknown
More Comments	: Taxa is not in commercial trade, but the local habitants are using the taxa for Timber, Fuel purposes.
Status	: Endangered (EN)
Collection in case of plant	: Non-destructive

Is the trend in population : As per Table
If declining % over years : As per Table
Data Quality : Census and field survey
Recommendations : M – Monitoring
HM – Habitat Monitoring
Is cultivation/captive breeding required : Yes
Does cultivation/captive breeding already exist : No

Sonneratia apetala

Name of the species : *Sonneratia apetala*
Family : *Sonneratiaceae*
Taxonomic status : Species
Local Name : Cheep
Habit : Tree with dense crowns.
Habitat : Inter tidal, lower and middle region.
Macrogeographic area : West coast of Maharashtra.
Microgeographic area : Ratnagiri and Sindhudurg districts
Study Duration : 1998-2006
Extent of occurrence : < 100 Sq. km
Area of occupancy : A = < 10 km^2 (0.0204 Km^2)
Number of locations : 6 Fragmented
Number of mature individuals : 18399
D-2 population estimation in area of occupancy less than 100 Km^2.
Habitat structure:
(a) Change in the habitat : Yes
Trade : Unknown
More Comments : Deforested at Mumbra, Purnagad and Vetye
Status : Endangered (EN)
Collection in case of plant : Non-destructive
Is the trend in population : As per Table
If declining% over years : As per Table
Data Quality : Census and field survey

Recommendations : M – Monitoring
HM – Habitat Management
Is cultivation/captive breeding required : Yes
Does cultivation/captive breeding already exist : No

Sonneratia caseolaris

Name of the species : *Sonneratia caseolaris*
Family : *Sonneratiaceae*
Taxonomic status : Species
Local Name : Cheep
Habit : Tree, tall with drooping branches with long pneumatophores.
Habitat : Eumangrove, upstream.
Macrogeographic area : West coast of Maharashtra
Microgeographic area : Ratnagiri and Sindhudurg districts
Study Duration : 1998-2006
Extent of occurrence : < 100 Sq. km
Area of occupancy : A = < 10 km^2 (Negligible)
Number of locations : 4 Fragmented
Number of mature individuals : 205
D-2 population estimation in area of occupancy less than 100 Km^2.
Habitat structure:
(a) Change in the habitat : Yes
Trade : Unknown
More Comments : The riped fruits are tasty and consumed by the local habitants.
Status : Critically Endangered (CR)
Collection in case of plant : Destructive
Is the trend in population : As per Table
If declining % over years : As per Table
Data Quality : Census and field survey
Recommendations : M – Monitoring
HM – Habitat Management
Is cultivation/captive breeding required : Yes
Does cultivation/captive breeding already exist : No

Aegiceras corniculatum

Name of the species	:	*Aegiceras corniculatum*
Family	:	*Myrsinaceae*
Taxonomic status	:	Species
Local Name	:	Kharfuti
Habit	:	Small sized tree with stilt roots.
Habitat	:	Inter tidal, Eumangrove
Macrogeographic area	:	West coast of Maharashtra
Microgeographic area	:	Ratnagiri and Sindhudurg districts
Study Duration	:	1998-2006
Extent of occurrence	:	< 100 Sq. km
Area of occupancy	:	A = < 10 km^2 (0.1751 Km^2)
Number of locations	:	29 Fragmented
Number of mature individuals	:	272752

D-2 population estimation in area of occupancy less than 100 Km^2.

Habitat structure:

(a) Change in the habitat	:	Yes
Trade	:	Unknown
More Comments	:	Taxon is not in commercial trade as local habitants using the taxa for the fuel purpose.
Status	:	Endangered (EN)
Collection in case of plant	:	Non-destructive
Is the trend in population	:	As per Table
If declining% over years	:	As per Table
Data Quality	:	Census and field survey
Recommendations	:	M – Monitoring HM – Habitat Management
Is cultivation/captive breeding required	:	Yes
Does cultivation/captive breeding already exist	:	No

Lumnitzera racemosa

Name of the species	:	*Lumnitzera racemosa*
Family	:	*Combretaceae*

Taxonomic status	:	Species
Local Name	:	Tivar, Kharfuti
Habit	:	Small tree/shrub.
Habitat	:	Inter tidal, downstream
Macrogeographic area	:	West coast of Maharashtra
Microgeographic area	:	Ratnagiri and Sindhudurg districts
Study Duration	:	1998-2006
Extent of occurrence	:	< 100 Sq. km
Area of occupancy	:	A = < 10 km^2 (0.0501 Km^2)
Number of locations	:	13 Fragmented
Number of mature individuals	:	53255

D-2 population estimation in area of occupancy less than 100 Km^2.

Habitat structure:		
(a) Change in the habitat	:	Yes
Trade	:	Unknown
More Comments	:	Species is exposed to changed habitat
Status	:	Endangered (EN)
Collection in case of plant	:	Destructive
Is the trend in population	:	As per Table
If declining% over years	:	As per Table
Data Quality	:	Census and field survey
Recommendations	:	M – Monitoring HM – Habitat Management
Is cultivation/captive breeding required	:	Yes
Does cultivation/captive breeding already exist	:	No

Xylocarpus granatum

Name of the species	:	*Xylocarpus granatum*
Family	:	*Meliaceae*
Taxonomic status	:	Species
Local Name	:	Samudraphal, Bhelandi
Habit	:	Tree
Habitat	:	Inter tidal, middle, distal zones, drier soils.

Macrogeographic area	:	(Regional distribution) East and West coast of India.
Microgeographic area	:	Ratnagiri and Sindhudurg districts. Achara, Vijaydurg, Purnagad, Jaigad.
Study Duration	:	1999-2006
Extent of occurrence	:	< 100 Sq. km
Area of occupancy	:	A = < 10 km^2 (Negligible)
Number of locations	:	4 Fragmented
Number of mature individuals	:	< 250 (133)
Habitat structure:		
(a) Change in the habitat	:	Yes
Trade	:	Local
More Comments	:	Very few individuals are recorded during the investigation. The taxon is highly medicinal and exploitated by the locals. The young fruits are very much favoured by monkeys. From the literature and from locals it is came to know that the seeds are used for treating the fever, cough in the newly born childs. The fruits, seeds and bark is used in dysentery, tonic, astringent, for breast cancer, cholera, diarrhoea.
Status	:	Critically Endangered (CR)
Collection in case of plant	:	Destructive
Is the trend in population	:	As per Table
If declining% over years	:	As per Table
Data Quality	:	Census and monitoring, Critical field Studies, collections.
Recommendations	:	Survey, Monitoring, Taxonomic studies, Life history study, habitat management, Genetic studies, others.
Is cultivation/captive breeding required	:	Yes
Does cultivation/captive breeding already exist	:	No

Population Density

The term population is used in a specific sense in the Red list criteria. Population is defined as the total number of individuals of the taxon, measured as number of mature individuals only.

The number of mature individuals is the number of individuals known, estimated or inferred to be capable of reproduction. For estimation of this quantity IUCN has suggested following points to remember.

1. Mature individuals that will never produce new recruits should not be counted.
2. In the case of populations with baised adult or breeding sex ratios, it is appropriate to use lower estimates for the number of mature individuals which take this into account.
3. Where the population size fluctuates, use a lower estimate. In most cases this will be much less than the mean.
4. Reproducing units within a clone should be counted as individuals, except where such units are unable to survive alone (e.g. corals)
5. In the case of taxa that naturally loss all or a subset of mature individuals at some point in their life cycle, the estimate should be made at the appropriate time, when mature individuals are available for breeding.
6. Re-introduced individuals must have produced viable offspring before they are counted as mature individuals.

IUCN has given the range to decide the status of the species, it is given as < 50, < 250, < 2500, > 2,500 in all populations based on numbers. In the present study the number of mature individuals of all the mangroves in the study area are attempted. It gives the idea about the number of mature individuals of the taxon. It helps to decide population size (criteria A, C & D) and also the mature individuals (criteria A, B, C, & D).

Area Under Each Species

Area covered by each species is called as 'Area of occupancy' in Red list criteria. Area of occupancy is defined as the area within its 'Extent of occurrence' which is occupied by a taxon. The extent of occurrence is defined as the area contained within the shortest continuous boundary which can be drawn to encompass all the known, inferred or projected sites of present occurrence of a taxon. The measure reflects the fact that a taxon will not usually occur throughout the area of its extent of occurrence, which may contain unsuitable or unoccupied habitats. The area of occupancy is also defined as, 'smallest area essential at any stage for the survival of existing populations of a taxon.' The size of area of occupancy will be a function of the scale at which it is measured and should be appropriate to relevant biological aspects of the taxon, threats and available data. This criterion is to be considered in the range of < 100 sq. km, < 5,000 sq. km., < 20,000 sq. km. and > 20,000 sq. km.

Threats to the Species

The factors which adversely affect the vegetation directly or indirectly in a large or small scale are considered as threats. The mangrove ecosystems are under threat as they are affected by direct and indirect factors. Threats are classified into those affecting the taxon population and those affecting habitat. But some of the factors affect both habitat and taxon population.

Ahmad (1999) accounted the major human impacts on the mangroves of Arabian Gulf region include oil pollution, solid and liquid waste disposal, coastal development, marine dredging, recreation activities, over grazing, wood harvest, diversion of fresh water runoff and pest control. Similar threats are recorded in the study area.

During the field study some of the threats affecting the mangroves are recorded and explained as below:

(A) Natural Threats

Mangroves face problem in the course of natural processes leading to destruction. Such events are referred to as Natural Threats.

1. Diseases

At many places like Kolamb, Kalavali, Achara, Vijaydurg, Bhatye it is found that fruits of *S. alba, S. apetala* are infested by the fruit borer insects, which cause rotting of the fruits from inside. The leaves of *Avicennia* are favoured by Grasshoppers.

2. Wild Animals

In the estuaries like Achara, Vijaydurg, Purnagad, Kolamb, Tarkarli, the fruits of *S. alba, S. caseolaris* and *X. granatum* are much favoured by the monkeys. Half eaten fruits are found under the tree in fruiting season.

(B) Man made threats

These threats can be considered under following titles.

(A) Affecting Taxon Population

1. *Grazing:* Heavy grazing in mangroves is observed during field survey. *Avicennia* are excellent feed for cattle. It is believed by the locals that the buffalos when fed by *Avicennia* leaves produce more milk. The grazing of *Avicennia* seedlings reduces regeneration rate.
2. *Fire wood:* The mangroves have high calorific value and are used all over the study area as a fire wood. The species preferred are *Rhizophora, Avicennia, Aegiceras* and *Sonneratia.*

3. *Timber:* Some species like *Rhizophora* yield good quality timber as they develop straight boles which are used for the construction purpose. Well grown *Aegiceras* is cleared for the fencing for the houses. Same is true for *Cynometra.*
4. *Siltation:* Siltation is the indirect effect of cutting the mangroves. At many places like Kolamb, Achara, Terekhol, Shiroda, Vengurla the cutting of mangroves caused loosening and disturbance of the sediments.
5. *Local medicines:* Some species like *X. granatum* are used by the local people against child cough and fever at Achara, Vijaydurg and Purnagad.

(B) Affecting Habitat and Taxon Population

1. *Human interference:* With the growing human population pressure, mangroves are cleared and the areas are used for construction purpose and for agriculture. The reclaimed areas are used for the rice, coconut and vegetable cultivation.
2. *Pollution:* The mangrove lands are used as liquid and solid waste disposal sites. At many places like Dabhol the industrial effluents are discharged in the estuaries. The estuaries around the Ratnagiri city are affected by this problem.
3. *Reclaimation of mangrove land:* Mangrove areas are reclaimed for many purposes. The local people clear mangroves for their settlements. Now-a-days Kharland Development Board is active in bunding the mangrove area. Large areas are reclaimed by the Board at Achara, Deogad, Mumbra, Kolamb, Vijaydurg. This practice has been responsible to eliminate the rare and endangered species.
4. *Aquaculture ponds:* The mangroves are also destroyed for the aquaculture ponds. Most of mangroves from Kolamb, Kalavali, Tarkarli, Achara, Deogad are cleared for this purpose. These ponds are constructed as small as 50 m^2 and as big as 31 ha. At Deogad an aquaculture pond of 8 ha is constructed by cutting the huge, pure stands of *B. gymnorrhiza.*
5. *Dredging:* Dredging is increasing water turbidity as the current patterns are not considered. Dredging on potential acid sulphate soils accelerates their acidification and salts are rising the surface rich in chlorides and sulphates, forming a whitish powder, at many places like Tarkarli, Kalavali and Savitri. It is observed that the dredging has been made at large scales for removing the sand for construction purpose. Huge amount of sand is continuously removed from the estuaries which result in continuous movement

of sediments. The dredging sites are near to the mangroves like *S. caseolaris* and *K. candel*. Due to continuous dredging these species are exposed to heighest degree of threat.

6. *Hypersalinity:* The flushing of fresh water is essential for the germination, sprouting of seeds and seedlings in mangroves. But at many sites it is observed that flushing of freshwater is blocked by constructing bunds and the flow is diverted. This causes no mixing of fresh water into estuaries and causing elimination of fresh water loving mangroves due to hypersalinity.
7. *Tourism:* Tourism near the estuaries like Tarkarli, Malgund, Kolamb creates the problems to mangroves in that area.

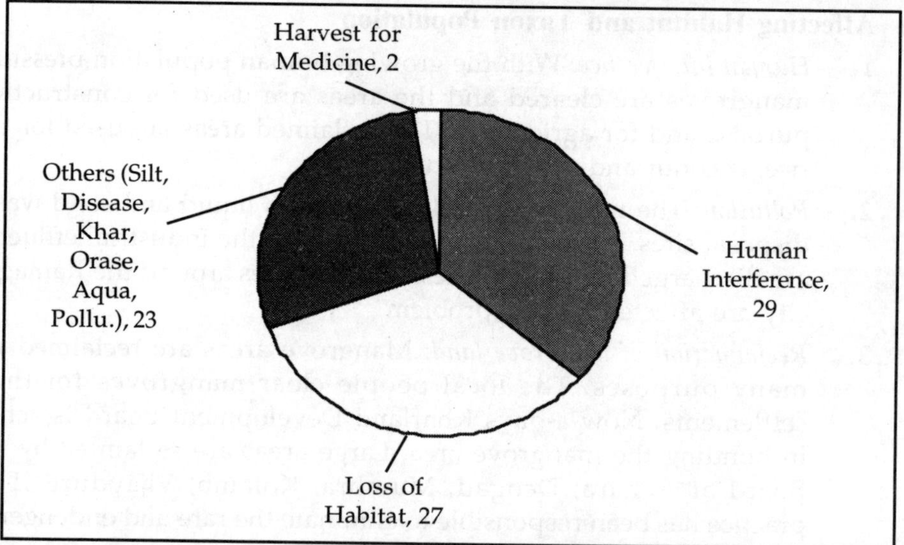

Fig. 1.3: Threats Affecting Mangroves in the Study Area

Total estuaries studied = 29

Number of threatened mangroves = 24

In short threats are the factors due to which the survival of the species in question is in danger. It has been found that most of the mangroves in the study area are under threat. The main threats are habitat loss, human interference, trade etc. Threats can be classified as those affecting the habitat and those affecting the taxon population, some threats can affect both. The threats at macro level can be enrolled as bunding or reclaimation, human encroachment, harvest, grazing, pollution, over exploitation, local medicinal importance etc. These threats are assessed for two districts.

Table 1.28: Threats to the Mangroves Recorded during the Present Study

Name of Estuary	1	2	3	4	5	6	7	8	9
Sindhudurg District									
Terekhol	–	–	+	+	–	+	+	–	–
Aronda	–	+	+	+	–	+	–	–	–
Mochemad	–	–	+	+	–	+	–	+	–
Vengurla	–	+	+	+	+	+	–	+	–
Vaingani	–	+	+	+	+	+	–		
Kalvi	–	–	+	+	–	+	–	–	–
Khavane	–	+	+	+	–	+	–	+	–
Nlvti	–	+	+	+	–	+	–	+	–
Tarkarli	–	+	+	+	–	+	+	–	–
Kolamb	+	+	+	+	+	+	+	+	–
Kalavali	–	+	+	+	+	+	+	+	–
Achara	+	+	+	+	–	+	+	+	+
Mithbav	–	–	+	+	–	+	–	–	–
Mumbra	–	–	+	+	–	+	–	+	–
Deogad	–	+	+	+	–	+	+	+	–
Vijaydurg	–	–	+	+	–	+	–	–	+
Ratnagiri District									
Rajapur	–	–	+	–	–	+	–	+	–
Vetye	–	–	+	+	–	+	–	+	–
Purnagad	–	+	+	+	–	+	–	–	–
Pavas	–	–	+	+	+	+	–	–	–
Bhatye	–	+	+	+	+	+	–	+	–
Kalabadevi	–	–	+	+	+	–	–	–	–
Are	–	+	+	+	–	+	–	–	–
Kelye	–	+	+	+	–	+	–	–	–
Malgund	–	–	+	+	+	+	–	–	–
Jaigarh	–	–	+	–	–	+	–	–	–
Dabhol	–	–	+	+	+	+	–	–	–
Harnai	–	–	+	+	–	+	–	–	–
Savitri	–	–	+	+	+	+	–	–	–

Legends:

1. Disease
2. Siltation
3. Human interference
4. Loss of Habitat
5. Pollution
6. Kharland bunding
7. Aqua culture ponds
8. Cattle grazing
9. Exploitation for medicinal use.

Biodiversity: Status and Conservation

Mangroves have no substitute either as ecosystem or the component species. Mangrove ecosystem forms bridging ecosystem between freshwater (terrestrial) and marine ecosystem. They represent great biodiversity which plays important role in livelyhood security of coastal people. The usefulness of the ecosystem is beyond doubt and has been realised across the globe. Each of the component in the ecosystem has its place and a role to play in sustaining not only the coastal people but the entire population as a whole. The mangrove ecosystem has got three zones of components namely aquatic, marshy and terrestrial (mesophytic). Because of tidal function there is considerable influx to and outflux from these three zones. Each zone is characterized by its biotic and abiotic components. As the mangrove ecosystem is a combination of three zones which are diversed in the type of habitat and nature of habitat the diversity of the life is great, obviously mangroves represent unique ecosystem of the tropical and sub-tropical coasts hence it is to be conserved. The International Council for Local Environmental Initiatives (ICLEI) (1996), putforth 'Agenda 21'. This act has proved that the present generation of the globe should preserve the biodiversity of the planet for future generation. This is true for the mangroves also.

Status

The forgoing result on IUCN categories has projected the status of mangroves in the study area. Bhosale and Mulik (1991) have reported threatened mangrove areas of Maharashtra. According to Selvam (1998) the mangrove forest cover in India has gone down to 2 to 3 lakh hectares in 1989 from 6 lakh hectares in 1953. The pressure on mangrove ecosystem is continuously increasing parallel to increase in population. NRSA has recorded a decline of 7000 hectare mangroves from India within a period of six years from 1975 to 1981. Bhosale (2005) has stated that Indian mangrove suffer from several types of pressures such as agriculture, aquaculture, industries, fuel wood extraction, diversion of freshwater and increase in salinity. Mangrove destruction in Maharashtra ingeneral and in study area in particular or has led to severe losses of some species like *L. racemosa, B. gymnorrhiza, S. caseolaris, X. granatum* (it was observed that a colony of *X. granatum* was totally felled in Vijaydurg estuary), *B. cylindrica* etc. There are consequences of mangrove destruction such as soil acidification, loss of nutrients, soil erosion, and decline in fishing potential. This situation demands conservation strategy for mangroves for sustainable development of mangrove resources.

Conservation

Conservation of Biodiversity depends on and respects for people including their needs, for its sustainable use. Spellerberg (1992) suggested that appropriate biological priorities be determined for action.

Reid (1994) explained that the ecological management is to maximize human capacity to respond changing ecological conditions for which maintenance of biodiversity is pre-requisite.

Gadgil (1996) summarized as biodiversity is a complex and cannot be conserved adequately to special areas or reserves but all the nature must be managed for biodiversity by considering species as a fundamental unit of diversity.

According to Ajmal Khan (2002) biodiversity conservation should be considered on the basis of biological representatives, uniqueness, naturalness, richness, valuable species, socio-economic value and conservation feasibility.

It indicates that it is necessary to conserve habitat diversity for maintaining the biological diversity. The conservation programme aims at:

1. Germplasm preservation.
2. Sustainable use of bioresources.
3. Maintenance of ecological balance.
4. Maintenance of ecotone characteristics
5. Protection and preservation of value added species.
6. Maintaining land use pattern.

Conservation strategy depend upon the degree of threatenment of species and the management plan adopted. Bhosale (1989 and 2005) has suggested management plan for mangroves of India and Maharashtra. The first and foremost thing is the awareness building, in public as well as decision makers and planners. It needs as a pre-requisite, fact finding where biological resources are quantified along with the significance. Precisely, present study putforth this aspect i.e. fact finding.

There are several reports which indicate that conservation measures planned by the Governments do not work successfully. The reason indentified is that the local people are least interested. Therefore a participatory management is emphasized. The participatory management of mangrove ecosystem is given by Bhosale (2005), as shown in the Fig. 1.4:

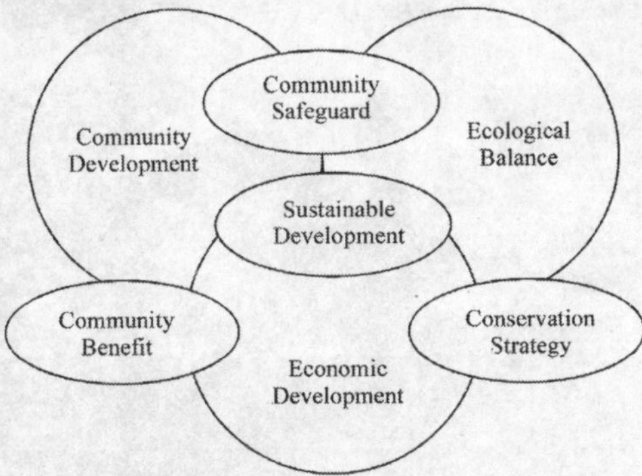

Fig. 1.4

As a conservation strategy Government of India has notified the regulation as CRZ notification on 19th Feb. 1991. It is supposed to take care of mangroves, however the development of pressures on the coastal areas do not allow the regulation to give results. It is the need of the day that the state Governments should take it more seriously and should see that the regulation is implemented effectively that is the only solution in present situation.

Full Grown Tree of Sonneratia Alba

Typical Mangrove Rhizophora Mucronata

Mangrove Colony

Ceriops Tagal

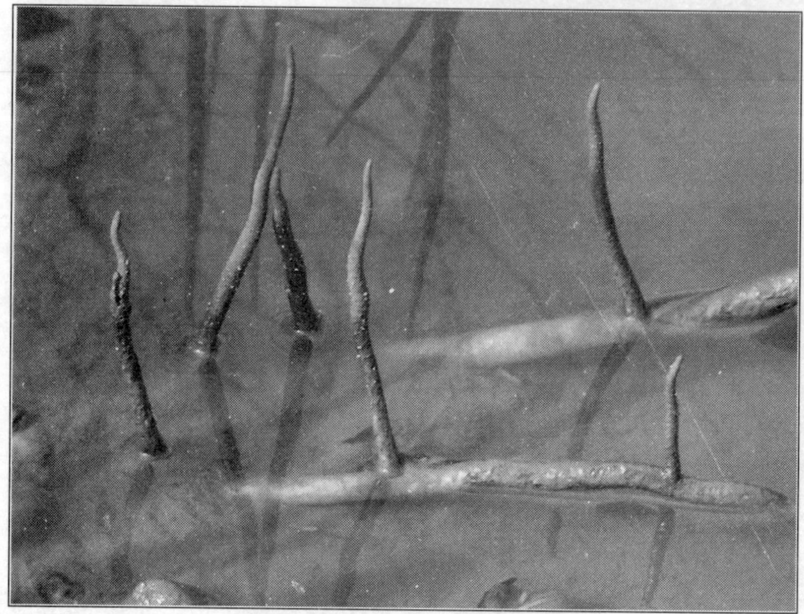

Breathing Roots of Avicennia

Avicennia Officinalis

SUMMARY AND CONCLUSION

Mangroves are defined as tropical and sub-tropical forests with a diverse floristic composition bordering the sea on muddy or peaty low lands periodically submerged or influenced by the tides. These ecosystems are proved important for many reasons.

In India mangroves have covered area of several thousand hectars all along the coast. Maharashtra is one of the coastal states of India, with many rivers emerging from Sahyadri ranges and meeting the Arabian sea. The coast line available for Maharashtra state is 720 km. Ratnagiri and Sindhudurg are the two coastal districts of the state of Maharashtra. Both the districts together have 29 estuaries. The estuaries in both the districts exhibit rich mangrove flora. However, in last few decades this fragile and sensitive ecosystem has been over exploited. All the mangroves in both the districts are exposed to severe anthropogenic pressure.

By considering all these aspects the present study has been undertaken. The emphasis is given to understand the biodiversity component of mangroves in study area. The data has been collected by extensive field surveys. The data is further analysed for species composition, species distribution pattern, diversity indices, faunal components, phenological observations, height and girth analysis, analysis of mangrove soil, remote sensing studies, threats and the IUCN categorization of the species found in the study area.

The survey, mapping and remote sensing studies are carried out by collecting the data from ground visits and from various sources. The studies on remote sensing, data is carried out with the help of the data collected from the remote sensing Agencies like NRSA, Hyderabad and MRSAC, Nagpur. The study revealed that this data is useful in analysing the mangrove area of the concerned region. The data of IRS 1B Liss – II is used for the present study. It is found from remote sensing data that estuaries like Vijaydurg shows maximum mangrove area of 639.5 ha and Kelye shows minimum of 6.25 ha area. The mangroves of Achara show 94.5 ha area. The mangrove area analysed by the ground surveys in present study, at Achara equals to 150.96ha. The ground surveys are carried out in all the estuaries. It is found that ground surveys are essential to record the ground facts which are not known by the aerial device during the ground surveys. Attempts are made to collect the data required for various purposes including IUCN categorization. The study reveals that the mangrove vegetation in the study area is diverse with respect to and follows the normal pattern of species distribution/occurrence. It also reveals that the species like *E. agallocha*, *A. ilicifolius*, *R. mucronata*, *A. officinalis* and *A. marina* show maximum percentage of occurrence as compared to the species like X. *granatum*,

C. iripa, B. cylindrica, S. caseolaris and *T. gallica*. The average canopy area is greater in the species like *A. alba, A. officinalis, S. alba* and *C. iripa* and lower in species like *K. Candel, C. tagal* and *L. racemosa*. The study also shows that the data collected during the ground surveys and RS studies shows considerable variations. It suggests that the high resolution RS data can help in such type of studies.

The studies on mangrove biodiversity in both the districts show the major variations. The study gives importance to both the districts to investigate different mangrove species. The study found 20 typical mangroves, 10 halophytic species, 13 border line mangroves and 15 mangrove associates from both these districts. The mangrove biodiversity is also studied with the help of various diversity indices. The vegetation in the study area is analysed for various indices like species diversity index (D), diversity index (Di), alpha and beta diversity indices. It indicates that the Simpson's Index of Diversity (Di) is greater for the estuaries like Achara, Khavane, Purnagad, Dabhol and Savitri estuaries. The diversity index (Di) shows variation in values for the mangrove stands in the study area. The analysis of alpha and beta diversity indicates that these values are variable for different estuaries. These values are obtained by using the Jaccard's Index of species diversity. The alpha and beta diversity profile indicates that there is positive correlation between the estuarine area and the area occupied by the mangroves of concerned area.

During the present study the vegetation is also analysed to understand the possible Correlation between height and girth with that of canopy cover. It is found that the species like *A. officinalis* and *A. corniculatum* show more positive correlation in case of girth and height. The positive correlation is observed between girth and canopy cover is more or less 0.7 except *A. marina* (dwarf), *E. agallocha* and *A. corniculatum*.

Mangrove supports variety of animal life. These animals become a part of the energy flow in the ecosystem. The important animal groups which are associated with the mangroves are macro and meiobenthos, pisces, mammals, reptiles and birds. Some of the bird group observed in the study area are Herons, Egrets, Lapwings, plover, Gulls, Terns, Storks, Hawks, Kites, Hornbills and King fishers. Among these the uncommon and threatened greet pied Hornbill (Buceros bicornis) have been found at some sites. Some of the common crab species are *Uca roseus, Uca lactea annulipes* and *Uca vocans*. The species like *Scylla serrata* and *Portunus pelagius* are edible. In the present study 13 sp. of molluscs, 25 species of edible fish, 9 species of reptilia, 45 sp. of birds and 10 species of mammalia are found.

Mangroves exhibit specific zonation pattern. During the present study the mangrove zonation and distribution across and along the estuaries are studied. It is found that the species like *Avicennia* occur along the seaward zone flooded by all medium high tides. The second zone is dominated by *R. mucronata* and *S. alba*. The third zone or mixed zone is composed of *A. alba, S. apetala, A. ilicifolius, B. gymnnorrliza, A. cornicnlatum* and *C. tagal*. The landward fringe is limited by *S. persica, C. inerme* and *I. Pes-caprae*. The study revealed that habitat adaptation and microclimate of species decides its zone and succession in the community. From this study it is found that all sites being under human pressure the natural zonation pattern is not seen. The existing zonation pattern is a result of natural distribution and human disturbances.

The mangroves exhibit unique reproductive behaviour or functional diversity. Which is governed by tidal amplitude, and latitude amongst various factors such as soil, temperature and salinity. The present attempt has studied the flowering and fruiting in the mangroves with respect to periodicity. It is observed that in most of the species the early phenophases initiate in the early summer season. Members of family *Rhizophoraceae* show flowering throughout the year. The species like *R. mucronata, C. tagal* and *K. candel* show early stages in the month of April and May and blooming is observed from September to November. The mature propagules are found upto May and June. The species like *Avicennia* show flowering from March to July and matured fruits are formed in June – July. It is found that some phenophases overlap in the species like *C. tagal*. The present study differs from that for Ratnagiri because of latitudinal difference. It is observed that flowering is delayed from lower to upper latitude. The period of delay depends upon the distance between two locations.

The characteristics of the mangroves soils play key role in vegetation development. In the present study the mangrove soil from 28 sites, randomly collected is analysed for various parameters like texture, pH, EC, chlorides and minerals like Na, K, Ca. It is found that soil characteristics show fluctuations in different sites. The soil samples studied so far show the greater sand component as compared to gravel, silt and clay. The lower pH value recorded is 5.15 from two sites of Achara estuary and greater value recorded is 7.75 from one site of Kalabadevi estuary. The values of EC show 1.29 ms/cm as lower and 5.76 ms/cm as the greater value, from a site from Achara estuary and a site from Kolamb estuary, respectively. The chloride content ranges from 0.16% to 1.84%. The Na content ranges from 0.22 to 1.85 gm/100 gm. The K values show a range of 0.13 to 0.97 gm/100 gm. The values for Ca ranges from 0.11 to 0.57 gm/100 gm. The study reveals that the physical and chemical characteristics of mangrove soil show variations on the basis of site of collection in the estuary, time of collection and dominant vegetation.

IUCN has given Red list criteria. These criteria are used for assessing the status of mangroves in the study area. The categorization process requires the data like number of mature individuals, area under each species, threats affecting taxon population etc. this information is helpful to decide the status of the species. During the present study the data required for categorization of mangroves for both the districts has been collected. From these studies it is found that out of twenty four species analysed, some species are analysed as Critically Endangered (CR), some are found Endangered (EN). The study also reveals that all the mangroves from the study area are found under severe anthropogenic threats. The mangroves in the study area are threatened due to loss of habitat, due to fragmentation (LF), Harvest for Food (HF), pollution (Pu), loss of habitat (L), Human interference (I) and trade (T). These threats are listed as per IUCN (2000) version of Red list guidelines.

It is the last aspect of study to deal with conservation aspect. The threatened species indicate priorities for conservation. It is suggested that for conservation of mangroves there is need to implement the CRZ Notification (1991) quite effectively. Moreover, peoples participation is a must and therefore, participatory management of mangrove areas is suggested.

The study concludes that:

(a) the ground surveys lead to record of 20 typical mangroves along with 10 halophytes12 borderline species and 15 associates;

(b) the data from R.S. though is very useful is far from ground surveys,

(c) alpha and beta diversity indices serve as better measure of biodiversity;

(d) though the faunal components do not represent complete list, but added dimensions to biodiversity;

(e) distribution and zonation pattern is indicative of disturbances in the original structure;

(f) the parameters like height and girth also are indicative of disturbance mainly by prunning;

(g) the growth of the species proceeds simultaneously along the increase in girth and canopy area;

(h) phenological observations in present study differ from those earlier reported because of latitudinal differences which amounts to difference of about a week in the phenophase;

(i) the soil characters with respect to physical and chemical nature are within the reported data, however, the granulometry indicates erosion of fine grained layer leaving behind coarse, sandy soil;

(j) all the mangrove species are threatened to a great degree;

(k) for conservation of mangroves participatory approach and effective implementation of CRZ regulation are required.

REFERENCES

Ahmad, A. (1990). Impact of Human Activities on Marine Environment and Guidelines for its Management: Environmentalist View Points. In : Recent Trends in Limnology (eds.) Agrawal, V. P. and P. Das, Muzaffarnagar, India Soc. Of Bio. Sci. 49-60.

Ajmalkhan, S. (2002). Marine Biodiversity Values. Lecture Manual. UNU-UNESCO Inter. Train. Course on Mangrove Biodiversity. Centre of Adv. Study in Mar. Bio. Anna University, India. 10-16.

Aksornkoae S. (1980). Distribution, Growth and Survival of Seedlings of Mangrove Forest in Thailand. In : Symp. Forest Regeneration in Southeast Asia Biotrop. Special Publ., No. 13: 23-27.

Aksornkoae, S. (1976). Structural Characteristics of Natural Forests in Ranong, Southern Thailand. Res. Pap. Fac. Of Forestry, Kasetsart Uni. Bangkok, Thailand 29 p.

Aksornkoae, S. (1976). Structure of Mangrove Forest at Amphoe Khlung, Changwat Chantaburi, Thailand, Kasetsart Univ. For. Bull., 38-42.

Aksornkoae, S. (1982). A Comparison of Structural Characteristics of Mangrove Forest Near Mininf Area and Undisturbed Natural Forests in Ranong. Paper Presented to NRCT-JSPS Seminar, Aug. 2-6, Phuket, Thailand. 29 p.

Annonymous, (1987). A Long Term Multidisciplinary Research Approach and Report on Mangrove Ecosystems of Sunderbans (Publ.) Marine Science Department, Calcutta University, India.

Arnold, C.Y. (1960), Maximum Minimum Temperatures as a Basis for Computing Neat Units. Proceedings of the American Society of Horticultural Science 76: 682-692.

Bacon, P.R. (1970). The Ecology of Caroni Swamp. *Special Publ. Central Statistical Office.* Trininad, 68 p.

Bahuguna, A., and S. Nayak (1994). Coastal Landuse Mapping of Brackish Water Aquaculture site Selection on Orissa Coast. Sci. Note SAC (ISRO), Ahmedabad. RSAM/SAC/CMASS/SN/04.

Bahuguna, A., and S. Nayak (1994C). Coastal Landuse Mapping for Brackish Water Aquaculture site Selection on Orrisa Coast. RSAM/SAC/CMASS/SN/04/94. 13 p.

Bahuguna, A., Chauhan, H.B., and S. Nayak (1995). Coastal Landaus Mapping for Brackish Water Aquaculture site Selection of the Andaman and Nicobarr Group of Islands. RSAM/ SAC/ SMASS ISN/ 08/95.

Bannerjee, L.K. and T.A. Rao (1990). Mangroves of Orissa Coast and Their Ecology. Bishen Singh and Mahendrapal Singh (Publ.) Dehra Dun, India.

Bannerjee, L.K., D.Ghosh and A.R.K. Sastry (1998). Mangroves, Associates and Salt Marshes of the Godavari and Krishna Delta. (A.P.). India, B.S.I., ENVIS, Calcutta, 128 p.

Baskerville, G.L. and Emin, P. (1969). Rapid Estimation of Heat Accumulation from Maximum and Minimum Temperatures. *Ecology,* 50: 514-517.

Bhosale L.J., and Mulik N.G. (1991). Strategies of Seed Germination in Mangroves. Proc. Inter. Seed Symposium, Jodhpur, India, (eds.) David. N. Sen and S. Mohammed (1991). 201-205.

Bhosale L.J.; Banik, S., Gokhale, M.V. and Jayappa, M.A. (2002). Occurrence of *Xylocarpus granatum Koen* and *Cynometra iripa* Kostel Along the Coast of Maharashtra J. Econ. Taxon. Bot. 26(1): 82-87.

Bhosale, L. J. (1974). Physiology of Salt Tolerance of Plants. Ph.D. Thesis, Shivaji University, Kolhapur (MS) India.

Bhosale, L.J. (1978). Ecophysiological Studies of the Mangroves from the Western Coast of India. Final Report, Shivaji University, Kolhapur, India. 81 p.

Bhosale, L. J. (1983). Adaptive Strategies in Mangroves. *Proc. Natl. Symp. Adv. Front. Pl. Sci. Jodhapur,* 81: 82 p.

Bhosale, L.J. (1986). (ed.) The Mangroves. *Proc. Nat. Symp. Biol. Util. And Cons. Of Mangroves.* (ed.) Shivaji University, Kolhapur. 558 p.

Bhosale, L. J. (1987). Mangrove Regeneration. Brochure. Shivaji University, Kolhapur (India), 12 p.

Bhosale, L.J. (1987). The Mangrove Ecosystems of India. In: C.D. Field and A.J. Dartnall (eds.) Mangrove Ecosystems of Asia and The Pacific. Status, Exploitation and Management. Proc. Of the Res. for Development Seminar, Australian Institute of Marine Science, Townsville, Australia, 18-25 May, 1985, 24-29.

Bhosale, L.J. (1989). Mangroves of Maharashtra – An Overview. In: Wetlands, Mangroves and Biosphere Reserves. *Proc. Indo-US Workshop, New Delhi, Jan, 1989*: 187-196.

Bhosale, L.J. (1990). Human Impact on Primary Productivity and Regeneration of Mangroves of Maharashtra, Final Report, Submitted to DOEN, New Delhi, 278 p.

Bhosale, L.J. (1990a). Effect of Water Pollution in the Areas Near Sea on Eustarine Ecosystem. Final Report Submitted to Department of Ocean Development, Govt. of India, New Delhi. 146 p.

Bhosale, L. J. (1990b). Mangrove Management Plan for India. *Proc. First Nat. Sem. On Wetlands, April, 1989*: 42-48.

Bhosale, L. J. (2002). Categorization of Mangroves of Maharashtra Based on IUCN Red List Guideline and Germplasm Preservation of Threatened Species. Final Report Submitted to Ministry of Environ. and Forest, Govt. of India, New Delhi. 155 p.

Bhosale, L.J. (2002). New Mangrove Records for the Coast of Maharashtra: A Note. *Seshaiyana*, Vol. 10(2), ENVIS, Annamalai University, Tamilnadu, India.

Bhosale, L.J. (2003). Malvan. In: *Bioresource Status in Select Coastal Location*. (Publ.) NBBD, New Delhi and MSSRF, Chennai, India: 63-82.

Bhosale, L.J. (2005). Field Guide to Mangroves of Maharashtra. Shivaji University, Kolhapur. 315 p.

Bhosale, L.J. and Mulik, N.G. (1995). Environment Adaptive Biology: The Mangroves Environ. and Adaptive Bio of Plants. Prof. D.N.Sen Commemoration Volume (ed) D.D. Chawan, Scientific Publishers, Jodhapur. 143-150.

Bhosale, L.J. and N.G. Mulik (1991). Endangered Mangrove Areas of Maharashtra. In: Proc. Symp. On Significance of Mangroves, Pune (eds.) Agate, A. D., S.D. Bonde and K.P.N. Kumaran, India, Mah. Asso. Cultiv. Sci.: Res. Inst., 8-10.

Blasco, F. (1975). The Mangroves India. Inst. Fr. Pondichery Trav. Sec. Sc. Tech. N XIV 175 p.

Blasco, F. (1977). Outline of Ecology, Botany and Forestry of the Mangals of the Indian Subcontinent. In : V.J. Chapman (ed.) *Ecosystems of the World 1: Wet Coastal Ecosystems.* Elsevier Scientific Publ. Co., New York, 241-260.

Blasco, F., T. Gauguelin., M.Rasolofo-Harrinoro, J. Denis., M. Aizpuru., and V.Caldairou (1998). Recent Advances in Mangrove Studies Using Remote Sensing Data. *Mar. Fresh water. Res.* 49: 287-296.

Braun and J. Blanquet (1932). *Plant Sociology*: The Study of Plant Communities. McGraw Hill, New York.

Bunt, J. S. (1992). In: Coastal and Estuarine Studies: Tropical Mangrove Ecosystem (eds.) A.I. Robertson and D.M. Alongi American Geophysical Union, Washington DC, USA, 101-136.

Bunt, J.S. (1996). Mangrove Zonation: An Examination of Data from Seventeen Riverine Estuaries in Tropical Australia. *Annals of Botany*, 78: 333-341.

Bunt, J.S. (1999). Overlap in Mangrove Species Zonal Patterns: Some Methods of Analysis. Mangroves and Salt Manshes. 3: 155-164.

Bunt, J.S. and E.D. Bunt (1999). Complexity and Variety of Zonal Pattern in the Mangroves of the Hinchinbrook Area, Northeastern Australia. *Mangroves and Salt marshes*, 3: 165-176.

Bunt, J.S. and Thomas, S.S. (1999). Indicators of Mangrove Zonality: The Normanby River, N.E. Australia. *Mangroves and Salt marshes*, 3: 177-184.

Caprio, J.M. (1974). The Solor Thermal Unit Concept in Problems Related to Plant Development. In: Phenology and Seasonally Modeling. Ecological Studies 8: Syn. Thesis and Modelling (ed) H. Leith. Springler, Verlog, New York.

Caprio, S.M. (1971). The Solar-thermal Unit Theory in Relation to Plant Development and Potential Evapo-transpiration. Montana States University Agricultural Experiment Station Circular 251, Missoula, Montana, U.S.A.

Cawkell, E.M. (1964). *Ibis*. 106: 251-253.

Champion, H. G. (1936). A Preliminary Survey of the Forest Types of India and Burma, Indian For Rec, 1: 365 p.

Champion, H.G. and S.K. Seth (1968). A Revised Survey of Forests of India. Manager and Publ. 6. Delhi, India.

Chapman V.J. (1960). Salt Marshes and Salt Deserts of the World. Leonard Hill (Book), Ltd. 392 p.

Chapman V.J. (1976). *Mangroves vegetation* J. Cramer, Vaduz. 447 p.

Chapman, V.J. (1944-1939). Cambridge University Expedition to Jamaica *J. Linn. Soc. Bot.* (Land), 52: 407-533.

Chapman, V.J. (1954). The Halophytic Vegetation of the World. *VIII Congress International Botanique Report Sec.* 1(5): 24-30.

Chapman, V.J. (1964). *Coastal Vegetation*. Pergamom Press, Oxford: 245 p.

Chapman, V.J. (1970). Mangrove Phytosociology. *Trop. Ecol.* 11: 01-10.

Chapman, V.J. (1974). *Salt Marrshes and Salt Deserts of the World*. 2nd Edition, Vertigo Von J. cramer. Germany. 392 p.

Chapman, V.J. (ed) (1977). Wet Coastal Ecosystems (Ecosystems of the World, I) Amsterdam, Elsevier.

Chatterjee, D. (1958). Symposium on Mangrove Vegetation. *Sci. Cult.* 23: 329-335.

Chhapquar, B.T. (1959). Adding the Crab Fauna of Bombay. *J.B.N.N.S.* 55: 582-585.

Chirputkar, M.B. (1969). Physiological Studies in Marine Plants of Bombay. Ph. D. Thesis. Univ. of Bombay.

Clark, C.D., D.J. Mumby,. E.P. Green., A.J. Edwards, and A.C. Ellis. (1998). Remote Sensing Techniques for Mangrove Mapping. *Int. J. Remote Sensing*., 19(5): 935-356.

Cody, M.L. (1986). Diversity, Rarity and Conservation in Mediterranean-climate Regions. In: Soule, M.E. (ed.). *Conservation Biology*: The Science of Scarcity and Diversity. 123-152. Sinquer Associates, Sunderland, Mass.

Cooke, T. (1901). The Flora of the Presidency of Bombay. *Bot. Survey of India*, Culcutta.

Cornell, H.V. (1985). Local and Regional Richness of Cynipine Gall Wasps on California Oaks. *Ecology*. 66: 1247-1260.

Dagar, J.C. (1987). Mangrove Vegetation, its Structure, Ecology, Management and Importance with Special Reference to Andaman and Nicobar Islands. Proc. Symp. on Management of Coastal Ecosystems and Oceanic Resources of the Andamans. (eds.) Singh, N.T., B. Gangwar., G.C.Rao and R. Sounderrajan, 8-23.

Davies, J.L. (1977). *"The Coasts"*. In: D.N. Jeans (ed.) *Australia Geography.* Sydney Univ. Press, Sydney. 134-151.

Deshmukh, S. (1991). *Ecological* Studies of Mangroves Nearby Bombay, Ph.D. Thesis Submitted to University of Bombay.

Diops, E.S., Gordon, C., Semesi, A.K., Soumare, A., Diallo, N., Guisse, A., Diouf, M. and Ayivor, J. S. (2000). Mangroves of Africa. In : *Mangrove Ecosystems,* Edited by L.D. de Lacerda (Springer, Berlin). 63-121.

Dwivedi, S.N.; A.H. Parulekar, S.C. Goswami and A.G. Untawale, (1975). Ecology of Mangrove Swamps of the Mandovi Estuary, Goa, India. In: G. Walsh, S. Snedaker and H. Teas (eds.) *Proceedings of Intl. Symp. On Biol. And Manag. of mangroves Honolulu, Hawaii.* Oct. 1974 I: 115-125.

Efrenel, G.D. (1966). *Ibis,* 108: 423-424.

ENVIS Publication (1997). Mangroves of India; State of the Art-report Published by Environmental Information System Center. Center of Advanced Study in Marine Biology, Annamalai University, Parangipettai, Tamil Nadu, India.

Farnsworth, E.J. and Ellison, A.M. (1997). The Global Conservation Status of Mangroves. *Ambio,* 26 (6): 328-334.

Fiedler, P.L. and Ahouse, J.J. (1992). Hierarchies of Cause: Towards an Understanding of Rarity in Vascular Plant Species. In Fiedler, P.L. and Jain, S.K. (eds.) *Conservation Biology.* The Theory and Practice of Nature Conservation, Preservation and Management, 23-47. Chapman and Hall, New York.

Field, G.D. (1968). Utilization of Mangroves by Birds on the Freetown Peninsula Sierra Leone. *Ibis,* 110: 354-357.

Franklin, J.F. (1993). Preserving Biodiversity: Species, Ecosystems or Landscapes. *Ecological Applications.* 3: 202-205.

Gadgil, M. (1996) Documenting Diversity: An Experiment. *Current Science.* 70(1): 36-44.

Galloway, R.W. (1982). Distribution and Physiographic Patterns of Australian Mangroves. In : *Mangrove Ecosystems in Australia. Structure, Function and Management.* (ed.) B.F. Clough,ANU Press, Canberra: 31-54.

Gaykar, B.M. (1991). Studies on Zinc from Mangroves and Their Environment. Ph.D. Thesis, Shivaji University, Kolhapur (MS) India.

Ghewade, K.S. and G.V. Joshi. (1980). Photosynthetic and Photorespiratory Carbon Metabolism in the Seagrass. *Halophilla beccarii* Aschers. Indian J. Exp. Biol., 18: 1344-1345.

Gill, A.M. and Tomlinson, P.B. (1969). Studies on the Growth of Red Mangrove (*R. mangle*). I. Habit and General Morphology. *Biotropica,* 1: 1-9.

Graham, M.J. and *et al.* (1975). Cairns Wetlands a Preliminary Report *Operculam,* 4: 117-148.

Green, E.P., P.J. Mumby. A.J. Edwards., C.P.Clark. and A.C.Ellis. (1998). The Assessment of Mangrove Areas Using High Resolution Multispectral Airborne Imagery *Jour. of Coastal Res.* 14(2): 433-443.

Gunasekaran, S.A., Jayapaul, and P.M. Raju (1992). Distribution of Mangrove Plants in Relation to the Chemical Characteristics of the Soil, Muthupet, Tamil Nadu, India. *Asian Environ.* 14(3): 59-69.

Hartog, C. den (1967). The Structural Aspects in the Ecology of Seagrass Communities. Halgolander Wiss. Meere-Sunters, 15: 648-659.

Huston, M.A. (1994). Biological Diversity – The Coexistence of Species on Changing Landscapes. Cambridge University Press, Cambridge.

Imoh E. Ukpong (1992). The Structure and Soil Relations of *Avicennia* Mangrove Swamps in Southeastern Nigeria. *Tropical Ecology* 33(1): 1-16.

IUCN (1993). Draft IUCN Red List Categories. IUCN, Gland, Switzerland.

IUCN (1994). IUCN Red List Categories. Prepared by the IUCN Species Survival Commission. IUCN, Gland, Switzerland.

IUCN (1996). Resolution 1.4. Species Survival Commission. Resolution and Recommendations, pp. 7-8. World Conservation Congress, 13-23 October 1996, Montreal, Canada. IUCN, Gland, Switzerland.

IUCN/SSC (1997). Unpublished Biological Information Sheet for Mangroves.

IUCN/SSC (1999) Criteria Review Working Group. IUCN Red List Criteria Review Provisional Report: Draft of the Proposed Changes and Recommendations. Species 31 & 32: 43-57.

IUCN/SSC (2000). Criteria Review Working Group (version 3.1), IUCN, Gland, Switzerland.

IUCN/SSC (2001) Criteria Review Working Group (version 3.1), IUCN, Gland, Switzerland.

Jagtap, T.G. (1985). Ecological Studies in Relation to the Mangrove Environment Along Goa Coast, India. Ph.D. Thesis, Shivaji University, Kolhapur, India.

Jagtap, T.G., A.G. Untawale and S.N. Inamdar (1994). Study of Mangrove Environment of Maharashtra Coast Using Remote Sensing Data. *Indian J. Mar. Sci.* 23: 90-93.

Jagtap, T.G. (1986 b). Structure and Composition of Mangrove Forest Along the Goa Coast. In: Bhosale, L.J. (ed.) *The Mangroves: Proc. Nat. Symp. Biol. Util. Cons. Mangroves.* Nov. 1985, Shivaji University, Kolhapur, India. 185-195.

Jagtap, T.G. (1987). Seasonal Distribution of Organic Matter in Mangrove Environment of Goa. *Indian J. Mar. Sci.* 16(2): 103-106.

Japar, A. (1994). Mangrove Plant Resource in the ASEAN Region. In: Proc. of ASEAN- Aust. Symp. On Liv. Coast. Resources. Vol. 1 : Status Review (eds.) C. Wilkinson, S. Sundara and C.L. Ming, (Aus. Inst. Mar. Sci.) 123-138.

Jones, W.T. (1971). The Field Identification and Distribution of Mangroves in Eastern Australia. *Queensland Naturalist*, 20: 35-51.

Joshi, G.V. (1976). Studies in Photosynthesis Under Saline Condition. PL. 480 Project Submitted to Shivaji University, Kolhapur.

Joshi, G.V. (1976). Studies on Photosyuthesis Under Saline Conditions. (Publ.) Shivaji University, Kolhapur.

Joshi, G.V. and L.J. Bhosale (1982). Estuarine Ecosystems of India. In: D.N. Sen and K.S. Rajpurohit (eds.) *Contribution to the Ecology of Halophytes T: VS2*. Dr. W. Junk, the Hague, 21-23.

Joshi, G.V. and S.D. Shinde (1978). *Ecogeographical Studies on Terekhol and Vashisthi Rivers*, Shivaji University Publ. Kolhapur, India, 56 p.

Joshi, G.V., B. B.jamale and L.J. Bhosale (1975). Ion Regulation in Mangroves. In: G. Walsh, S. Snedaker and H. Teas. (eds.) Proc. Int. Symp. Biol. of Manag. of Mangroves. Honolulu, Hawaii Oct. 1974. Gainesville, Florida. 595-607.

Julius, A. (1997). A Study of the Microbial Population and the Decomposition of Leaf Litter in the Mangrove Ecosystem Along the Dar es Salaam Coast, Dissertation, University of Dar es Salaam, Tanzania.

Kadam, S.D. and L.J. Bhosale (1986). Variation in Different Physical and Chemical Parameters of Estuarine Water and Soil at Different Places in Ratnagiri District. In: L.J. Bhosale (ed.) *The Mangroves: Proc. Nat. Symp. Biol. Util. Cons. Mangroves.* Nov. 1985. Shivaji Univ. Press, Kolhapur. India. 356-361.

Kadam, S.D. and L.J. Bhosale (1987). Chlorophyll, Carbohydrate and Polyphenol Contents from the Leaves of *Avicennia officinalis* in Response to Water and Soil Quality. *J. Mar. Biol. Ass.* India. 29(1 & 2) : 373-376.

Kannan, L. (2002). Understanding Biodiversity. Lecture manual, UNU-UNESCO Inter. Train-course on Mangrove Biodiversity, Centre of Adv. Study in Mar. Bio. Anna. University, India. 2-8.

Kasinathan, R. and A. Shanmugam (1985). Molluscan Fauna of Pitchavaram Mangroves, Tamil nadu. In : L. J. Bhosale (ed.) The Mangroves : *Proc. Nat. Symp. Biol. Util. Cons. Mangroves.* Nov. 1985. Kolhapur, India. 438-443.

Kathiresen, K. (2002). Global Bio-diversity of Mangroves in Relation to India. *Lecture Manual.* UNU-UNESCO Inter. Train. Course on Mangrove Bio-diversity. Centre of Adv. Study in Mar. Bio. Anna University. 106-122.

Kathiresen, K. and R. Rajendran (2005). Mangrove Ecosystems of the Indian Ocean Region. *Ind. J. Mar. Sci.* 34(1): 104-113.

Kathiresen, K. and S.Z. Quasim (2005). Biodiversity in Mangrove Ecosystems, (Hindustan Publisher, New Delhi). 252 p.

KjerFve, B. (1990). Manual for Investigation of Hydrological Processes in Mangrove Ecosystem. UNESCO/UNDP Regional Project, New Delhi.

Kotmire, S.Y. (1983). Ecophysiological Studies in the Mangroves of Western Coast of India. Ph.D. Thesis Submitted to Shivaji University, Kolhapur (MS), India.

Kotmire, S.Y. and L.J. Bhosale (1979). Some Aspects of Chemical Composition of Mangrove Leaves and Sediments. *Mahasagar*, 12(3): 149-154.

Kotmire, S.Y. and L.J. Bhosale (1980). Chemical Composition of Leaves of *Avicennia officinalis* Linn and *A. marina* var. *acutissima* Staff and Moldenke. *Ind. Jour. Mar. Sci.* 9: 299-301.

Kotmire, S.Y. and L.J. Bhosale (1985). A Study of Mangrove Vegetation Along Deogad Estuary. In: V. Krishnamurthy and A.G. Untawale (eds.) *Marine Plants.* Seaweed Research and Utilization Association, Madras, 225-230.

Krishnamurthy, K., A. Choudharry, and A.G.Untawale (1987). Status Report Mangroves in India, Ministry of Environment and Forest, Govt. of India, New Delhi, 150 p.

Kulkarni, P.K. (1990). Some Ecological and Physiological Aspects of *Rhizophora* Propagules. Ph.D. Thesis Submitted to Shivaji University, Kolhapur (MS) India.

Kulkarni, P.K. and L.J. Bhosale (1992). Growth Performance of *R. mucronata* in Field and Laboratory Conditions. *J. MAR. BIOL. ASSO. INDIA.* 34: 1-4.

Kurlapkar, D.D. (1993). Studies on the Mangrove Ecosystem of Western Maharashtra, Ph.D. Thesis Submitted to Shivaji University, Kolhapur (MS), India.

Kurlapkar, D.D., and L.J. Bhosale (1985). Preliminary Report on Ecology of *Rhizophora Apiculata.* In: Bhosale, L.J. (ed.) *The Mangroves: Proc. Nat. Symp. Biol. Util. Cons. Mangroves.* Nov. 1985. Shivaji University, Kolhapur, India. 205-209.

Lakshminarsimhan, P. (1996). Flora of Maharashtra State. Botanical Survey of India 337-339.

Lugo, A. F. and S. C. Snedaker (1973). Properties of Mangrove Forest in South Florida. In: G. Walsh, S. Snedaker and H. Teas (eds.) *Proc. Int. Symp. Biol. Mang. Mangroves. Honolulu, Hawaii.* Oct. 1974. Gainesvtille, Florida I : 170-211.

Mace, G.M. and *et al.* (1992). The Development of New Criteria for Listing Species on the IUCN Red List. Species 19: 16-22.

Mace, G.M. and Lande, R. (1991). Assessing Extinction Threats: Towards a Reevaluation of IUCN Threatened Species Categories. *Conservation Biology*. 5: 148-157.

Macnae, W. (1966). Mangroves in Eastern and Southem Australia. *Aust. Jour. Bot.*, 15: 67-104.

Macnae, W. (1968). A General Account of the Fauna and Flora of Mangrove Swamps and Forests in the Indowest Pacific Regions. *Advances in Marine Biology*, 6: 270-273.

Magurran, A.E. (1988). Ecological Diversity and its Measurement. Princeton University Press, Princeton, NJ. 149 p.

Mandal, A.K. and A. Mishra (1985). Mudflats of Lower Bengal with Special Reference to Macrobenthic Fauna. In: L.J. Bhosale (ed.) *The Mangroves: Proc. Nat. Symp. Biol. Util. Cons. Mangroves*. Nov. 1985. Kolhapur, India. 425-431.

Martinez, N.D. (1992). Constant Connectance in Community Food Webs. *American Naturalist* 139: 1208-1218.

Matilal, S.B., B. Mukherjee, Chatterjee, and M.D. Gupta (1986). Studies on Soil and Vegetation of Mangrove Forests of Sunderbans (India). *Indian J. Mar. Sci.* 15(3): 181-184.

McLusky D. S. (1974). Ecology of Estuaries. 144 p.

McNaughton, S.J. (1983). Serengeti Grassland Ecology: The Role of Composite Environmental Factors and Contingency in Community Organisation. Ecological Monographs. 53: 291-320.

McRoy, C.P. and C. Helfferich (1977). In: Seagrass Ecosystems. A Scientific Perspective (eds.) C.P. McRoy and C. Helfferich. (Publ.) Marcel Dekker, Inc. New York and Basel, 1-314 p.

Mishra, S.D. (1967). Physiological Studies in Mangroves of Bombay. Ph.D. Thesis Submitted to University of Bombay (India).

Misra, R. (1968). Ecology Workbook. Oxford and IBH Publishing Co.

Mulik, N. G. (1987). Studies on Some Aspects of Mangroves. Ph.D. Thesis, Shivaji University, Kolhapur (MS) India.

Mulik, N.G. and L.J. Bhosale (1987). Flowering Penology of the Mangroves from the West Coast of Maharashtra. *Jour. Bombay. Nat. His. Soc.* 86: 355-359.

Mulik, N.G. and R.D. Tare (1997). *Avicennia* an Ecological Perspective. *Ecol. Env. and Cons.* 3(3/4): 197-201.

Murthy Ramana, V.K. and B. Kondala Rao (1987). Survey of Meiofauna in the Gautami-Godavari Estuary. *J. Mar. Biol. Assoc. India*, 29(1&2): 37-44.

Murthy, M.S.R., Udaya Lakshmi. and C.B.S. Dutt (1998). Efficient Forest Resources Management Through GIS and Remote Sensing. *Curr. Sci.*, 75(3): 272-282.

Naidoo, G. and F. Raiman (1982). Some Physical and Chemical Properties of Mangrove Soils at Sipingo and Mgeni, Natal. *South African J. of Bot.*, 1 (4): 85-90.

Nair, B.N., K. Dharmaraj., P.K. Abdul Axis., M. Arunachalam., K. Krishnakumar and N.K. Balsubramanian (1984). Ecology of Indian Estuaries: VIII. Inorganic Nutrients of Ashtamudi Estuary. *Mahasagar* 17: 19-32.

Naskar, K. and D.N.G. Bakshi (1989). Stages of Land Formation and Comparative Studies of the Different Microecological Zones of Sundarbans (WB, India). *Fragm. Flor. Geobot.*, 34(3-4): 341- 354.

Naskar, K.R. and Guha Bakshi (1987). Mangrove Swamps of the Sunderbons. An Ecological Perspective. Publ. Naya prakash. Calcutta (India).

Navalkar, B.S. (1956). J. Univ. Nat. Hist. Soc. 53: 335-345.

Nayak, S. and *et al.* (1993). A Summary Report of Coastal Studies Project, Scientific Note, Space Application Center, Ahemedabad. SAC/RSA/RSAG/DOD-COS/SN/06/93.

Negi, H.R. (2001). Diversity and Dominance of Liver Worts of Chopta-Tunganath in the Garhwal Himalaya. *Int. Jr. of Eco. And Envirn. Sci.* 27: 13-21.

Noss, R.F. (1983). A Regional Landscape Approach to Maintain Diversity. *Bioscience.* 33: 700-706.

Odum, W.E. and E.J. Heald (1975). The Detritus Based Food Web of an Estuarine Mangrove Community. *Estuarine Research,* 1: 205-286.

Odum, W.E., C.C. McIvor and T.J. Smith (1982). The Ecology of the Mangroves of South Florida: A Community Profile. *Biological Service Programme* D.S. Dept. of the Interior. 145 p.

OTA (1987). Office of Technology Assessment. Technologies to Maintain Biological Diversity. OTA-F-350. Washington, DC.

Parulekar, A.H., Dhargalkar, V.K. and S.Y.S. Singhal (1980). Benthic Studies in Goa Estuaries: Part III. Annual Cycle of Macrofaunal Distribution, Production and Trophic Relations *I. J. M. S.* 9: 189-200.

Parulekar, A.H., G. Victor Rajamanickam and S.N. Dwivedi. 1975. Benthic Studies in Goa Estuaries : Biomass a Faunal Composition in the Zuari Estuary. *I.J.M.S.* 4: 202-205.

Patanapanpaliboon, P. (1979). Structure of Mangrove Forest at Amphoe Khao Saming, Trat, M.S. Thesis, Chualongkorn, Univ., Bangkok 88 p.

Percival, M. and J.S. Womerseley (1975). In Floristic and Ecology of the Mangrove Vegetation of Papua New Guinea. Botany Bull No. 8. Dept of Forests, Div. of Botany, LUE, Papu New Guinea, 94 p.

Pillai, G.N. (1977). Distribution and Seasonal Adundance of Macrobenthos of Cochin Backwaters. *I.J.M.S.,* 6: 1-5.

Puri, G.S. and S.K. Jam (1958). Mangrove Vegetation in Western India. Symp. On Mangrove Vegetation, *Sci. and Cult.,* 23: 332 p.

Radhakrishanan, N. (1985). Studies on the Mangrove Along the Central West Coast: Achara, Maharashtra).' In: Bhosale L.J. (ed). *The Mangroves Proc. of Natl. Symp on Bio. Uti. and Cons. of Mangroves* Nov. 1985, Shivaji University, Kolhapur, India, 222-226.

Rajagopalan, M.S. (1987). Mangroves as Component of Coastal Ecosystems of the Andamans. Proc. Symp. On Management of Coastal Ecosystems and Oceanic Resources of the Andamans (eds.) Singh, N.T., B.Gangar., G.C. Rao and R. Soundarragjan. 1-7.

Ramchandran, S.S. Sundaramoorthy, and R. Krishamoorthy, (1998). Application of Remote Sensing and GIS to Coastal Wetland Ecology of Tamil Nadu and Andaman and Nicobar Islands with Special ref. Erence to Mangroves. *Cur. Sci.* 75(3): 236-244.

Ramchandran, K.K., G. Balasubramanian, J. Kurian and J. Thomas (1985). The Mangrove Ecosystem of Kerala. Its Mapping, Inventory and Some Environmental Aspects. 47 p.

Rangnath, B.K., C.B.S. Dutt and B.Manikian (1989). Digital Mapping of Mangroves in Middle Adaman of India. Proc. 6th Symp. Coast. Zone 89, Charleston, South Carolina, American Society of Civil Engineers, New York. 1: 741-750.

Rao, B.K. and A.S.R. Swamy (1991). Sediment Characteristics of Environments in the Modern Krishna Godavari Deltas. *Quaternary Deltas of India* (ed.) R. Vaidyanadhan, Banglore, India. Geol. Soc. Of India., 121-138.

Rao, R.K. and B.B. Sharma (1992). A Manual for Herbarium Collections, B.S.I., Calcultta.

Rao, T.A. (1998). Flowering Phenology and Pollination of the Eumangroves and Their Associates to Plan Regeneration and Breeding Programmes. *Jour. of Econ. and Tax Bot.*, 22(1): 19-27.

Rao, T.A., A.K. Mukherjee and L.K. Bannerjee (1973). Is *Acrostichum aureum* L. Truly a Mangrove Fern? *Current Sci.*, 42(15): 546- 547.

Rao, T.A., K.R.Aggarwal and A.K. Mukherjee (1963). An Ecological Account of the Vegetation of Reameshwaram Islands, *Bull. Bot. Sur India*. 5(314): 301-323.

Rao, T.A., K.R.Aggarwal and A.K. Mukherjee (1966). Ecological Studies of Sarurashtra Coast and Neighbouring Islands: IV Piram Island. *Bull. Bot. Sur. India*. 8: 60-67.

Reid, W.V. (1994). Setting Objectives for Conservation Evaluation. In: Forey, P.L. Humphries, C.J. and Vane-wright, R. I. (eds.) Systematics and Conservation Evaluation. 1-14 Claredon Press, Oxford.

Reid, W.V. and Miller, K.R. (1989). Keeping Options Alive. World Resources Institute, Washington, DC.

Ricklefs, R.E. and Schluter, D. (1993). Species Diversity: Regional and Historical Influences. In: Ricklefs, R.E. and Schluter, D. (eds.) Species Diversity in Ecological Communities: Historical and Geographical Perspectives. University of Chicago Press, Chicago. 350-363.

RSAM, (1992). (Remote Sensing Application Mission), Coastal Environment Space Application Center (ISRO), Ahmedabad.

Rueda, L., Rogelio and Fritz Gosselk. (1986). Investigation of the Benthos of Mangrove Coastal Lagoons in Southern Cuba. *INT. REV. GESAANTTEN HYDROBIOL*. 71(6): 779-794.

Saenger, B., E.J.Hegerl and J.D.S. Davie (1983). Global Status at Mangrove Ecosystems. International Union for Conservation. of Nature and Natural Resources, Vol. 3: 88 p.

Saenger, P. (1982). Morphological, Anatomical and Reproductive Adaptations of Australian Mangroves. In: B.F. Clough (ed.), Mangrove Ecosystems in Australia Structure, Function and Management, Australian Institute of Mar. Sci. Cape Ferguson, 153-192.

Saenger, P. (1998). Mangrove Vegetation: An Evolutionary Perspective. *Mar. Freshwater Res.*, 49: 277-286.

Sah, K.D. (1986). Studies on Nutrient Status of Some Mangrove Muds of Sunderbans. In: L.J. Bhosale (ed.) *The Mangroves: Proc. Nat. Symp. On Biol. Util. Cons. Mang.* Nov. 1985. Shivaji University, Kolhapur, India. 375-377.

Samant, J.S. (1985). Avifauna of the Mangroves Around Ratnagiri, Maharashtra. In: L.J. Bhosale (ed.) *The Mangroves: Proc. Nat. Symp. Biol. Util. Cons.* Mangroves Nov. 1985. Kolhapur, India. 456-468.

Santisuk, T. (1983). Taxonomy of the Terrestrial Trees and Shrubs in the Mangrove Formation in Thailand. First UNDP/UNESCO Region. Train. Course on Introduction to Mangrove Ecosystems (National Res. Council, Bangkok, Thailand).

Sanyal, Pranabes (1992). Sunderbans Mangrove: Wild Life Potential and Conservation. In: K.P. Singh and J.S. Singh (eds.) *Tropical Ecosystems: Ecology and Management*. Wiley Eastern Ltd., New Delhi: 309-313.

Sathe, S.S. and L.J. Bhosale (1991). Physiology of Avicennia: A Review (eds.) Agate, A.D., S.D. Donde, and K.P.N. Kumaran. Proc. Symp. On Significance of Mangroves, Pune. Inst. Maha. Assoc. cultiv. Sci. Res. Inst. 47-51.

Sathe, S.S. and Bhosale, L.J. (1987). Comparative Study on the Leaf Constituents of Different Species of *Avicennia*., *J. Aqua. R.* 1(1): 30-34.

Satyanarayana B., A.V. Raman., F. Dehairs., C, Kalavati., and P. Chandramohan (2002). Mangrove Floristic and Zonation Patterns of Coringa, Kakinada Bay, East Coast of India. *Wetlands Ecology and Management*. 10(1): 25-39.

SCOR/COE (1981). Global Status of Mangrove Ecosystems. Paper No. 3 (eds.) Saenger, Hegerl. and Davis, Gland Switzerland.

Selvam, V. and *et al*. (1991). Plant Communities and Soil Properties of Three Mangrove Stands of Madras Coast. *Indian J. Mar Sci*., 20(1): 67-69.

Sharma, V.V., G.K.K. Raju and T.R. Babu (1982). Pollution Characteristics and Water Quality of Visakhapatnam Harbour. *Mahasagar*, 15: 15-22.

Shekhawat, M.S., and A.K. Dixit (2005). Mangroves can Save US from Tsunami. *Agrobios* 4(5): 57-59.

Sidhu, S.S. (1963). Studies on the Mangroves of India. I. East Godavari Region. *Indian Forester*, 89: 337-351.

Singh, V.P., and Ajay Garge (1993). Ecology of Mangrove Swamps of the Andaman Islands, 181 p.

Singh.V.P., Garge, A. Pathak, S.M. and L.P. Mall. (1986). Mangrove Forests of Andaman Islands in Relation to Human Interference *Environmental Conservation*. 13(2): 169-172.

Snedaker, S.C. (1978). *Nat and Resources*., 14 UNESCO PARIS, 6-13.

Spellerburg, I. F. (1992). Evaluation and Assessment for Conservation. Chapman and Hall, London.

Stevely, J. and L. Robinwitz (1982). Mangroves: A Guide for Planting and Maintenance. *Florida Co-operative Extension Marine Advisory Bulletin Map*. 25: 1-8.

Sukardjo, S. and S. AKhmad (1982). The Mangrove Forest of Java and *Bali*. *Biotrop. Spe. Publ*. No. 17: 113-116.

Sukardjo, S., K. Kartawinata, and I. Yamada (1984). The Mangrove Forest in Bungin River, Banyuasin South Sumantra. *Proc. As. Symp. Mangr. Env. Res. and Manag*. 121-141.

Supate, A.R. (1992). Study of Estuarine Ecosystem in Relation to Phytoplankton. Ph.D. Thesis, Shivaji University, Kolhapur (MS) India.

Swaminathan, M.S., S.V. Deshmukh and V. Balaji (1994). Establishment of an International Network for the Conservation and Sustainable Utilization of Mangrove Forest Genetic Resources. Final Report of Travelling Workshop to Mangrove Forests in South and Southeast Asia, Oceania and Central Africa. 61 p.

Tansley, A.G. (1935). The Use and Abuse of Vegetational Concepts. *Ecology* 67 : 1167-1179.

Tare, R.D. (1993). Ecology of Mangrove Species. M. Phil. Thesis Shivaji University, Kolhapur (MS) India.

Thomas, G. and T.V. Fernandez (1993). A Comparative Study on the Hydrographic and Species Composition in Three Mangrove Ecosystems of Kerala, South India. *J. Ecobiol*., 5(3): 181-188.

Tomlinson, P.B. (1986). The Botany of Mangroves. Cambridge Univ. Press. Cambridge, England. 413 p.

Untawale, A.G. (1985). Mangroves of Asia and the Pacific: Status and Usage. The Final Document of the UNDP, UNESCO Regional Research and Training Pilot Programme on Mangrove Ecosystem in Asia and the Pacific NIO. Dona, Paula, Goa, 20 p.

Untawale, A.G. (1985). Status of Mangrove Research in India. In: Bhosale L.J. (ed.) *The Mangroves: Proc. Nat. Symp. Biol. Util. Cons. Mangroves*. Shivaji University, Kolhaour. Nov. 1985. 127-134.

Untawale, A.G., S. Wafar, and T.G. Jagtap (1982). In: Brij Gopal, R.E.Turner, R.G.Wetzel and D.F. Whigham (eds.) *Wetlands: Ecology and Management*. NIE and ISP. New Delhi. 10-17.

Vannucci, M. (1989). The Mangroves and us. IAAS Publishers, New Delhi 203 p.

Volhard, A. (1956). Chlorides. In: Modern Methods of Plant Analysis. Peach K. and Tracy, M.V. (eds.) *Sprinter Verlog* (Berlin), I. 487 p.

Walsh, G.E. (1974). Mangroves: A Review. In R.J. Reimold and W.H.Queen (eds.), *Ecology of Halophytes*, Academic Press, New York, 51-174.

Walter, H. (1936 b). Her den was sevhau shalt dev mangrove. Schweiz, bot, Ges. 46:217-228 (orig. Ref. Not seen)

Walter, H. (1936a). der wasser-und salzgehalt der ost-Afrikanischen Mamgroven, Ber. Dtsch. Not Ges. 54:33-49. (English Summary)

Walter, H. (1977). Climate in: V.J. Champman (ed.) *Ecosystems of the World* 1: Wet Coastal Ecosystem. Elservier Scientific Publ. Co., New York Chapter 3: 61-67.

Walter, H. and Steiner, M. (1936). Die okologie des osta Friknischen Mangroves. Z. Bot, 30: 65-193 pp (English Summary).

Warick, R. P. (1960). Physiological and Ecological Studies of Halophytes, Ph.D. Thesis Submitted to Bombay University, India.

Watson, J.G. (1928), Mangrove Forest of the Malaya peninsula. Malaya for Rec. 6. Fraser and Neave, Singapore. 275 p.

Wells, A.G. (1982). Mangrove Vegetation of Northern Australia. In: Mangrove Ecosystems in Australia. In : Mangrove Ecosystems in Australia: Structure, Function and Management, (ed.) B.F. Clough, AIMS and AN Univ. Press, Canberra, Australia. 57-58.

Wells, F.E. (1986). Distribution of Molluscs Across Pneumatophore Boundary in a Small bay in North Western Australia. *J. Molluscan Stud.* 52(2): 83-90.

Whittaker, R.H. (1960). Vegetation of the Siskiyuo Mountains, Oregon and California. Ecological Monographs. 30: 279-338.

Whittaker, R.H. (1972). Evolution and Measurement of Species Diversity. *Taxon*. 21: 213-251.

Whittaker, R.H. (1977). Evolution of Species Diversity in Land Communities. *Evolutionary Biology*. 10: 1-67.

Whittaker, R.W. (1972). Evolution and Measurement of Species Diversity. *Taxon* 21: 213-251.

Williams, G. (1987). Techniques and Field Work in Ecology. Bell and Himan, London.

Assessment of Antimicrobial Activity, Microbial Quality and Effectiveness of Different Toothpastes on Reduction in Oral Bacterial Flora

M.S. Kadam and **A.R. Jagtap**

Department of Zoology, Yeshwant Mahavidyalaya, Nanded (Maharashtra), India.

ABSTRACT

Dental caries is a multi factorial disease where various products are used. Anti-microbial agents have been used as a chemotherapeutic agent to improve oral health. The aim of the present study was conducted to evaluate the efficacy of ten commercially available toothpastes and their effect on the salivary streptococcus mutans count level and laboratory evaluation of different toothpaste on antimicrobial activity against streptococcus mutans. The antimicrobial activities against different toothpastes were checked by on isolated culture of streptococcus mutans. The diameter of the zone of inhibition were measured in centimeter and recorded after 24 hours incubation at 37°C for each toothpaste and results were obtained. In conclusion the antimicrobial activity of Colgate Dantkanti and Anchor were better. For CFU counting micro-organisms were isolated by using different selective and enrichment media and then were identified by the various distinctive biochemical tests and the colonial and morphological characteristics. The focus of CFU counting was to check the activity of antibiotic in reduction of microflora, for which the students (26-28 years) were selected for the present study. The effect of different toothpastes was checked after brushing and overnight brushing. The total numbers of CFU's before brushing and after brushing were evaluated.

Keywords: Toothpaste, Antimicrobial Activity, CFU, Oral Cariogenic *Streptococcus mutans*.

INTRODUCTION

Teeth's are mineralized objects that will either dissolve or re-crystallize, depending on the acidity, enzymatic activity, and mineralization of their environment. After eating a meal with any almost any simple carbohydrate, dental plaque produces lactic and acetic acids for up to three hours. Most people eat about five to seven times a day (including snacks and sweetened drinks); therefore, people unfortunately allow their teeth to wallow in a slimy cesspool of acids and bacterial digestive enzymes for about 15 to 21 hours per day. Such environment favors demineralization of the teeth and eventually decay sets in. The decaying of teeth's starts by series of chemical reactions in an acidic oral environment, and then continues with enzymatic digestion of the dematerialized teeth, you can and must reserve direction and favor demineralization and repair of decayed teeth by maintaining a neutral or alkaline oral environment. The oral cavity is home to many different species of streptococci and is not surprising, considering they share the same habitat, that they have many features in common. This can pose problems in identification and in sorting out the relationship between the various species. One group of oral streptococci is closely related to S. mutans and is referred to as the mutans group1 or the mutans streptococci (Clarke, 1924; Gamboa et.al., 2004; Botelho et.al, 2007; Tsao et.al., 1982).

Each day in our life starts with the use of cleaning of teeth's by toothpastes for maintenance of good dental hygiene. Generally people are unknown about the potential efficacy of toothpastes. They are under the influence of the various advertisements of toothpastes. Some of these toothpastes however have undergone sophisticated and rigorous research concerning the effectivity of their products. The bacterial species of *Streptococcus* such as *Streptococcus mutans, Streptococcus salivarious, Streptococcus sanguis, Streptococcus sobrinus and Streptococcus mitis* causes dental diseases viz., Dental caries, Dental plague, Gingivitis and Periodontitis. The awareness of using toothpastes is increasing day by day in rural as well as in urban areas also. The toothpaste contains the antimicrobial substance that inhibits and kills the microorganisms that are responsible for dental diseases (Jagan et.al, 2012; Pannuti *et al.*, 2003; Zainab Dakhil Degiam, 2010).

The success of any toothpaste depends on its ability to remove oral microflora which causes the dental diseases. The toothpastes containing fluoride have been have been widely used in all over the world. The numbers of researchers are working on the efficacy of different toothpastes containing chemicals, that are working as antimicrobial agents functions as a inhibitory effect against plaque formation (Itthagarum & Wei, 1996; Fine *et al.*, 2006). The present investigation tries to fulfill gap on study of efficacy of various toothpastes against oral flora using Standard Agar Well Diffusion Method.

Toothpaste is classified as drugs not cosmetics. Because drugs should contain an ingredient to achieve the effect the consumer desires, it is important to determine if different brands of toothpastes contain effective antibacterial ingredients (Regos, 1974; Okpalugo et. al., 2009).

The purpose of oral hygiene using toothpaste is to reduce oral bacterial flora. Mouth bacteria have been linked to plaque, tooth decay and toothache. The most localized pathological infection is a dental caries which destructs the hard enamel tissue. Dental caries is a localized, transmissible infectious process that ends up in the destruction of hard dental tissue. It results from accumulation of plaque on the surface of the teeth and biochemical activities of complex micro-communities (Manupati Prasanth, 2011). The acidogenic and aciduric microorganisms colonizing the oral cavity such as *Streptococcus mutans* are found as a main cause for dental caries (Haraszthy et.al. 2010, Loesche, 1986). A variety of microbiological techniques used to characterize microorganisms present in the oral cavity of human. One of the important techniques to reduce oral bacterial flora is dental plaque which controls physical removal of plaque, use of antimicrobial toothpastes and mouthwashes (Collins et.al., 1998; Okpalugo et. al., 2009). The main purpose of use of toothpaste is to reduce oral flora and deliver fluoride to the teeth. The fluoride protects teeth against attack from bacteria found naturally in many things such as food and drinking water. The Toothpaste which efficiently reduces oral bacterial flora should contribute to dental health.

The aim of the present study was to assess the laboratory evaluation of different toothpastes on *Streptococcus mutans*. The different toothpastes were selected for handily Colgate strong teeth, Dabur Red, Pepsodent, Dabur Babool, Close-up, Anchor, Thermoseal, Colgate Max Fresh, Meswak, Colgate Cibaca, Dantkanti (Patanjali), Acasia Sticks, Mango Sticks, Neem Sticks, Laung, Vicco Vajradanti, Vitthoba Dantamanjan, Bitco Kala Dantamanjan, Dabur Red Dantamanjan, Nirmala Kala Danatamanjan. The present investigation deals with to check the activity of antibiotic reduction of microflora. The effects of different toothpastes were checked after brushing and overnight brushing and number of CFU's before and after brushing were calculated for condition.

MATERIALS AND METHODS

The aim of the present study was to investigate antimicrobial activity, microbial quality and effectiveness of different toothpastes on reduction in oral bacterial flora of different toothpastes on *Streptococcus mutans*. The different toothpastes were selected for handily Dabur Red, Anchor, Colgate strong teeth, Pepsodent, Thermoseal, Dantkanti (Patanjali Vicco Vajradanti), Close-up, Dabur Babool, Meswak, Colgate Cibaca, Colgate Max Fresh. The present investigation deals with to check the antimicrobial activity against microflora. The antimicrobial properties of the individual toothpastes were measured by testing the zones of inhibition on the bacteria strains *S. mutans casing* decay in oral cavity by demineralization and weakening of the enamel part of the tooth (Steinberg *et al.*, 2003).

ANTIMICROBIAL ACTIVITY

Sampling Technique

Eleven brands of toothpaste were randomly purchased from the market of Nanded (Maharashtra). The zone of inhibition of different toothpaste brands are shown in table (Table 2.2) and in figure. The selected toothpastes when checked for their activity on *Streptococcus mutans*, the zone of inhibitions obtained were as per the observation table.

The study of antimicrobial activity in the present paper was done by measuring the zones of inhibition by less time consuming, simple, and inexpensive viz., disc diffusion method. The method involves by applying a thin paper disc containing the antibacterial agent on a culture of bacteria grown on the agar media. The simple diffusion of the agent through the paper and onto the agar plate containing the bacteria provides an effective means to evaluate the differences among the toothpaste's antibacterial properties. This is the method I used to test and measure the zones of inhibition. The microbial culture was prepared by growing in the nutrient agar medium and broth was prepared with a bent glass rod spreading manner. The isolated culture of bacteria was spread by applying a thin film over agar plates. The sterile discs were placed on agar plated having 3 mm diameter disc on the central position of plates where antimicrobial slurry was applied consisting of toothpastes and water to the sterile disc. The agent was then allowed to diffuse through the disc and onto the plate, ultimately resulting in inhibition of growth of the bacteria. The resulting diameter in which the bacteria were inhibited was indicative of the toothpaste's antibacterial potential on the specific bacteria. The zones of inhibition on the growth of the test strains were observed by point where visible growth had been inhibited. The diameter of zone of inhibition was measured with a ruler in mm after 24 hours for test sample (Moran and Addy, 1988). The tests for zones of inhibition involved 6 replicates for different toothpastes used for the present study for bacterial culture. The averages for each toothpaste solution on bacterial strain were calculated, and the results were noted by measuring zones of inhibition

CFU COUNTING

Sampling Technique

Eleven brands of toothpaste were randomly purchased from the market of Nanded (Maharashtra). The labeled compositions of different toothpaste brands are shown in table (Table 2.1). Each toothpaste brand was assessed for microbial status, using growth on nutrient agar and broth. 10 volunteers were selected for the present study. Each volunteer used toothpaste 12-hourly on three consecutive occasions as the only means of oral hygiene, and then switched to another brand. Saliva and mouth swaps and before and after brushing were taken for further study. The saliva and mouth swaps samples were washed in 10ml of sterile saline, and counted on nutrient agar after 24h and per cent reduction in bacterial content calculated.

The present work was carried on the volunteers having age of 27-28 years. Before the test volunteers were observed and instructed on how to brush with the toothpastes. The volunteers having tooth infection mouth disease, or diabetic volunteers, pregnant or lactating or suffering from any other diseases were avoided during the present study. The samples were analyzed within 24hr after receipt at the laboratory. The time between brushing and swabbing; toothbrush type, amount of toothpaste used, brushing method, time period for brushing, and counting method for bacteria were constant during the study. Powders for preparing microbial media were rehydrated according to the manufacturer's instructions (Cochrane review, 2004). Sterile carrying cases (10ml opaque plastic containers with twist covers) were used for collecting oral bacteria. The carrying cases were labeled according to the volunteer's name.

METHOD OF ISOLATION FOR MICROORGANISMS

Ten-fold serial dilutions of 0.5mg of toothpaste were made up to 10-3 with sterile water. Samples were plated using the pour plate technique. The diluted samples were added to nutrient agar. Plates were incubated in an incubator at 37ºC for 24-48 hr.

MOUTH FLORA COUNT

Ten volunteers were selected for the study. Each volunteer used toothpaste 12-hourly on three occasions as a source of oral hygiene, before switching over to another brand. Mouth swaps (rolled over different sections of teeth and tongue) and saliva before and after brushing was taken. The cotton swabs were washed in sterile normal saline (10ml). Saliva (0.5 ml) was diluted with 9.5ml of sterile water. Ten-fold serial dilutions of both washed swab and saliva were made up to 10-6 with sterile normal saline and plated by using pour plate technique. The diluted sample was poured by pipette into nutrient agar. Plates were incubated in an incubator at 37ºC for 24 hrs. The oral bacterial floras were counted after 24 hrs. The bacterial reductions were calculated by differentiating the bacterial counts before and after brushing. Appropriate positive and negative control was plated in duplicate to observe for contamination source which is a useful guidance to identify bacterial colonies isolated from the mouth swab.

Table 2.1: Composition of Toothpastes Used for the Present Study

Sl. No.	Toothpaste	Key Ingredients as Listed on Packages
1.	Colgate Strong Teeth	Sodium Monoflurophosphate, Calcium Carbonate, Silica, Triclosan
2.	Pepsodent	Triclosan, Sodium Monoflurophosphate, Sorbitol and Flavor
3.	Dabur Babool	Calcium Carbonate, Sorbitol, Water, Silica, Sodium Lauryl Sulphate, Flavor, Babul Extract, Cellulose Gum, Carrageenan, Sodium Silicate, Sodium Saccharin, Formaldehyde, Foaming nonfloridated
4.	Close-up	Sorbitol, Water, Hydrade Silica, Sodium Lauryl Sulphate, PEG32, Flavor, Cellulose Gum, Sodium Fluoride, Sodium Saccharin, CL-16255, CL-17200
5.	Anchor	Calcium, Fluoride, Triclosan
6.	Thermoseal	Active ingredients- Strontium Chloride XahydrateInactive ingredients- Sorbitol, Glycerine, Hydrated Silica, Sodium Ethyl Cocoyl Taurate, Polysorbate, Flavor, Cellulose Gum, Sodium Saccharine, Sodium Benzoate, Purified water
7.	Colgate Max Fresh	Sorbitol, Silica, Sodium Bueryl Sulphate, Flavor, Cocamidopropyl Betane, Polyethylene Glycol 600, Sodium Monofluorophosphate, Sodium Carboxymethyl Cellulose, Sodium Saccharine, Whith Film, FD & C Red.
8.	Meswak	Calcium Carbonate, Sorbitol, Water, Silica, Sodium Lauryl Sulphate, Flavor, Meswak Extract, Cellulose Gum, Carrageenan, Sodium Silicate, Sodium Saccharin, Formaldehyde, Foaming, Non fluoridated toothpaste
9.	Dantkanti (Patanjali)	Anacyclus {Pyrethrum, Azadirachta Indica, Acacia Arabica, Xanthoxylum Alatum, Menthe Spicata, Syzygium Aromaticum, Piperlongum, Barferia Prionitis, Mimusops Elergi, Embelia Ribes, Cucuma Longel, Salvadara Persica, Querieus InfectoriaBase Material- Calcium Carbonate base, Sorbitol, SMFP, Sphatic BhosmaPreservatives- Sodium Benzoate and Perfume
10.	Colgate Cibaca	Sodium Monofluorophosphate, Sodium Carboxynetyl Cellulose, White Film, Sorbitol, Silica, Sodium Beuryl Sulphate, Flavour

Table 2.2 Table Showing Zone of Inhibition in Different Toothpastes

Sl. No.	Name of Toothpaste	Zone of Inhibition
1.	Dabur Red	0.6
2.	Anchor	2.0
3.	Colgate Strong Teeth	2.0
4.	Pepsodent	1.4
5.	Thermoseal	0.2
6.	Dantkanti (Patanjali)	1.7
7.	Close-up	0.5
8.	Dabur Babool	0.4
9.	Meswak	1.4
10.	Colgate Cibaca	1.5
11.	Colgate Max Fresh	1.4

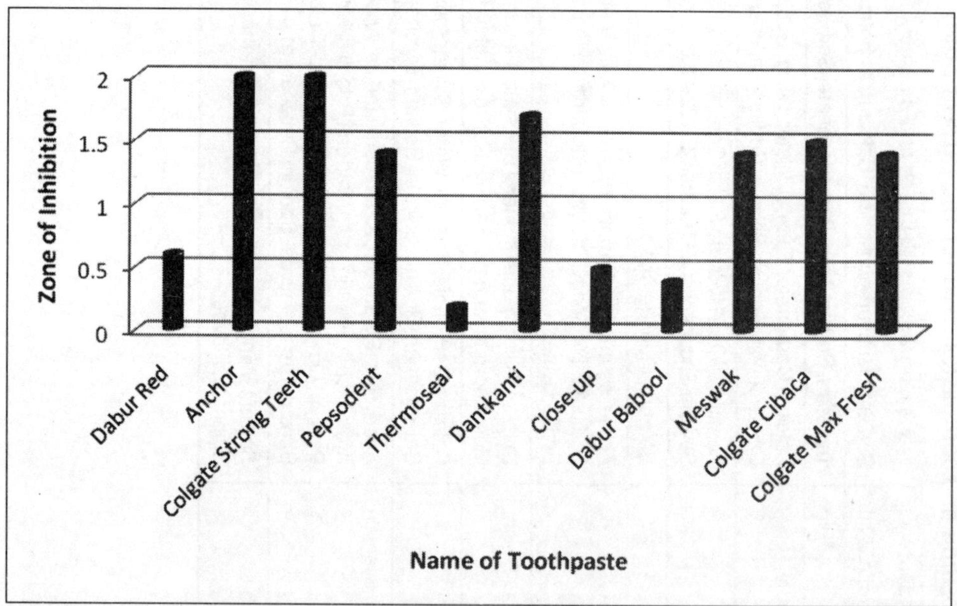

Fig. 2.1: The Graph Shows the Average Zones of Inhibition, Measured in mm, for Each Toothpaste Listed. The Zones of Inhibition were Measured 24 Hours after the Application of Each Toothpaste on the Test Bacteria *S. mutans*.

Table 2.3: Table Showing Numbers of Colony Forming Units (CFU) in Different Toothpastes

Sl. No.	Name of Toothpaste	Number of CFU
1.	Dabur Red	325
2.	Anchor	137
3.	Colgate Strong Teeth	50
4.	Pepsodent	225
5.	Thermoseal	320
6.	Dantkanti (Patanjali)	70
7.	Close-up	57
8.	Dabur Babool	138
9.	Meswak	87
10.	Colgate Cibaca	75
11.	Colgate Max Fresh	60

RESULTS AND DISCUSSION

The results of the present investigation showed that the bio efficiency of Colgate Strong Teeth, Dantkanti and Anchor is highest among all the toothpastes against the test organism. The zones of inhibition were less in Dabur Red, Pepsodent, Thermoseal, Close-up, Dabur Babool, Meswak, Colgate Cibaca and Colgate Max Fresh. The results obtained in this study suggest differences among the tested dentifrices regarding antimicrobial properties. Each test comparing zones of inhibition amongst the oral bacteria, *Streptococcus mutans*. The reason for this could be attributed to the differences in interactions between the bacteria and Colgate. Results of the present investigation of antimicrobial activity showed that triclosan containing toothpaste formulations were more effective in controlling the oral microflora compared to non-triclosan containing synthetic toothpastes.

Tooth brushing with toothpaste is the most widely practiced form of oral hygiene in most countries (Pannuti *et al*., 2003). The present investigation shows the investigation of antimicrobial activity of selected toothpastes against *Streptococcus mutans* viz., Dabur Red, Anchor, Colgate Strong Teeth, Pepsodent, Thermoseal, Dantkanti (Patanjali), Close-up, Dabur Babool, Meswak, Colgate Cibaca and Colgate Max Fresh.

Streptococcus mutans is one of the main opportunistic pathogens of dental caries, which plays a central role in fermenting carbohydrates resulting in acid production, and leading to the demineralization of the tooth enamel. *It* is considered to be one of the most important pathogens in the development of dental caries in humans. From sucrose, the organism synthesizes adhesive extracellular glucans that mediate the firm attachment of cells to the tooth surface (Gamboa et.al., 2004).

Maintenance of good oral hygiene is the key to the prevention of dental diseases. The formation of dental plaques in mouth is the primary symptoms of dental diseases which involves initial adherence of bacteria to the salivary pellicle and subsequent accumulation by growth and inter-bacterial adherence. This results in the accumulation of complex micro-organisms near the tooth surface which is hazardous for enamel tissues. The control of oral microorganisms is compounded as well by the ingested diet. The diet that contains sugar than the normal level is more likely to perpetuate the formation of a thicker bio-film. The individual bacteria are also responsible for the production of biofilm by increasing the chances for the dental diseases (Manupati Prasanth, 2011; Steinberg *et al.*, 2003).

Triclosan i.e. the content of toothpastes [5-chloro-2-(2, 4-ichlorophenoxy) phenol] has been used from several years as antibacterial and antifungal agent. Recent investigation suggests that triclosan blocks lipid biosynthesis by specifically inhibiting the enzyme enoyl-acyl carrier protein reductase (ENR) (McMurry et.al., 1998).

Tooth brushing with toothpaste is the most widely practiced form of oral hygiene in most countries (Pannuti *et al.*, 2003). The present investigation shows the counting of oral flora against the different toothpastes viz., Dabur Red, Anchor, Colgate Strong Teeth, Pepsodent, Thermoseal, Dantkanti (Patanjali), Close-up, Dabur Babool, Meswak, Colgate Cibaca and Colgate Max Fresh. With the selected toothpastes, the numbers of colony forming units (CFU) were obtained. The obtained results were compared by observation of bacterial count reduction in different eleven toothpastes. The results show that the bio-efficiency in the Colgate, Close up, Colgate Strong Teeth and Meswak showed less numbers of colonies after brushing with these toothpastes as compared to other toothpastes.

Clinical studies indicate that the use of a Triclosan/copolymer/fluoride dentifrice (Colgate Total Toothpaste) may provide oral health benefits beyond those associated with traditional toothpaste use, in a manner that is safe and effective. Studies presented in this supplement demonstrate that Colgate Total Toothpaste provides superior protection against plaque and gingivitis, caries, oral malodor, exhibits superior stain removal and provides protection against the progression of periodontal disease. For the reduction in oral bacterial flora counts by toothpaste brands, see (Table 2.3).

Streptococcus mutans is one of the main opportunistic pathogens of dental caries, which plays a central role in fermenting carbohydrates resulting in acid production, and leading to the demineralization of the tooth enamel. *It* is considered to be one of the most important pathogens in the development of dental caries in humans. From sucrose, the organism synthesizes adhesive extracellular glucans that mediate the firm attachment of cells to the tooth surface (Gamboa et. al., 2004).

Triclosan a low-toxicity, non-ionic phenolic derivative with a broad-spectrum antibacterial agent, has been successfully incorporated into toothpastes and mouthrinses, resulting in moderate but distinct positive effects on both dental biofilm and marginal inflammation or gingivitisis. It is usually used in gum. It is a constituent used to avert gum disease because of its antibacterial properties. The active ingredient sodium fluoride is also known to have antibacterial properties which is effective against both gram-positive and gram negative bacteria. PVM/MA is the non-proprietary designation for a polyvinyl methyl ether maleic acid copolymer. It has been demonstrated that there is a greater uptake of triclosan to enamel and buccal epithelial cells from the use of a fluoride dentifrice containing triclosan and the PVM/MA copolymer than from a dentifrice containing Triclosan alone. This supplement details reviews on the effect of a Triclosan/copolymer/fluoride dentifrice on peridontitis, calculus, caries, whitening and stain removal, oral malodor, and on the microflora (Moran et.al, 2000; Nogueira-Filho et.al., 2002; W.H.O., 1986) .

Although it is one of the most common ailments on the planet, dental caries, more commonly known as cavities, remains a poorly understood disease. Caries are caused by a complex interplay of factors, especially patient diet and the presence of the bacteria *Streptococcus mutans* on the teeth. In spite of the fact that poor dental health has been linked to multiple full-body conditions and diseases, such as Multiple Sclerosis and Heart Disease, and that 80% of all American adolescents will be diagnosed with caries, there are still few successful preventative treatments. Rampant caries diseases are especially common among lower-income populations, such as the devastating pediatric disease, early childhood caries, which has reported rates of as high as 90% in some subpopulations. Recent research into the intricate microbial ecology of the mouth and the other risk factors that may play a role in caries formation has provided insight into new treatment and prevention possibilities for this extremely common infectious disease.

REFERENCES

Botelho, MA, JG B Filho, L L Correa, S G Fonseca and D Montenegro et.al., (2007): Effect of Novel Essential Oil Mouthrinse Without Alcohol on Gingivitis: A Double-blinded Randomized Controlled Trial, J. Applied Oral Science., Vol. 15: pp. 175-180.

Clarke J K (1924): On the Bacterial Factor in the Etiology of Dental Caries. Brit J Exp Pathol; 5: 141-7.

Cochrane Review (2004): Manual Versus Powered Tooth Brushing for Oral Health. The Cochrane Library, Issue 3.

Collins W.J., Walsh T.F. (1998): Handbook for Dental Hygienists. pp. 272-273.

Fine, D H; Furgang, D; Markowitz, K; Sreenivasan, P K.; Klimpel, K & De Vizio, W (2006): The Antimicrobial Effect of a Triclosan/copolymer Dentifrice on Oral Microorganisms in vivo. J Am Dent Assoc; 137(10): 1406-13.

Gamboa F, Estupinan M, Galindo A (2004): Presence of *Streptococcus mutans* in Saliva and its Relationship with Dental Caries: Antimicrobial Susceptibility of the Isolates. Universitas Scientiarum; Vol. 9(2): pp. 23-7.

Haraszthy Violet I, Joseph J. Zambon (2010): Evaluation of the Antimicrobial Activity of Dentifrices on Human Oral Bacteria, The Journal of Clinical Dentistry, 21[Spec Iss.4]: pp. 96-100.

Itthagarun, A & Wei, S H (1996): Analysis of Fluoride ion Concentrations and in vitro Fluoride Uptake from Different Commercial Dentifrices. Int Dent J. 46(4); 357-361.

Jagan N Rao, K R Subash and K Sandeep Kumar (2012): Role of Phytotherapy in Gingivitis: A Review, Int. J. of Pharmacology, Vol. 8 (1): pp. 1-5.

Loesche, W.J. (1986): Role of Streptococcusmutans in Human Dental Decay, Microbiological Reviews, Vol. 50 (4), pp. 353-380.

Manupati Prasanth (2011): Antimicrobial Efficacy of Different Toothpastes and Mouthrinses: An In Vitro Study, Dent Res J (Isfahan). 2011 Spring; 8(2): 85-94.

Manupati Prasanth, (2011): Antimicrobial Efficacy of Different Toothpastes and Mouthrinses: An In Vitro Study, Dent Res J 2011; 8(2): 85-94.

McMurry LM, Oethinger M, Levy SB (1998): Triclosan Targets Lipid Synthesis. Nature; 394 (6693): 531-2. [PubMed]

Moran J, Addy M (1988): Determination of Minimum Inhibitory Concentrations of Commercial Toothpastes Using an Agar Dilution Method. *Journal of Dentistry*. 16 (1): 27-31.

Moran J, Addy M, Newcombe RG, Marlow I. (2000): A Study to Assess the Plaque Inhibitory Activity of a New Triclosan Mouthrinse Formulation. J Clin Periodontol; Vol. 27(11): 806-9.

Nogueira-Filho GR, Duarte PM, Toledo S, Tabchoury CP, Cury JA. (2002): Effect of Triclosan Dentifrices on Mouth Volatile Sulphur Compounds and Dental Plaque Trypsin-like Activity during Experimental Gingivitis Development. J Clin Periodontol; 29(12): 1059-64.

Okpalugo J, K Ibrahim, US Inyang (2009): Toothpaste Formulation Efficacy in Reducing Oral Flora, Tropical Journal of Pharmaceutical Research, Vol. 8 (1): pp. 71-77.

Pannuti, C M; Mattos, J P; Ranoya, P N; Jesus, A M; Lotufo, R F & Romito, G A (2003): Clinical Effect of a Herbal Dentifrice on the Control of Plaque and Gingivitis: a Double-blind Study. Pesqui Odontol Bras; 17(4): 314-8.

Regos J, Hitz HR. (1974): Investigations on the Mode of Action of Triclosan, a Broad-spectrum Antimicrobial Agent. Zentbl. Bakteriol. Parasitenkd. Infektkrankh. Hyg. Abt. 1 Orig. Reihe A; 226:390-401.

Steinberg D, Mor C, Dogan H, Kaufmann D, Rotstein, I (2003): Formation of *Streptococcus Mutans* Biofilm following Toothbrushing with Regular and Whitening Toothpastes. *American Journal of Dentistry*. 16(1): 58-60.

Tsao, T F, M G Newman, Y Y Kwok and A K Horikoshi (1982): Effect of Chinese and Western Antimicrobial Agents on Selected Oral Bacteria, J. of Dent. Res., Vol. 61: pp. 1103-1106.

World Health Organisation (1986): Appropriate use of Fluoride for Human Health, Geneva.

Zainab Dakhil Degiam (2010): An In Vitro Antimicrobial Activity of Six Commercial Toothpastes, Thi-Qar Medical Journal (TQMJ): Vol. (4) No(4): (127-133).

Status, Diversity and Threats to the Mangroves Along the Ratnagiri and Sindhudurg Coastal Districts of Maharashtra State

Narendra A.Kulkarni* and **Leela J.Bhosale****

* Department of Botany, R.P.College, Osmanabad (M.S.), India.

** Department of Botany, Shivaji University, Kolhapur (M.S.), India.

ABSTRACT

Mangroves are typical group of plants which are adopted for survival in sheltered brackish water habitats along coasts of tropical and sub-tropical regions. Mangroves play a key role in maintaining the quality and productivity of coastal waters. Mangroves are known as primary producers, shoreline protectors, nursery grounds and habitat for variety of animals, bridging components and unique biological resources. They provide erosion control and shoreline stabilization, they are also involved in complex detritus food webs. The Tsunami occurred on 26th Dec. 2004 along the East west of south India created a massive destruction in these areas and killed over thousands of people. It is also found that Tsunami has created greater destruction where there are no mangroves. On the other hand it is found that the areas with thick mangrove forests have received least impact of Tsunami. It is the need of time that the present mangrove ecosystem are to be protected first and rehabilitation of destructed mangrove areas is to be undertaken.

Keywords: Mangroves, Status, Diversity, Threats, Maharashtra.

INTRODUCTION

The study area is the coastal Maharashtra which lies between 15°44′ N to 20°08′ N and 72°44′ E to 73°39′ E. The study area has tropical climatic conditions. Three distinct seasons are observed as Monsoon (June to Sept.),

Winter (Oct. to Jan.) and Summer (Feb. to May). The maximum annual rainfall that occurs along the coast is 2500 mm. The relative humidity ranges between 60 to 80%. The temperature varies from 20° C to 35° C.

The pressure on mangrove ecosystem is continuously increasing parallel to increase in population. NRSA has recorded a decline of 7000 hectare mangroves from India within a period of six years from 1975 to 1981. Bhosale (2005) has stated that Indian mangrove suffer from several types of pressures such as agriculture, aquaculture, industries, fuel wood extraction, diversion of freshwater and increase in salinity. Mangrove destruction in Maharashtra has led to severe losses of some species like *Lumnitzera racemosa, Bruguiera gymnorrhiza, Bruguiera cylindrical, Sonneratia caseolaris,* and *Xylocarpus granatum*. There are consequences of mangrove destruction such as soil acidification, loss of nutrients, soil erosion, and decline in fishing potential. This situation demands conservation strategy for mangroves for sustainable development of mangrove resources.

There are several reports which indicate that conservation measures planned by the Governments do not work successfully. The reason indentified is that the local people are least interested. Therefore a participatory management is emphasized. The participatory management of mangrove ecosystem is given by Bhosale (2005).

As a conservation strategy Government of India has notified the regulation as CRZ notification on 19th Feb. 1991. It is supposed to take care of mangroves, however the development of pressures on the coastal areas do not allow the regulation to give results. It is the need of the day that the state Governments should take it more seriously and should see that the regulation is implemented effectively that is the only solution in present situation.

METHODOLOGY

IUCN red list categories and criteria are used for assessing status of the species for conservation. These are as *CR* - Critically endangered, *EN* – Endangered, *VU* – Vulnerable, *LR* - Lower risk, *DD* - Data Deficient, *NE* - Not Evaluated.

For understanding the diversity the plant samples are collected from the study area. These samples were pressed and herbarium sheets were prepared. A record of species occurring at each site was prepared. The field survey is based on maps of the area. During the field surveys the vegetation was critically observed for its Floristic Composition. Detailed field notes were prepared. The flowering twigs were brought to the laboratory and were identified with the help of published literature on identification keys.

The threats to the mangroves in the study area were recorded on the basis of threat categories given by IUCN such as *Al* = Artificial lighting,

L = Loss of habitat, *Lf* = Loss of habitat due to fragmentation, D = Diseases, *E* = Edaphic factors, *H* = Harvest, *Hf* = Harvest for food, *I* = Human interference, *P* = Predation, *Ps* = Pesticides, *Pu* = Pollution, *R* = Road kills, *Sf* = Fire as catastrophic event, *Sn* = Situation, *T* = Trade, *Tp* = Trade of parts.

Conservation strategy depend upon the degree of threatenment of species and the management plan adopted. The study has suggested management strategies for mangroves of Maharashtra.

RESULTS AND DISCUSSIONS

Status

The results on IUCN categories (IUCN 2002) has projected the status of mangroves in the study area. Bhosale and Mulik (1991) have reported threatened mangrove areas of Maharashtra. According to Selvam (1998) the mangrove forest cover in India has gone down to 2 to 3 lakh hectares. The pressure on mangrove ecosystem is continuously increasing parallel to increase in population. Bhosale (2005) has stated that Indian mangrove suffer from several types of pressures such as agriculture, aquaculture, industries, fuel wood extraction, diversion of freshwater and increase in salinity. Mangrove destruction in Maharashtra has led to severe losses of some species like *Lumnitzera racemosa, Bruguiera gymnorrhiza, Sonneratia caseolaris, Xylocarpus granatum*, and *Bruguiera cylindrica* etc. There are consequences of mangrove destruction such as soil acidification, loss of nutrients, soil erosion, and decline in fishing potential. This situation demands conservation strategy for mangroves for sustainable development of mangrove resources.

CONSERVATION

Conservation of Biodiversity depends on and respects for people including their needs, for its sustainable use. Spellerberg (1992) suggested that appropriate biological priorities be determined for action. Reid (1994) explained that the ecological management is to maximize human capacity to respond changing ecological conditions for which maintenance of biodiversity is pre-requisite. Gadgil (1996) summarized as biodiversity is a complex and cannot be conserved adequately to special areas or reserves but all the nature must be managed for biodiversity by considering species as a fundamental unit of diversity. According to Ajmal Khan (2002) biodiversity conservation should be considered on the basis of biological representatives, uniqueness, naturalness, richness, valuable species, socio-economic value and conservation feasibility. It indicates that it is necessary to conserve habitat diversity for maintaining the biological diversity. The conservation programme aims at : Germplasm preservation, Sustainable use of bioresources, Maintenance of ecological balance, Maintenance of ecotone characteristics, Protection and preservation of value added species, Maintaining land use pattern.

Conservation strategy depends upon the degree of threatenment of species and the management plan adopted. Bhosale (1989 and 2005) has suggested management plan for mangroves of India and Maharashtra. The first and foremost thing is the awareness building, in public as well as decision makers and planners. It needs as a pre-requisite, fact finding where biological resources are quantified along with the significance. There are several reports which indicate that conservation measures planned by the Governments do not work successfully. The reason indentified is that the local people are least interested. Therefore a participatory management is emphasized. As a conservation strategy Government of India has notified the regulation as CRZ notification on 19th Feb. 1991. It is supposed to take care of mangroves, however the development of pressures on the coastal areas do not allow the regulation to give results. It is the need of the day that the state Governments should take it more seriously and should see that the regulation is implemented effectively that is the only solution in present situation.

CONCLUSION

Mangroves are defined as tropical and sub-tropical forests with a diverse floristic composition bordering the sea on muddy or peaty low lands periodically submerged or influenced by the tides. These ecosystems are proved important for many reasons. In India mangroves have covered area of several thousand hectars all along the coast. Maharashtra is one of the coastal states of India, with many rivers emerging from Sahyadri ranges and meeting the Arabian sea. The coast line available for Maharashtra state is 720 km. All the coastal districts of the state of Maharashtra exhibit rich mangrove flora. However, in last few decades this fragile and sensitive ecosystem has been over exploited. All the mangroves in both the districts are exposed to severe anthropogenic pressure.

It is found that ground surveys are essential to record the ground facts. Attempts are made to collect the data required for various purposes including IUCN status. The study reveals that the mangrove vegetation in the study area is diverse with respect to and follows the normal pattern of species distribution/occurrence. It also reveals that the species like *Excoecaria agallocha, Acanthus ilicifolius, Rhizophora mucronata, Avicennia officinalis* and *Avicennia marina* show maximum percentage of occurrence as compared to the species like *Xylocarpus granatum, Cynometra iripa, Bruguiera cylindrica, Sonneratia caseolaris* and *Tamarix gallica*. The studies on mangrove biodiversity show the major variations.

IUCN has given Red list criteria (IUCN, 2001). These criteria are used for assessing the status of mangroves in the study area. From these studies it is found that out of twenty four species analyzed, some species are analyzed as Critically Endangered (CR), some are found Endangered (EN). The study also reveals that all the mangroves from the study area are found under severe anthropogenic threats. The mangroves in the study area are threatened due to loss of habitat, due to fragmentation (LF), Harvest for Food (HF), pollution (Pu), loss of habitat (L), Human interference (I) and trade (T). These threats are listed as per IUCN (2001) version of Red list guidelines.

The threatened species indicate priorities for conservation. It is suggested that for conservation of mangroves there is need to implement the CRZ Notification (1991) quite effectively. Moreover, peoples participation is a must and therefore, participatory management of mangrove areas is suggested. The study concludes that all the mangrove species are threatened to a great degree.

REFERENCES

Ajmalkhan, S. 2002. Marine Biodiversity Values. Lecture Manual. UNU- UNESCO Inter. Train. Course on Mangrove Biodiversity. Centre of Adv. Study in Mar. Bio. Anna University, India. 10-16.

Bhosale, L.J. 2005. Field Guide to Mangroves of Maharashtra. Shivaji University, Kolhapur. 315 p.

Bhosale, L. J. 1989. Mangroves of Maharashtra – An Overview. In : Wetlands, Mangroves and Biosphere Reserves. *Proc. Indo-US Workshop, New Delhi, Jan, 1989*: 187-196.

Bhosale, L.J. and N.G. Mulik 1991. Endangered Mangrove Areas of Maharashtra. In: Proc. Symp. On Significance Of Mangroves, Pune (eds.) Agate, A.D., S.D. Bonde and K.P.N. Kumaran, India, Mah. Asso. Cultiv. Sci.: Res. Inst., 8-10.

Gadgil, M. 1996. Documenting Diversity: An Experiment. *Current Science*. 70(1): 36-44.

IUCN/SSC 2001. Criteria Review Working Group (Version 3.1), IUCN, Gland, Switzerland.

Reid, W.V. 1994. Setting Objectives for Conservation Evaluation. In: Forey, P.L. Humphries, C.J. and Vane-wright, R.I. (eds.) Systematics and Conservation Evaluation. 1-14 Claredon Press, Oxford.

Selvam, V. 1998. Plant Communities and Soil Properties of Three Mangrove Stands of Madras Coast. *Indian J. Mar Sci.*, 20(1): 67-69.

Spellerburg, I.F. 1992. Evaluation and Assessment for Conservation. Chapman and Hall, London.

Tomlinson, P.B. 1986. The Botany of Mangroves. Cambridge Univ. Press. Cambridge, England. 413 p.

Spectroscopic Investigations of Kaolinite

Bhaskar J. Saikia
Department of Physics, A.D.P. College, Nagao -782 002, Assam, India.

ABSTRACT

Clay plays an important role as natural adsorbents to immobilize different types of contaminants (heavy metals, organic pollutants and nuclear elements) from ecosystem. Herein, the compositional and structural studies of some selected clays (kaolinite) were carried out at room temperature by using X-ray diffraction (XRD), X-ray fluorescence (XRF), electron microprobe (EPMA) analyses, Differential thermal analysis (DTA) and Fourier transform infrared (FTIR) spectroscopic techniques. The physicochemical analysis of the samples also performed using standard procedure. This study demonstrates usefulness of the spectroscopic techniques in determining characterization of natural kaolinite from the Assam and Meghalaya, North-eastern India.

Keywords: Clay, kaolinite, spectroscopic characterization.

INTRODUCTION

The clay minerals are considered as excellent indicators of environment because of their sensitivity to slight changes in the composition, temperature, and pH of their surroundings (Frederickson, 1952; Grim, 1953). Different clay minerals indicate different environments of formations e.g. kaolinite usually develops in an acidic environment; montmorillonite forms in the presence of certain alkalies and alkaline earths whereas illites are the dominant clay minerals in marine sediments. Kaolinite is an economically important clay mineral that is common in the weathering, diagentic, hydrothermal, and very low grade metamorphic environments. Kaolinite is one of the most abundant aluminosilicate minerals, occurring primarily as clay sized particles with high surface-area to volume ratios. Hence kaolinite weathering may play an important role in controlling the chemical characteristics such as degree of crystallinity, concentration of impurities, particles size distribution. Despite its economic and geological importance, the spectroscopic characterization is not well documented. Clay is widely utilized for different industrial applications, and as such any of its occurrences is worth proper chemical, mineralogical and technological investigations. Its current market price (about US $ 0.04-0.12/kg) is considered to be 20 times cheaper than that of activated carbon (Babel and Kurniawan, 2003). In recent years, there has been an increasing interest in utilizing kaolin for its capacity to absorb not only inorganic but also organic molecules. It showed that kaolinite and some other naturally occurring clay mineral (such as bentonite, smecttite ,diatomite and fullers earth) could use as a substitute for activated carbon as an adsorbent due to its availability and low cost, and its good sorption properties (Nayak and Singh, 2007).

Structure of Clay Minerals

Clay minerals are classified as phyllosilicates because of their layered structure (Neese, 1986). The basic structural units in clays consist of the silica sheet formed of silica tetrahedra and the octahedral units formed of octahedrally coordinated cations with oxygens or hydroxyls octahedra (Norton, 1970). Tetrahedral sheets are made up of oriented corner-shared Si–O tetrahedra (Figure 1a) (Grim, 1962).The basic structure of kaolinite is shown in figure 1(b) (Brindley, 1958). Each tetrahedron contribute to three of its corners with three adjacent tetrahedra, resulting in a structural formula of $(Si_2O_5)_n$ for the sheet (Kingery et al, 1976). In the same way, octahedral sheets are composed of Al bonded to O or OH anions, resulting in an effective chemical formula of $AlO(OH)_2$ (Gastuche, 1963; Kingery et al, 1976). The repeat unit or layer of the structure is composed of alternating octahedral and tetrahedral sheets. These repeat units are bonded by covalent bonding and making the layers strong. But in presence of excess water, the bonding between repeat units is became relatively weak and allowing the layers to separate. Complex clay minerals are produced when Mg^{2+} or Fe^{3+} substitute onto the octahedral Al^{3+} sites in either the kaolinite or the pyrophyllite structures (Velde, 1985). Along with the substitution onto the octahedral sites, Al^{3+} can substitute onto the tetrahedral sites. It produces a net negative charge on the structural units, which can be compensated by alkali (Na^+, K^+) or alkaline earth (Ca^{2+}, Mg^{2+}) cations that attach to the structure either between the layers of the structural units or within the relatively large open space inside the Si–O tetrahedra (Brindley,1958). In other words, their layers consist of TO_4 tetrahedra (T = Si^{4+}, Al^{3+}, etc.) and MO_6 octahedra (M = Al^{3+}, Fe^{3+}, etc.). Phyllosilicates contain isomorphous substitutions on Al^{3+} and/or Si^{4+} sites are micas and chlorites. An almost infinite number of clay minerals can be imagined by varying site occupancy and layer orders. These structures can be complex and difficult to determine by experimental methods. The structural complication of clays arises when clays are made up of layers with different structural units e.g. chlorites are similar to the pyrophyllite-type structures with two tetrahedral sheets and an octahedral sheet making up each layer.

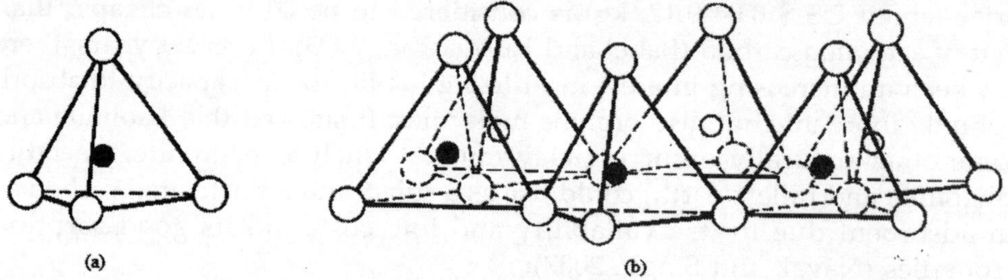

Fig. 4.1: (a) A Single Si–O Tetrahedron and (b) the Structure of the Tetrahedral Sheet

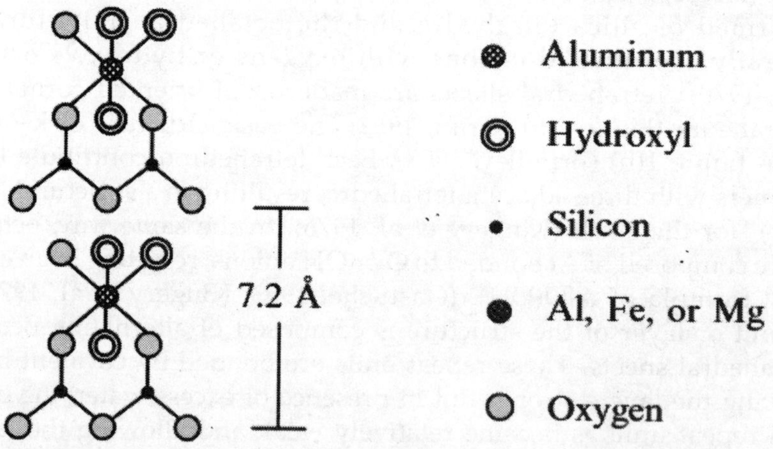

Fig 4.1(b): Schematic Representation of the Structure of Koalinite

Clays are layered aluminosilicate minerals forming important components of soils and sedimentary rocks. A natural clay consists of one or different type of clay minerals together with some impurities. The most common impurities in natural clay are quartz, calcite, feldspar, mica and organic matter while hydrated iron oxide, ferrous carbonate and pyrite are being the minor impurities. The factors that affect most of the physical properties of clay are particle size, shape, cation exchange capacity and the type of impurities present. Clay particle sizes are in the micrometer to nanometer range length scale.

Kaolinite Properties

The ideal composition of the kaolinite $Al_2(Si_2O_5)(OH)_4$ is 46.54% SiO_2, 39.5% Al_2O_3, 13.96% H_2O, however, in nature, this exact composition is rare. Fe_2O_3, TiO_2, MgO and CaO are nearly always present in kaolinite samples and K_2O and Na_2O are usually present. Most samples have an excess either of SiO_2 or Al_2O_3. Mineral impurities such as quartz, feldspar, mica, montmorillonite, pyrite and various iron and titanium oxides are commonly present in addition to a number of other minerals. Si and Al in the form of hydroxides, apparently can occur as coating on the kaolinite layers. The cation exchange capacity (CEC) of kaolinite is generally low. Kaolinite shows a perfect cleavage along the (001) plane. The particles are white in color, sometimes with reddish, brownish or bluish tints; and colorless in thin sections. The refractive index values for kaolinite are: n_α = (1.553 - 1.563), n_β = (1.559 - 1.569), and n_1 = (1.560 - 1.570)

Mechanism of Kaolinite Formation

The most common clay mineral is kaolinite. Geologically, clay minerals are classified based on the conditions under which they form. Clay minerals can form at or near the surface of the Earth by weathering due to water. It can also form under pressure at greater depths due to the action of heated (~100–450°C) liquid-water or liquid-vapor mixtures (Kerr, 1956). Generally for both formation condition, three different mechanisms have been proposed for the conversion of aluminosilicate minerals to clays, these are: (*i*) the direct reaction with water; (*ii*) dissolution and removal of carbonate minerals, leaving insoluble clay impurities behind; or (*iii*) the action of water on compacted shale sediments (Ries, 1927). Feldspars are considered as the most common group of mineral which convert to clay, but it is recognized that many other minerals also convert to clays. Feldspars are common aluminosilicate minerals that are present in many different igneous rocks including granites and rhyolites. When exposed, these rocks are susceptible to physical and chemical weathering. The classic chemical reaction for clay formation is simple but in nature, the formation of clays is more complex. One complexity is due to the variable composition of feldspar and the other is due to minerals that can react to form clays. Even when only feldspars are considered, the composition can vary significantly among the end-members of the system (Klein and Hurlbut, 1993). The different feldspars along with many other aluminosilicate minerals can undergo conversion to kaolinite. Another complexity is due to the fact that feldspars and other aluminosilicates are present in nearly all igneous rocks (Neese, 1986). Generally, the formation of clay is considered in the context of the decomposition of granite, a rock that contains feldspar, quartz, and mica (Ryan, 1978). Quartz and mica, which form due to incomplete decomposition of feldspar, are much more resistant to hydration than feldspar and are often left unaltered by the formation of clays from granite. As a result, quartz and mica are common impurities in primary clays.

Clay Deposition

Generally clays can be found either in the same location where they were formed or they can be found in a location where they were transported after formation. Clay deposits that are found where they were formed are termed as primary or residual deposits and those that have been transported after formation are said to be in secondary or sedimentary deposits. Primary clays are formed from rocks due to the chemical weathering of water. The size and shape, mineral constituents and impurities of a primary clay deposit are depends on the composition of the parent rock and the degree of completion of the reaction (Norton, 1970). Secondary or sedimentary clays are formed in one location and then transported to the location of the deposit by the action of wind or water. Generally, mineral impurities present in the primary deposit are left behind during transport. Impurity minerals such as quartz and mica are almost completely removed in some cases and some other impurities such as TiO_2 and Fe_2O_3 are often picked up during transport (Norton, 1970). Secondary deposits are generally larger than the primary deposits and contain a wider variety of clay mineral types, since clay can be transported in from different primary deposits.

A number of works has been carried out on the quantitative clay mineral analysis using infrared spectroscopy. Vibrational spectroscopic investigations yield useful information about hydration characteristics, interlayer cations and moisture content in clays. The structural differences of kaolin can be detected by spectroscopic method. The FTIR spectroscopy applied to clay mineralogy lies in its ability to characterize the functional group and fingerprint region of very small quantities of samples (Tan, 1998). The studied samples are collected from clay occurrence locations of Assam and Meghalaya. This study demonstrates the complementary role of both FTIR and XRF spectroscopy in characterizing the kaolin of Assam and Meghalaya.

EXPERIMENTAL

Mechanical analysis is executed by pipette method, cation exchange capacity (CEC) by sodium saturation method, while pH and electrical conductivity (EC) were determined by glass electrode and electrical conductivity device, respectively (Black et al. 1985). Anion exchange capacity (AEC) is determined using the standard method proposed by Wilson (1994). The composition of the clays was determined by using Philips X-ray fluorescence (XRF) machine with a Mo-target tube operated at 50 Kv and 30 mA. A series of natural standard clay samples were used for quantitative determination. A LiF 200 analyzing crystal (2d = 4.028 °A) and a flow proportional counter together with a scintillation counter for detection used. Pulse height analysis with the lowest permissible base lines and channel width used to avoid interference. Each powdered sample (5g) pressed into pellets using aluminum cups for trace element analysis. Analyzed trace elements include Ba, Cu, Nb, Rb, Sr, Pb, Zn, V, Zr, Cr, Co, Ni, Ga and Y. The samples were powdered in dry conditions using agate mortar and pestle. The chemical composition of the calumetite was also determined by electron probe micro-analyzer (EPMA). Energy Dispersive X-ray (EDAX) measurements were carried out by using scanning electron microscope (JEOL JSM-840 A) in EDAX mode with a filament current of 100 μA and an accelerating voltage of 20 kV. Five independent measurements were carried out and the average composition of the calumetite sample is presented here. The chemical constituents and LOI at 800°C were determined by the Indian standard method (Indian Standard Methods of Chemical Analysis of Fireclay and Refractory Materials, 1960) and differential thermal analyses. Differential thermal analysis (DTA) and thermo gravimetric studies were performed on powder samples using a Mettler Toledo star System apparatus. The temperature was measured with platinum sensors. Temperature precision and accuracy are ± 0.1°C. Thermo gravimetric method is used to quantify the percentage of hydroxyl/water content in the sample. The calibration and reproducibility of this apparatus is discussed elsewhere (Parthasarathy, 2002). In X-ray fluorescence method, typical uncertainty involved in oxide analyses was about 0.01 wt%. Thin slurry of the clay samples deposited on a glass slide, air dried at room temperature and subjected to X- ray diffraction analysis. Philips X-ray unit (PW 3710) with a generator model PW 1830 fitted with a scintillation counter model PW 3020 was used. The tube operated at 40 kV and 20 mA with a CuKα (λ = 1Å"54 Å) radiation and a graphite monochromator. A PW 1877 Automated Powder Diffraction, X'PERT Data Collector software package was employed to capture raw data, and a Philips X'PERT Graphics & Identify software package was used for qualitative identification of the minerals from both the data and patterns obtained by scanning at a speed of 1°2θ/min. Samples were scanned from 2°2θ to 60° 2θ and their diffractograms recorded. The XRD analysis carried out on their clay fractions (< 2 microns). The clay samples were crushed into fine powder for analysis. The powdered sample was homogenized in spectroscopic grade KBr (1: 20) in an agate mortar and pressed into 3 mm pellets with a hand press. We tried to minimize the grinding time to avoid the deformation of the crystal structure, the ion exchange and the water absorption from atmosphere as suggested by Hlavay et al (1977 and 1978). The infrared spectra was acquired using Perkin-Elmer system 2000 FTIR spectrophotometer, with He–Ne as the reference, at a resolution of 4 cm^{-1}. The spectra were taken in the region 400-4000 cm^{-1}. The room temperature was 28°C during the experiment.

RESULT AND DISCUSSION

Physicochemical Analysis

The general physicochemical characteristics of the studied clay samples are listed in the Table 4.1. The cation exchange capacity (CEC) of clay minerals is a fundamental property of these materials and can be determined routinely. Methods of the measurements are based on a determination of the quantity of a particular exchangeable cation, by a variety of means, expressed per 100 g of dry clay. The CEC of a clay mineral is generally understood to be equivalent with the layer charge.

The sample–water ratio is considered as 1:5 for analysis. The textural classes was clayey, this attributed to the geological nature of the parent rocks. The value of cation exchange capacity (CEC) and anion exchange capacity (AEC) are 3-15 Meq/100g and 7-20 Meq/100g respectively for kaolinite (Wilson, 1994). The observed CEC and AEC value has in same range with this reference value.

DTA, Compositional and Trace Element Analysis

The compositional analysis of the clay samples are performed by XRF analysis (Table 4.2). It is obvious from Table 4.2, that improvement on the chemical composition of kaolin as result of beneficiation was marginal. The XRF result shows the major constituents of the samples are silica, alumina, which confirms the chemical analysis of clay. The infrared and compositional analyses indicate that the clay samples belong to kaolin. The loss on ignition (LOI) was determined at 800°C. The measured DTA curves of tested kaolinites showed the following endothermic effects: desorption of surface water at low temperature interval 105-110 °C and releasing of constitution water and breaking of crystal lattice at higher temperature interval 550-580 °C. The recrystallization and transformation of dehydrated substance to mullite, cristobalite and quartz was observed as the exothermic effect at about 970-1000 °C. From obtained data it is evident that with increasing of decomposition peak temperature value, respectively with increasing of orderliness, the transformation exothermic peak temperature also increases. The relatively large difference in the LOI values between the sample-1 (10.32 wt%) and sample-3 (4.10 wt%) indicates that greater loss on ignition took place during the calcination step. This is largely due to the giving off of structural hydroxyl water and volatile organic components.

The data of the trace elements analysis for the studied kaolin samples are presented in Table 4.3. The observed data is compared with the results of trace elements analysis by Mason, (1966). The observed trace elementai data has good agreement with the compared data except for the element Ga and Ba. It is worthwhile to mention that the high content of V in the studied samples may render them to be natural resources. The high abundance of Ba and Zr may be due to the presence of barite and zircon minerals respectively as accessory minerals in the studied samples.

Table 4.1: Basic Physicochemical Characteristics of the Studied Clay Samples

Sample	pH	ECmS/m	CECMeq/100g	AECMeq/100g	Mechanical Analysis (in %)				Textural Classes
					Coarse Sand	Fine Sand	Silt	Clay	
Sample 1	7.1	0.49	13.4	10.2	3.05	10.75	23.65	62.55	Clay
Sample 2	7.2	0.46	13.1	10.6	3.35	10.65	22.87	63.13	Clay
Sample 3	7.2	0.43	12.8	11.5	3.11	11.42	23.51	61.96	Clay
Sample 4	7.1	0.48	12.3	13.8	3.47	11.44	23.67	61.42	Clay
Sample 5	7.2	0.43	12.8	12.7	3.29	11.49	23.65	61.57	Clay
Sample 6	7.2	0.44	12.9	13.6	3.35	10.75	23.09	62.81	Clay

Table 4.2: Composition of the Studied Kaolin Samples (in Weight (%))

Sample	SiO_2	Al_2O_3	Fe_2O_3	TiO_2	CaO	MgO	K_2O	Na_2O	LOI
Sample 1	44.71	36.34	2.03	1.01	0.37	–	0.07	0.01	10.32
Sample 2	46.81	32.59	4.18	–	3.04	0.71	–	–	9.47
Sample 3	43.79	37.37	1.94	0.38	0.77	0.89	1.11	0.02	4.10
Sample 4	44.66	34.04	0.95	1.23	1.56	–	–	–	6.51
Sample 5	42.96	33.71	1.17	1.45	1.25	0.36	–	–	4.54
Sample 6	45.58	36.33	1.97	0.18	0.49	–	0.02	–	7.11

Table 4.3: Trace Elements Analysis of the Studied Clay Samples in (ppm)

Element	Sample 1	Sample 2	Sample 3	Sample 4	Sample 5	Sample 6	Standard Data *
V	131	140	139	137	141	134	130
Cr	77	86	84	79	77	81	90
Co	16	21	21	18	18	19	19
Ni	54	73	62	69	60	78	68
Cu	46	38	40	37	40	33	45
Zn	84	88	81	87	86	89	95
Ga	1	4	1	1	2	1	19
Sr	205	287	201	264	281	217	300
Y	8	17	19	10	17	9	26
Zr	184	209	201	206	201	173	160
Nb	5	3	2	7	5	3	11
Ba	903	779	712	696	991	910	580
Rb	10	9	12	7	12	11	140

* Trace Element Results are compared with Mason (1966)

X-ray Diffraction and Infrared Spectroscopy

XRD is used to determine the mineralogical composition of the raw material components as well as qualitative and quantitative phase analysis of multiphase mixtures. The occurrences of minerals in clay were identified by comparing '*d*' values. Structurally, kaolin minerals consist of a sheet of corner-sharing tetrahedra, sharing a plane of oxygens and hydroxyls (inner hydroxyls) with a sheet of edge-sharing octahedral with every third site vacant (dioctahedral). This T-O layer has no charge, and interlayer cations are unnecessary to form the crystal. The T-O layer has two different surfaces: A surface of oxygens and a surface of hydroxyls (external hydroxyls). Kaolinite structures are based on a similar sequence of layers, and would be identical if trioctahedral. In kaolinite, the vacant octahedral site is in the same place in all layers. The structural differences in kolinite with other clays are clearly reflected in the X-ray pattern. The XRD patterns of the studied samples are illustrated in Figure 1 indicated that the sample contains kaolin, quartz and less amounts of alunite and montmorillonite. The XRD pattern of the samples are shown in Figure 4.2 with a sharp peaks at *d*=7.15 Å, 3.58 Å, and other reflections.

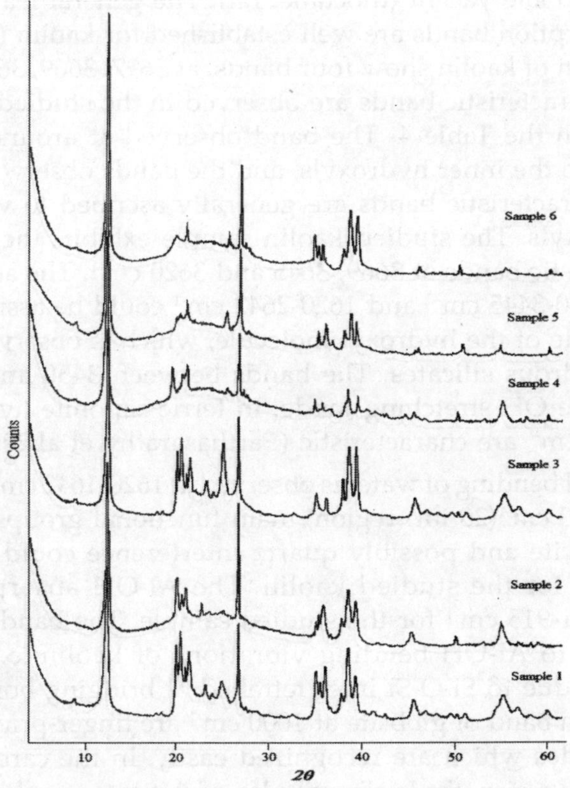

Fig. 4.2: X - ray Diffraction Patterns of the Studied Kaolinite Sample

The distinctive 7 Å reflections (001) of kaolin are showing that it is the primary clay mineral. The intensive kaolin peaks are displaced in the <2 µm fraction where the montmorillonite peak become more obvious indicating that it is the ancillary clay species in the ore matrix. Reflections at *d*=3.35 Å, 4.35 Å, 4.06 Å, for low alpha- quartz (SiO_2), indicating the later is the more associated non-clay mineral with kaolinite. The XRD patterns of studied clays indicate the presence of kaolinite with quartz and associated mineral phases as the major phases. Further the occurrence of the above minerals in the abovementioned adsorbents was confirmed by FTIR study.

The infrared spectrums of six kaolin samples are presented in the Figure 4.3. The FT-IR technique investigates OH vibrations, whose absorption bands appear at different frequencies depending on the cations directly linked to the hydroxyls. This permits the determination of cation distribution around hydroxyls and thus allows assessing short-range cation ordering. The band position is compared with the Gadsden (1975) and possible assignments of the samples are presented in the Table 4.4. The structure of kaolin minerals consist of a sheet of corner-sharing tetrahedra, sharing a plane of oxygens and hydroxyls (inner hydroxyls) with a sheet of edge-sharing octahedral with every third site vacant (dioctahedral). The general features of the OH stretching absorption bands are well established for kaolin (Farmer,1974). A typical spectrum of kaolin show four bands, at 3697, 3669, 3645 and 3620 cm^{-1}, and these characteristic bands are observed in the studied kaolin samples as mentioned in the Table 4. The band observed at around 3620 cm^{-1} has been ascribed to the inner hydroxyls, and the bands observed at around the other three characteristic bands are generally ascribed to vibrations of the external hydroxyls. The studied kaolin sample exhibits the bands near the three characteristic bands at 3669, 3645 and 3620 cm^{-1}. The absorption bands observed at 3420-3445 cm^{-1} and 1620-2642 cm^{-1} could be assigned to the OH vibrational mode of the hydroxyl molecule, which is observed in almost all the natural hydrous silicates. The bands between 3450 and 3670 cm^{-1} are attributed to the OH stretching mode. In ferric saponite hydroxyl peaks at 3610 and 3400 cm^{-1} are characteristic (Parthasarathy et al,2001).

The H-O-H bending of water is observed at 1620-1642 cm^{-1}. In the 1000cm^{-1}(10 ìm) and 500 cm^{-1}(20 ìm) region, main functional groups were Si-O and Al-OH. Muscovite and possibly quartz interference could be observed at 1031-1038 cm^{-1} for the studied kaolin. The Al-OH absorption peak was identified at 891-915 cm^{-1} for the studied sample. The band at 914-936 cm^{-1} corresponding to Al-OH bending vibrations of kaolinite, the doublet at 780-798 cm^{-1} is due to Si-O-Si inter tetrahedral bridging bonds in SiO_2 and OH deformation band of gibbsite at 1000 cm^{-1} are finger-prints of the typical vibrational modes which are recognized easily. In the carbonate and C-H bending vibration region, the kaolin samples exhibit some weak peaks (Table 4.4).

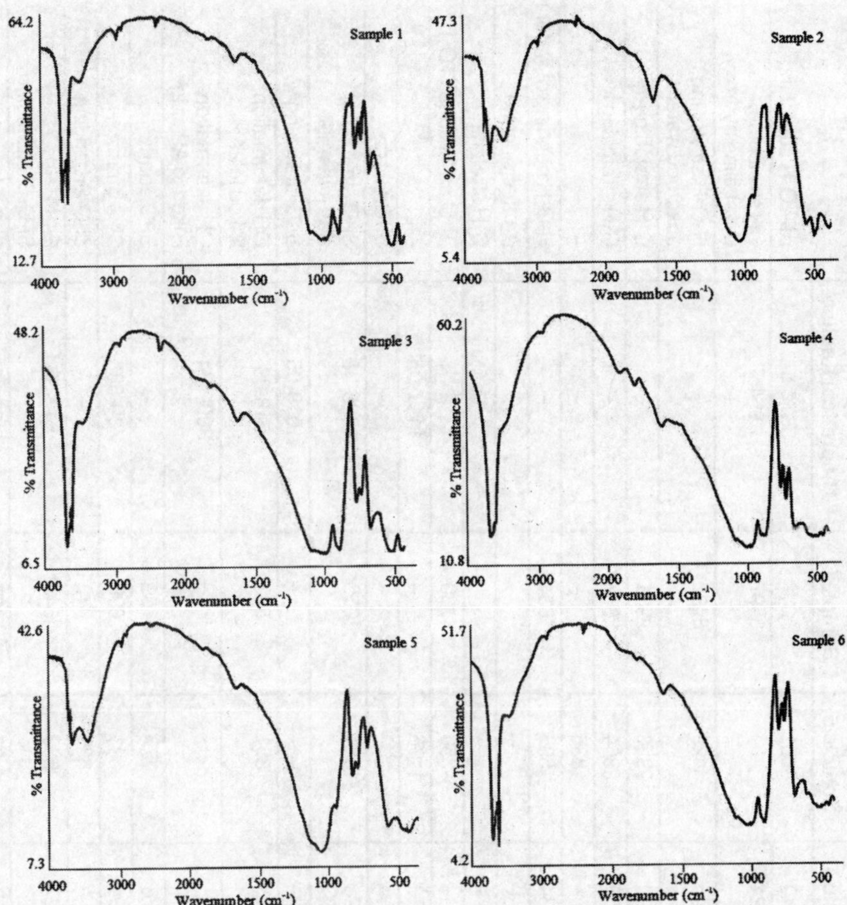

Fig. 4.3: The Mid Infrared Spectra of the Studied Kaolin Samples

The band found at 1347-1360 cm^{-1} arises due to 2vs, overtone of Al-O as Si cage (TO4). The carbonate structure contains isolated CO_3^{2-} group with a doubly degenerate symmetric stretch (ν3) at the region 1508-1560 cm^{-1} (Parthasarathy et al, 2002a). This band is observed in the studied kaolin at 1520cm^{-1}. Another band found at 1470-1475 cm^{-1} is arising due to Na+....CO_3^{2-} vibration (McMillan et al, 1992). The OH deformation of water is found in between 1620-2642 cm^{-1}. The kaolin samples exhibits the C-H stretching bands in between 2850–2958 cm^{-1} indicating polyatomic C_n-H-O entitles with C bonded to two or three H. The strongest υ_{CH} band in between 2920-2931 cm^{-1} assigned to symmetrical stretch of C-H mode of –CH_2-group. The bend between 2850-2867 cm^{-1} is assigned to anti symmetrical stretch of –CH_2-group. Another peak is found at 2954cm^{-1} in one kaolin sample due to symmetric stretch of –CH_3 group.

Table 4.4: Infrared Band Positions of the Studied Kaolin Sample

Wave Numbers (cm^{-1})							Assignments
Sample 1	Sample 2	Sample 3	Sample 4	Sample 5	Sample 6	Theoretical Kaoline	
–	–	–	3640	3661	–	3670-56	Al—O-H stretching
3630	3630	3634	3624	–	3597	3645	OH stretching, Crystalline hydroxyl
3420	3440	3435	3445	3429	3432	–	H-O-H stretching, absorbed water
2925	2958	2920	2920	2926	2931	–	C-H stretching
2850	2854	2855	2855	2864	2867	–	C-H stretching
–	1875	–	–	1835	–	–	–
1620	1642	1637	1634	1635	1634	–	H-O-H bending of water
–	1520	–	–	–	–	–	Aromatic nitrate
1470	1475	–	–	–	–	–	C-H stretching
–	–	1347	–	1356	1360	–	Al-O as Si cage (TO_4)
–	1175	–	1179	1175	–	1117-05	–
–	–	1079	–	–	–	–	Si-O quartz
1038	–	1038	1038	1031	1033	1035-30	Si-O stretching, clay minerals
–	1005	1008	–	–	–	1019-05	Si-O stretching
912	910	–	915	891	893	918-09	OH deformation, linked to $2Al^{3-}$
840	840	847	–	–	–	800-784	OH deformation linked to Al^{3-}, Mg^{2-}
788	779	797	778	777	799	–	Si-O quartz
693	690	–	694	691	696	700-686	Si-O quartz
–	635	673	–	635	642	–	Si-O-Si bending
544	535	535	527	539	543	542-35	Fe-O, Fe_2O_3, Si-O-Si stretching
470	468	470	467	469	467	475-68	Si-O-Si bending

CONCLUSION

The XRD patterns of the studied clay samples revealed that kaolinite are the sole clay mineral. Its percentage reached 80% while the rest of the sample is quartz 5% and 15% others oxides and accessory minerals. The compositional analysis (XRF) exhibits that kaolin of the study area are constituted of alumina and silica in major quantities. The minor and trace oxide compositions are iron, calcium, magnesium and other elements. The elemental results indicated that the samples are safe and free from any hazardous materials or toxic metals and had suitable cation and anion capacity, low salinity; clayey fraction. The DTA results imply that the studied kaolinite belongs to well-ordered group. It is evident, that XRD diffraction data set a reasonable agreement with the data obtained by FTIR spectroscopy method. The infrared spectra of the kaolin samples exhibits, the Si–O stretching vibrations at around 778 cm^{-1}, 695 cm^{-1} and 468 cm^{-1} which is indicative of the presence of quartz in the kaolin samples. The presence of quartz and organic matter as minor phases were confirmed by FTIR analysis.

REFERENCES

Babel, S and Kurniawan, T.A., 2003. Low Cost Adsorbents for Heavy Metals Uptake from Contaminated Water: A Review, *Journal of Hazard Mater*, B97, 219-243.

Benco,L, Tunega,D., Hafner, J. and Lischka, H., 2001. A Binitio Density Functional Theory Applied to the Structure and Proton Dynamics of Clays, *Chemistry Physics Letter*, 333, 479-484.

Brindley, G.W.,1958. Ion Exchange in Clay Minerals, in *Ceramic Fabrication Processes*, W.D. Kingery (ed.), John Wiley, New York, 7-23.

Black, C.A., D.D. Evans, L.E. Ensminger, J.L. White and F.E. Clark, 1985. *Methods of Soil Analysis*, Am. Soc. Agronomy. In., Madison, Wisconsin, U.S.A.

Farmer, V. C., 1974. *The Infrared Spectra of Minerals*, Mineralogical Society.

Gadsen, J.A., 1975. *Infrared Spectra of Minerals and Related Inorganic compounds*, Butterworths.

Gastuche, M.C., 1963. The Octahedral Layer, in *Clays and Clay Minerals, Proceedings of the Twelfth National Conference on Clays and Clay Minerals*, W.F. Bradley (ed.), Pergamon Press, Oxford, 471-493.

Grim, R.E., 1962. *Applied Clay Mineralogy*, McGraw-Hill, New York.

Hlavay, J.; Jonas, S. ; Elek, S. and Inczedy, J. 1977. Characterization of the Particle Size and the Crystallinity of Certain Minerals by IR Spectrophotometry and other Instrumental Methods-I, Investigation on Quartz and Feldspar, *Clays and Clay Minerals*, 25, 451-456.

Hlavay, J.; Jonas, S. ; Elek, S. and Inczedy, J. 1978. Characterization of the Particle Size and the Crystallinity of Certain Minerals by IR Spectrophotometry and Other Instrumental Methods-II, Investigation on Quartz and Feldspar, *Clays and Clay Minerals*, 26, 2, 139-143.

Indian Standard Methods of Chemical Analysis of Fireclay and Refractory Materials, 1960. IS: 1527.

Kingery, W.D.; Bowen, H.K. and Uhlmann, D.R., 1976. *Introduction to Ceramics*, 2nd edn., John Wiley, 77-80.

Kerr, P.F., 1955. Formation and Occurrence of Clay Minerals, in *Clays and Clay Technology, Proceedings of the First National Conference on Clays and Clay Technology*, J.A. Pask and M.D. Turner (eds.), California Division of Mines, San Francisco, 19-32.

Klein, C. and Hurlbut, C.S., 1993. *Manual of Mineralogy*, 21st edn., John Wiley, New York.

Mason, B., 1966. *Principals of Geochemistry*. 3rd Edit., John Wiley, New York, pp: 310.

McMillan, P.F.; Wolf, G.H. and e Poe, B.T., 1992. Vibrational Properties of Silicate Liquids and Glasses, *Chemical Geology*, 96, 351-356.

Nayak, P.S. and Singh, B.K., 2007. Instrumental Characterization of Clay by XRF, XRD and FTIR, *Bulletin of Materials Science*, 30, 235-240.

Neese, W.D., 1986. *Introduction to Optical Mineralogy*, Oxford University Press, New York, 234-251.

Norton, F.H., 1970. *Fine Ceramics*, McGraw Hill, New York.

Parthasarathy, G., 2002. Effect of High-Pressures on the Electrical Resistivity of Natural Zeolites from the Deccan Trap, Mahrashtra, India, *Journal of Applied Geophysics* 58, 321-329.

Parthasarathy, G., Kunwar, A.C., and Srinivasan, R., 2001. Occurrence of Moganite-Rich Chalcedony in Deccan Flood Basalts, Killari, Maharashtra, India, *European Journal of Mineral*, 13, 127-134.

Parthasarathy, G.; Chetty, T.R.K, and Haggerty, S.E., 2002a. Thermal Stability and Spectroscopic Studies of Zemkorite: A Carbonate from the Venkatampalle Kimberlite of Southern India, *American Mineralogist*, 87, 1384-1389.

Ries, H.,1927. *Clays: Their Occurrence, Properties, and Uses*, 3rd edn., John Wiley, New York.

Ryan, W., 1978. *Properties of Ceramic Raw Materials*, 2nd edn., Pergamon Press, Oxford, 42-72.

Tan, K.H., 1998. *Principles of Soil Chemistry*, Mariel Dekker Inc.

Velde,B; 1985. *Clay Minerals: A Physico-Chemical Explanation of Their Occurrence*, Elsevier, Amsterdam, 1-44.

Wilson, M.J., (editor), 1994. *Clay Mineralogy Spectroscopic and Chemical Determinative Methods*. Chapman & Hall, London, New York, Tokyo, 300-327.

A Brief Introduction to Ecosystem, its Structure and Functions

Fouzia Ishaq[1] and **Amir Khan**[2*]

1. Limnological Research Lab, Department of Zoology and Environmental Science, Gurukula Kangri University, Haridwar, India. UK, India.

2.* Glocal School of Life Science, The Glocal University, Mirzapur pole, Saharanpur, 247 001, U.P., India.

ABSTRACT

The ecosystem concept is fundamental to examination of human impacts on life on earth. It provides a way of looking at the functional interactions between life and environment which helps us to understand the behaviour of ecological systems, and predict their response to human or natural environmental changes. Ecosystems are found throughout the biosphere. The ecosystem concept provides a convenient means of structuring and understanding the highly complex system which is our world. Plants and animals live where they have water, food, and shelter. An ecosystem contains all the plants, animals, and nonliving things in an environment. The different parts of an ecosystem work together. Change to ecosystems may be caused by human actions. One of the issues that give rise to the greatest concern among scientists concerned with the environment, and among the public at large, is the effects that humans are having upon ecosystems and their functioning.

Keywords: *Ecosystem, Ecosystem functioning, Human Impacts, Environment.*

INTRODUCTION

An ecosystem has been defined in two ways:

1. It is an energy-driven complex of a community of organisms and its controlling environment.

2. An ecosystem is a community of living organisms together with the physical processes that occur within an environment.

These two definitions, nearly 25 years apart, provide consistent statements on the key attributes of ecosystems. These key attributes are directly related to the concepts of functional ecology. In particular, interactions between the physical environment and organisms and between organisms and other organisms direct the evolutionary trends of competition, tolerance of stress, and tolerance of disturbance. These interactions are central to the functional processes specified in the definitions of ecosystems. (Pullin, 2002).

ENERGY FLOW IN ECOSYSTEMS

All organisms need energy to grow, move, repair, and reproduce. Most organisms get their energy from sunlight. This can happen either directly or indirectly. Lettuce and most other plants, get energy directly from sunlight through photosynthesis. During photosynthesis, plant leaves produce glucose. The plants use the chemical energy in glucose to carry out life functions (DeAngelis, 1980). In an ecosystem, plants are called producers because they use energy from sunlight to make, or produce, their own food. A rabbit, however, cannot get energy directly from sunlight. But as the rabbit eats the lettuce, it indirectly gets energy from the Sun that is stored in the leaves. Organisms that get energy by eating other organisms are called consumers. The fungus cannot make its own food from sunlight, but it doesn't eat other organisms either. It gets it by breaking down the remains of organisms that were once alive, such as trees that have fallen down. Organisms such as the fungus are called decomposers. They release materials from dead plants and animals back into the environment, where other consumers can use them. Without decomposers, nothing would decay. Most living things on Earth depend on the Sun's energy either directly or indirectly. The leaves of a berry bush use energy from the Sun to make food known as glucose. Plants use the chemical energy in glucose as energy for their life functions. Plants are producers; organisms that can make their own food (Ulanowicz, and Kay, 1991). Animals cannot use sunlight to make their own food. Animals are consumers; organisms that get energy by eating other organisms. When a bear eats berries, it gets the energy stored in them. The bear uses energy from the Sun indirectly. Toadstools cannot make their own food. But they cannot eat other organisms either. When organisms die and fall to the ground, their bodies decay. A decomposer is an organism that gets energy by breaking down the remains of dead organisms. Toadstools are decomposers. Decomposers return the materials from the dead organism's body back into the environment. Decomposers help provide materials that other organisms can use. Without decomposers, nothing would ever decay. Dead organisms would just pile up forever (Jonsson, and Malmqvist, 2000).

FOOD CHAINS

As you know, organisms either use energy from sunlight to produce their own food or they eat other organisms that have energy. A food chain shows one possible path of how organisms within an ecosystem get their food. Because the original source of energy is sunlight, a food chain begins with plant life and ends with an animal. Notice that the arrows in a food chain always point toward the organism that receives the energy (Post, *et al.*, 2000). *E.g.*, in the food chain, the food chain that connects the path of energy from wheat, to the mouse, to the snake, and on to the owl. In an ecosystem, some organisms produce food, while others consume food. This is how energy travels in an ecosystem. A food chain shows a path of energy through an ecosystem. Follow the food chain from the microscopic organisms to the common mussel, then to the herring gull (Krause, *et al.*, 2002).

FOOD WEB

Every chain has a producer that makes its own food and consumers that eat other organisms. Most organisms are part of more than one food chain and eat more than one kind of food (Dunne, *et al.*, 2002). Because organisms in an ecosystem often belong to more than one food chain, the food chains become interconnected, or mixed. These interconnected food chains form a food web. Study the food web is given here. Wheat, clover, and dandelions are the producers at the bottom of this food web. The owl and the hawk are the consumers at the top because no animals in this ecosystem eat them (Berryman, 1993). Many different food chains exist in an ecosystem. Food chains have producers and consumers. Consumers often eat other consumers. Organisms may be part of several food chains. A food web is made up of several food chains that are interconnected.

ENERGY PYRAMIDS

A food chain shows the path that energy takes from producers to consumers. However, it does not give any information about how much energy moves from organism to organism. Not all of the energy that plants receive from sunlight is available to be passed on to animals that eat the plant. This is because the plant uses some energy to stay alive. The same is true for animals. They use energy to grow, move, and reproduce (Polis, and Strong, 1996). They pass on only the energy that is left over.

An energy pyramid shows how energy moves through an ecosystem. In an energy pyramid, the greatest amount of energy is available from the trees and bushes on the bottom level. Giraffes eat these plants then use most of the energy they get to carry out life processes. When a lion eats a giraffe, there is little energy stored in the giraffe's body to pass on to the lion. Because of this, an ecosystem needs many giraffes to support a small number of lions. A food chain shows how energy travels from producers to the top consumer. But a food chain does not show how much energy moves from one organism to another. Not all of the energy that a green plant takes in from the Sun moves to other organisms. The plant uses some of the energy for its own life processes. Some energy is lost as heat. This repeats throughout a food chain. A snake uses energy to slide along the ground. A wood mouse uses energy to dig itself a hole. Organisms must use energy to grow, move, and reproduce. So, only part of the energy can move to the next level of the food chain. An energy pyramid is a model that shows how energy moves through an ecosystem. The pyramid gets smaller as it nears the top. There is more energy at lower the levels (Levine, 1980). There is less energy towards the top of the pyramid because most of it has been used by organisms for life processes or has been given off as heat. Only energy stored in the tissues of an organism can pass from one level to the next.

COMPETITION BETWEEN ORGANISMS FOR RESOURCES

All plants and animals need food, water, and space. Within an ecosystem, these resources are limited, so there is always a competition for them. Animals with different needs can live side by side with little competition. This is because the birds eat different foods. These birds do not need to compete for food in this ecosystem. Competition occurs only when organisms of an ecosystem have the same needs. Sometimes competition is between members of the same species, such as two herons. If there is a drought and the marsh becomes dry, the herons that can survive with less food and water have a better chance of survival than those who need more. Sometimes competition is between different species. Suppose a stork came to this marsh to find food. Since storks and herons eat the same kind of fish and frogs, the two species would compete for the same resources (Downing, and Leibold, 2002).

ECOSYSTEMS CHANGE

All ecosystems sustain natural changes over time. People also cause changes to ecosystems. Sometimes ecosystems change. First, one part of the ecosystem changes. Then the other parts change too. Long ago, many wolves lived in Yellowstone National Park. The wolves ate elk and other animals. People wanted to get rid of the wolves. They killed many of them. When the wolves were gone, there were not enough animals to eat the elk. Yellowstone's elk population grew out of control. There were too many elk and not enough food. Many of the elk died. Finally, people divided to bring wolves back to the park (Knops, *et al.*, 2002)

NATURAL CHANGES

In the summer of 1988, raging forest fires burned throughout Yellowstone National Park. The fires, which were started by lightning, charred one-third of this national park. The park follows a "natural burn" rule. This means that fires started accidentally by humans are put out, but fires started by a natural event, such as lightning, are allowed to burn unless they threaten people's lives and property. Park managers know that natural disasters, such as forest fires, volcanic eruptions, and floods, are an important part of ecology. They change ecosystems by killing old plants and allowing new ones to grow. Succession is a series of changes that occur in an ecosystem (Jørgensen, *et al.*, 2000). This is how succession worked in Yellowstone after the fires. Plants called pioneer species began to grow on the damaged land. Pioneer plants can grow under difficult conditions. The following spring, about two dozen different kinds of plants began to grow out of the ashes. Many of these plants had existed before the fires, but only as roots. The forest floor had been so thick that they could not compete for the resources necessary to grow stems and leaves. As the pioneer plants died each season, their bodies decomposed and built up the soil. After enough soil formed, other organisms were able to live in the ecosystem. Seeds took root and formed new plants in the rich soil. Some of these seeds may have survived the fire because they were buried deep in the ground. Others blew in from unburned areas. For the most part, park rangers did not replant Yellowstone. Yellowstone's forests replanted themselves.

COMPETITION

Competition is the struggle between organisms to survive when resources are limited. Like all organisms, the animals on the African savannah need food, water, and shelter. The animals that survive get these resources. Organisms that have different needs can live together without competing. Zebras eat the tall, coarse grass. After the zebras eat, the wildebeests eat the shorter grass left behind. Competition takes place between organisms that have similar needs. Resource, such as food, water, and shelter are limited in an ecosystem (Dierssen, 2000). Organisms can survive when their adaptations are best suited to their conditions. Organisms with adaptations not well suited to their conditions will not survive. Some competition takes place between members of the same species. For instance, lack of rainfall can make water scarce. Only some zebras that compete for water will survive. The successful ones will be those who can live on less water. Competition also occurs between different species. Wildebeests and gazelles both eat short, tender grass. If drought kills many grass plants, gazelles and wildebeests must compete for what is left. All organisms, not just animals, compete for resources. Plants compete for water, space to grow, minerals, and sunlight. Some plants even have ways to reduce competition. They release chemicals into the soil that kill other species around them (Fath, *et al.*, 2004).

HUMAN IMPACT ON ECOSYSTEMS

People have an enormous impact on the ecosystems we live in. Our daily activities change ecosystems in ways that make it difficult, and sometimes even impossible, for other animals and plants to survive. Landfills that we build to hold our trash change ecosystems. Each person in the United States creates about four pounds of trash every day. Together, we create about 600,000 tons per day. Some is recycled, some is burned, but most is taken to landfills. An advantage of landfills is that they reduce health hazards created by open-air dumps. However, hazardous materials, such as paint, acid from batteries, and chemicals, can leak out of landfills and harm ecosystems. People often harm the environment without even realizing it (Marques, *et al*., 2003). When fossil fuels are burned, they create air pollution. Many of our everyday activities, such as driving cars and using electricity, depend on the use of fossil fuels. Think about how many times you rode in a car or a bus this week, and how many times you used electricity. Another way people harm the environment without realizing it is by using too much water. Water is an important resource in every ecosystem. People in the United States use more water every year than people in any other country. Humans are part of the ecosystem where they live. Human activity can change the environment. Some organisms cannot survive these changes. Think of the trash you threw away so far today. In 2001 each American produced about four pounds of trash a day. Much of it ends up in landfills. The advantage of using landfills is that they reduce odor. They are safer than open dumps. But they can cause problems too. Unsafe waste, such as paint and batteries, can leak and harm ecosystems. Building landfills can cause some organisms to lose their habitats and die. Over time, landfill space gets used up, and new areas must be found for the waste. People may cause harm without even knowing it (Hall, and Raffaelli, 1993). Pollution enters the air when people drive their cars. Power plants cause pollution too. Even ranching and farming can have harmful results. When livestock overgraze, plants die. The soil erodes. Fertilizers can enter the water cycle and pollute lakes and rivers.

SAVING ECOSYSTEMS

During a winter storm in 1996, an oil barge ran aground off the coast of Rhode Island. About 828,000 gallons of oil spilled into the ocean. The oil spill killed more than nine million lobsters, two thousand marine birds, and about one million pounds of clams, oysters, and scallops in the ecosystem. The oil also damaged the habitat of a bird called the piping plover, which was already on the list of endangered species (Ho, and Ulanowicz, 2005). Crews of workers tried to soak up the oil from the water's surface and the beaches. Ninety-seven volunteers spent hundreds of hours in an effort to seed new scallop beds. They carefully placed about eight thousand healthy scallops in the area to try to grow a new scallop population. Similar projects are underway to replace the oyster population. Unfortunately, even with the efforts of scientists and volunteers, much of the damage done to the animals and the ecosystem they live in cannot be undone. In 1989 an oil spill damaged the coast of Prince William Sound in Alaska. Millions of gallons of oil leaked from an ocean oil tanker. It polluted the land and water and put a great strain on the ecosystem. Thousands of workers helped to clean up the mess. Many washed oily animals, such as otters, with soap and water. They scrubbed oil from the rocks. But even with all the work and money spent, much of the damage could not be undone. Billions of animals died, including 22 orca whales and 250,000 sea birds. The area still has not fully recovered (Herendeen, 1981).

PREVENTING PROBLEMS

Crews of workers tried to soak up the oil from the water's surface and the beaches. Ninety-seven volunteers spent hundreds of hours in an effort to seed new scallop beds. They carefully placed about eight thousand healthy scallops in the area to try to grow a new scallop population. Similar projects are underway to replace the oyster population (Hannon, 1973). Unfortunately, even with the efforts of scientists and volunteers, much of the damage done to the animals and the ecosystem they live in cannot be undone, environment healthy for all its organisms. Become a recycling "watchdog" at home and at school. More than four billion individual drink boxes are thrown away each year in the United States. These can sit in a landfill for more than three hundred years before they decompose. Setting up a programme to recycle just these small items is a good way to begin. It's better to prevent problems before they happen in the first place. Here are ways you can help:

- Understand how you affect your ecosystem.
- Learn how to reduce the harm you cause.
- Reuse, recycle, or reduce your use of natural resources.
- Know how ecosystems work.
- Get involved. Join environmental groups to help.

As an adult, you will make decisions that affect yourself and your community. And what your community does will affect other regions in your state and country. These choices may even affect the world at large. Learn to be an informed citizen now. It will make it easier for you to become a responsible adult (Gunderson, *et al.*, 2000).

FRESHWATER ECOSYSTEMS

Some ecosystems have fresh water. Other ecosystems have salt water. In some places fresh water and salt water come together. Lakes, ponds, rivers, and streams are all freshwater ecosystems. Lakes and ponds have land all around them (Reynolds, 1984). In rivers and streams, the water moves from one place to another. The water in some lakes and rivers comes from under the ground. The water in others comes from rain or melting snow. A wetland is land that is covered by water most of the time. Trees, grasses, and plants grow in a wetland. Many animals live there too. Some wetland birds have long legs that help them walk in the water. They have beaks for catching fish to eat. Wetland frogs and toads can live in the water and on the land. The largest freshwater wetland is in Brazil. Many large rivers run through Brazil. When it rains, these rivers can overflow, flooding the surrounding land. The flooded land becomes a wetland habitat for many plants and animals. Many birds stay in the wetlands of Brazil for a short time while they are traveling to other places. Many fish live there too. The wetlands of Brazil are also home to capybaras. They have webbed feet, like a duck. Their webbed feet help them swim (Simon, and Townsend, 2003).

SALTWATER ECOSYSTEMS

Earth's oceans contain almost all of its salt water. They cover most of the planet. Near the land, the ocean is not very deep. Clams, crabs, and some kinds of fish live there. Far from land, the ocean water is deep. Large fish, sharks, and whales can live in deep water. The deepest parts of the oceans are dark and cold. Very few plants can grow there because there is little sunlight (Shugart, 1998). Rivers flow into oceans. The fresh water from rivers mixes with salt water from the ocean. When this happens, salt marshes are formed. A salt marsh is a type of wetland. Most of the salt marsh is covered with water. Many grasses grow in the salt marsh. These grasses can live in water and soil that is salty. Some of the animals in the salt marsh are so small that you can't see them. Many sea animals start their life in salt marshes before moving out to the ocean (Engelhardt, and Ritchie, 2002).

CONCLUSION

Ecosystems are conceptual and functional units of study that entail the ecological community together with its abiotic environment. Implicit in the concept of any system, such as an ecosystem, is that of a system boundary which demarcates objects and processes occurring within the system from those occurring outside the system. Furthermore, as open systems, energy–matter fluxes occur across the boundary; these in turn provide the ecosystem with an available source of energy input such as solar radiation and a sink for waste heat. All ecosystems are open systems embedded in an environment from which they receive energy–matter input and discharge energy–matter output. The earth is a non-isolated system. There is almost no exchange of matter with the outer space. To be able to utilize the matter many times during the evolution or from one year and decade to the next, cycling is necessary. Cycling implies that the ecosystem components are linked in an interacting network. The flow of energy from the sun to the ecosystems is also limited. It is important that an ecosystem captures as much sunlight as possible to cover its energy needs. Therefore, ecosystems, with increased biomass, can increase net primary productivity. The development of the life forms that we know from the earth has been possible because the earth has the elements that are needed to build the biochemical compounds that explain the life processes. As ecosystems are valuable commodity, it is important to protect them with all its species and prevent them from the harmful impacts of humans.

REFERENCES

Berryman, A.A. (1993). Food Web Connectance and Feedback Dominance, or does Everything Really Depend on Everything Else? Oikos 68, 183-185.

DeAngelis, D.L. (1980) Energy Flow, Nutrient Cycling and Ecosystem Resilience. *Ecology*, 61, 764-771.

Dierssen, K. (2000). Ecosystems as States of Ecological Successions. In: Jørgensen SE, Müller F (eds.), Handbook of Ecosystem Theories and Management. Boca Raton, FL, pp. 427-446.

Downing, A.L. & Leibold, M.A. (2002) Ecosystem Consequences of Species Richness and Composition in Pond Food Webs. *Nature*, 416, 837-840.

Dunne, J.A., Williams, R.J., and Martinez, N.D. (2002). Food-web Structure and Network Theory: The Role of Connectance and Size. Proc. Natl. Acad. Sci. USA 99, 12917-12922.

Engelhardt, K.A.M. & Ritchie, M.E. (2002) The Effect of Aquatic Plant Species Richness on Wetland Ecosystem Processes. *Ecology*, 83, 2911-2924.

Fath, B.D., Jørgensen, S.E., Patten, B.C. and Stra□kaba, M. (2004). Ecosystem Growth and Development. BioSystem 77, 213-228.

Gunderson, L.H., Holling, C.S. and Peterson, G. (2000). Resilience in Ecological Systems. In: Jørgensen SE, Müller F (eds.), Handbook of Ecosystem Theories and Management. Boca Raton, FL, pp. 385-394.

Hall, S.J. & Raffaelli, D.G. (1993) Food Webs: Theory and Reality. *Advances in Ecological Research*, 24, 187-239.

Hannon, B. (1973). The Structure of Ecosystems. J. Theor. Biol. 41, 535-546.

Herendeen, R.A. (1981). Energy Intensity in Ecological and Economic Systems. J. Theor. Biol. 91, 607-620.

Ho, M.W. and Ulanowicz, R. (2005). Sustainable Systems as Organisms. BioSystems. 82, 39-51.

Jonsson, M. & Malmqvist, B. (2000) Ecosystem Process Rate Increases with Animal Species Richness: Evidence from Leaf-eating, Aquatic Insects. *Oikos*, 89, 519-523.

Jørgensen, S.E., Patten, B.C. and Stra□kraba, M. (2000). Ecosystems Emerging: 4 Growth. Ecol. Model. 126, 249-284.

Knops, J.M.H., Bradley, K.L. & Wedin, D.A. (2002) Mechanisms of Plant Species Impacts on Ecosystem Nitrogen Cycling. *Ecology Letters*, 5, 454-466.

Krause, A.E., Frank, K.A., Mason, D.M., Ulanowicz, R.E. & Taylor, W.W. (2002) Compartments Revealed in Food-web Structure. *Nature*, 426, 282-285.

Levine, S.H. (1980). Several Measures of Trophic Structure Applicable to Complex Food Webs. J. Theor. Biol. 83, 195-207.

Marques, J.C., Nielsen, S.N., Pardal, M.A. and Jørgensen, S.E. (2003). Impact of Eutrophication and River Management within a Framework of Ecosystem Theories. Ecol. Model. 166, 147-168.

Polis, G.A. and Strong, D. (1996) Food Web Complexity and Community Dynamics. *American Naturalist*, 147, 813-846.

Post, D.M., Pace, M.L. and Hairston, N.G. Jr. (2000) Ecosystem Size Determines Food-chain Length in Lakes. *Nature*, 405, 1047-1049.

Pullin, A.S. (2002). *Conservation Biology*. Cambridge University Press, Cambridge.

Reynolds, C.S. (1984). The Ecology of Freshwater Phytoplankton. Cambridge University Press, Cambridge, MA, 384 pp.

Shugart, H.H. (1998). Terrestrial Ecosystems in Changing Environments. Cambridge University Press, New York, NY, 534 pp.

Simon, K.S. and Townsend, C.R. (2003) The Impacts of Freshwater Invaders at Different Levels of Ecological Organisation, with Emphasis on Ecosystem Consequences. *Freshwater Biology*, 48, 982-994.

Ulanowicz, R.E. and Kay, J.J. (1991). A Package for the Analysis of Ecosystem Flow Networks. Environ. Software 6, 131-142.

Effect of Zinc Cyanide on the Behaviour and Oxygen Consumption in Air Breathing Fish *Channa Gachua*

Qaisur Rahman[1] and **S.A. Choudhary**[2]

1. Post Graduate, Department of Zoology, Vinoba Bhave University, Hazaribag - 825 301 Jharkhand, India.
2. Department of Zoology, Gandhi College of Women, Gandhi Nagar, Jammu, J&K, India.

ABSTRACT

Gills are vital respiratory and osmoregulatory organs in fishes. Cyanide is a fast acting poison because it binds to key iron containing enzymes required for cells to use oxygen as a result the tissue are unable to take oxygen from the blood. In the present investigation an attempt has been made to study the impact of zinc cyanide on the behaviour and oxygen consumption in air breathing fish, *Channa gachua*. Short term acute toxicity test was performed by static renewal bio-assay test over a period of 96 hours, using different concentrations of zinc cyanide and LC50 value was found to be 343 ug/liter. It was observed that the normal respiratory activity (oxygen consumption) was significantly affected due to the depression in the metabolic rate at the end of the exposure periods i.e. 24, 48, 72 and 96 hours respectively. The fish *Channa gachua* in different toxic media shows passive drift, active upstream movement, loss of balance, hyper excitability, moving in spiral fashion with sudden jerky movement and rapid flapping of the opercular movement was recorded. The variation in the oxygen consumption in zinc cyanide treated fish is probably due to impaired oxidative metabolism and cyanide induced respiratory stress. Hence, dysfunction of behaviour and respiration can serve as index of toxicity in *Channa gachua*. The details will be dealt in this chapter.

Keywords: Zinc cyanide, Behaviour, oxygen consumption, *Channa gachua*.

INTRODUCTION

The rapid industrialization of streams, lakes and rivers are receiving an increasing load of industrial wastes. Beside water pollution in many cases these waters kills the fish and other aquatic organisms. Fresh water are highly vulnerable to pollution since they act as immediate sinks for the consequences of human activity and always associated with the danger of accidental discharges. The ability to detect, identify and properly respond to natural chemical stimuli is an important component of the environmental physiology of fishes. Cyanide is fast acting poison because it binds to key iron containing enzymes required for cells to use oxygen and as results tissues are unable to take up oxygen from the blood Ballantyne (1975). In the absence of first aid poisoning from gas inhalation ingestion or absorption through the skin can kill within minutes Gosselin *et al.,* (1976). Some of the cyanide is changed to thiocyanate, which is less harmful and leaves the body urine. Some can also combine with hydroxo cobalamine to from B12. A small amount of cyanide is converted in the body to carbon dioxide, which leaves the body within the first 24 hours after exposure (WHO, 1996). Cyanide is considered as a potent suicidal, homicidal, genocidal and chemical warfare agent. Cyanides may be released into the aquatic environment through waste effluents the organic chemical and gold mining and milling industries, as well as from industrial processes such as gas works, coke ovens gas scrubbing in steel plant, metal cleaning and electroplating. Cyanide in the aquatic environment may also be associated with non-point sources including runoff from application on land and water of salt containing cyanide compounds as anti-caking agent ATSDR, (1988). Many cyanide containing compounds are highly toxic, but some are not. Nitriles [which do not release cyanide ions] and Hexa cynoferrates [Ferrocyanide and Ferricyanide where the cynide is already tightly bound to an iron] have low toxicities, while most other cyanides are deadly poisonous. These cyanides when dissolved in water they get dissociated and highly toxic free cyanide ion gets released, which get binds to the transition viz. copper and zinc forming the metal cyanide complex. Cyanide complex exits in solution as an ionic cyano metallates and is highly stable. Zinc cynide is an inorganic chemical compounds with the formula Zn(CN)2 . It adopts a polymeric structure consisting of tetrahedral zinc centers linked by bridging cyanide ligands. It is employed as a catalyst for the cyanosilylation of aldehydes and ketones Rasmussen and Heilman (1990). It is also used to introduce the formy1 groups in organic synthesis 2-Hydroxy-1–Naphthaldehyde has been prepared from 2-Naphthol, zinc cyanide and anhydrous hydrogen chloride. Fish have become an indispintate model system for the evaluation of the extent of aquatic pollution. Fishes is used as biomarker of not only acute toxic effect but also of the consequence of long term exposure to low concentration of pollutants Whitfield and Elliot (2002) and Rotchell and Ostrander (2003) respectively. Information on the acute toxic effects of metal cyanide on complexes in fishes is limited and its effects forms an important links in the aquatic food chain, are not known. The objective of the present study was to determine the acute toxicity of zinc cyanide in *Channa gachua* and its effect on behavioral and oxygen consumption. The reported result would be useful contribution in the ecotoxicity risk assessment studies of zinc cyanide on this fish species.

MATERIALS AND METHODS

Live specimens of *Channa gachua* were procured from local fish dealers at Hazaribag (Latitude 25° 59′N and Longitude 85° 22′E) and maintained in large glass aquaria size (90×60×60cm) with continuous flow of water. The specimens were fed on chopped goat liver daily during a minimum acclimation period of 15 days in the laboratory. Routine oxygen consumption from air and still water was measured in a closed glass respirometer containing 3 litres of water (initial O2 content = 6.5 mg O2/Iitre; pH = 7.2) and 0.51 ML of air (Fig. 6.1). The fish had free access to air through a small semi circular hole (10 cm diameter) in a disc float. Carbosorb (B.D.H) or KOH in a petridish placed on the float absorbed CO2. Thus the fish could exchange gases with water by way of its gills as well as with the air using the suprabranchial chamber. The air phase of respirometer was connected to a differential manometer. Movement of the manometer fluid follow uptake of oxygen when the CO2 is absorbed by "Carbosorb" (KOH). The fish were acclimatized to the respirometers for at least 12 hours before the readings were taken. The concentration of dissolved oxygen in the water was estimated by Winklers volumetric method (Welch, 1948). The oxygen uptake through gills was calculated from the difference between the oxygen levels of the ambient water in the respirometer before and after the experiment and the reading of volume of water in the respirometer. Oxygen uptake from air was measured and calculated from the reading of volume change in the manometer and by the use of the combined gas law equations and vapour pressure (Dejours, 1975). Mean values of VO2 of a series of observations, on each fish at standard temperature pressure dry and standard errors were calculated. The experiments were conducted at 29.0 ± 1.5°C. The desired degree of concentrations was prepared by adopting the dilution techniques of APHA *et.al.*,(1971). The 96 hours bio assay tests were performed employing the technique of static bioassay tests (Doudoroff *et. al.*, 1951). Five fish were used for each set of experiment and mean values of oxygen uptake of all the fish of each set of experiment were taken and compared. The experimental fishes including controls were divided into different groups each containing ten fishes. The animals of control group got the treatment of normal saline. The difference of significance, if any between the control and experimental groups of fish was calculated by students 't' test at the level of 5%.

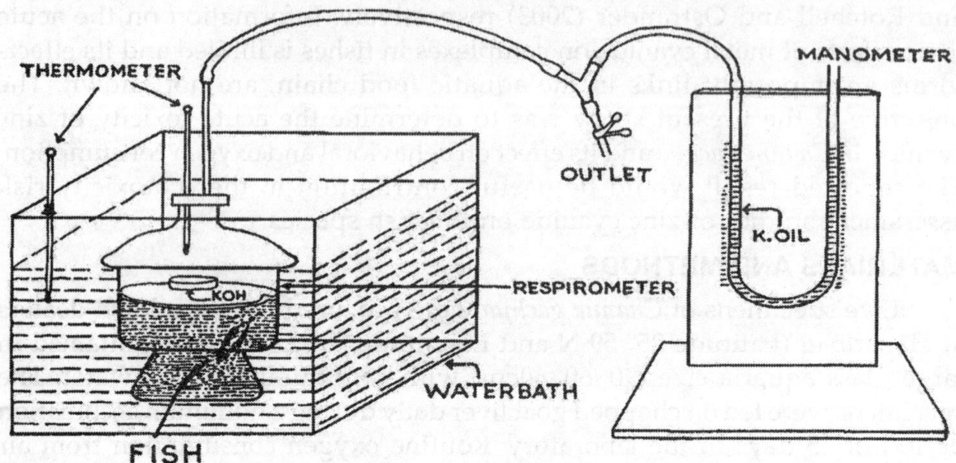

Fig. 6.1: Experimental Set up for the Measurements of Dual Mode of Oxygen Uptake in *Channa gachua*

RESULTS

No mortality was observed in the control ones however, mortality increased with an increase in the concentrations and the exposure of duration. The concentration at which there was zero per cent mortality was (335ug/L) in Table 6.1. The analysis of data from the present investigation evidenced that zinc cyanide is highly toxic and had profound impact on behaviour and respiration in *C. gachua*. Variation in the oxygen consumption in treated fish is probably due to impaired oxidative metabolism and cyanide induced respiratory stress, copious mucus secretion and bulging of gills were also observed. The drop in the oxygen consumption rate in *C. gachua* exposed to zinc cyanide can also be attributed to clogging of gills by mucous. These findings clearly suggest decreased respiratory surface dysfunction of behaviour and respiration can serve as index zinc cyanide toxicity.

Table 6.1: The Mortality of *Channa gachua* in 96 Hours at Different Concentration of Zinc Cyanide

Conc (ug/l)	Log Conc.	No. Fish Exposed	Death	Mortality	Emp. Probit
280	2.5250	10	1	10	3.72
285	2.5314	10	2	20	4.16
290	2.5327	10	3	30	4.48
291	2.5340	10	4	40	4.75
292	2.5352	10	5	50	5.00
293	2.5378	10	7	70	5.84
294	2.5403	10	8	80	5.93
295	2.5415	10	9	90	6.28
296	2.5440	10	10	100	8.09

The behaviour and condition of fishes in both the control and treated solution was noted in every 24 h to 96 h. The fishes showed marked changes in their behaviour when exposed to the test solution of different concentrations. In lower concentrations of zinc cyanide [335ug/L] the fishes showed rapid swimming than in control ones. Behavioural manifestations of acute toxicity like hyperactivity, loss of balance and rapid swimming increased surfacing activity was seen. For fish acclimatized to the 27°C temperature, the specific oxygen consumptions decreases with increase in zinc cyanide concentration. The oxygen consumption of fish exposed to zinc cyanide for 24, 48, 72 and 96 h of median lethal concentration was 0.3561, 0.3102, 0.2836 and 0.1837 (mg O2/ L/h) respectively. Oxygen consumption increased in the initial 24 h of exposure to zinc cyanide concentrations. The oxygen uptake in *C. gachua* for 24, 48, 72 and 96 h was 0.3561, 0.3102, 0.2836 and 0.1837 (ml/kg/hr) the O2 up take increased in the initial 24 h of exposure to zinc cyanide concentration. However, an average O2 consumption in different time intervals of zinc cyanide exposure was significantly different from the control 0.4812 (mg/L). The decrease in O2 consumption in *C. gachua* exposed to zinc cyanide indicates the onset of acute hypoxia under cyanide stress because of the drop in metabolic rate in fishes.

DISCUSSION

In the course of 96 h toxicity test in zinc cyanide to *C. gachua*, there was no mortality observed in control fish. The oxygen saturation of water neither drop below 60 per cent in any concentration test, nor in the control groups. Presence of the substance tested [above 80 per cent of the nominal concentration] was provided by the means of daily exchange of the testing bath. Where as in the present study the acute toxicity of zinc cyanide to *C. gachua* may be attributed the fact that cyanide induced changes in the physiological and survival of aquatic organisms under stress is complicated because such changes differ from compound to compound, species to species and from one experimental condition to another. The exact causes of death due to cyanide poisoning are multiple and depend mainly on time concentration combinations. However, there is no explanation on the exact mode of action of different metals causing the mortality in aquatic animals. Behavioral changes are most sensitive indication of potential toxic effects when studied. In the control groups the behavioural and swimming patterns of the fishes were normal and there was no mortality. The initial periods of exposure to zinc cyanide, the fishes stay in motion less and settled to the bottom. This can be attributed to the fact that, the sudden shock caused by the toxicant. The fishes began to swim naturally after an hour of exposure and the behavioural response started appearing only after 3 h of treatment.

The shoaling behaviour was disrupted in the first day itself and they were spread out and appeared to be swimming independent of one another.

The disturbance in the shoaling behaviour of the fish in the treated media indicates the loss of group hydrodynamic effect of fish Zuyev and Bolyayen (1970) increased swimming activity and entails high expenditure of energy Murthy (1987) respectively. Erratic swimming of the treated fish indicates the loss of equilibrium. Cyanide has profound effect on the central nervous system. This is strongly supported by the changes in the neurotransmitter levels in the corpus striatum and cerebellum Mathangi and Namasivayam (2000). It is likely that the region of the brain which is associated with the maintenance of equilibrium might have been affected by the cyanide intoxication. Surfacing phenomena as observed in the fish treated with lethal concentration of zinc cyanide indicates hypoxic condition. Such surfacing might be to procure definite proportion of its oxygen requirement from the atmosphere Rajasekaran *et al.*, (2009). Loss of equilibrium follows erratic and darting swimming movements, which might be due to the inhibition of brain cytochrome C-oxidase activity, causing the brain damage to the region of the associated with the maintenance of equilibrium David *et al.*, (2007). Ferrando *et al.*, (1991) in the study on the effects of eight selected organochlorine pesticides such as endosulphan, diazinone, phenyltrithian and methylparathion on eels, determined their 96 h LC50 values and reported behavioral changes in the fish. They observed anxiety, disorders in swimming pattern, loss of balance, excessive mucus secretion and lightening in colour. Although the modes of function of these insecticides are markedly different than zinc cyanide, behavioural changes observed are similar to our study. Bardbury and Coast (1989) reported signs of fenvelerate poisoning in fish, which included loss of schooling behaviour, swimming near the water surface, hyperactivity, erratic swimming, seizures, loss of buoyancy, elevated cough rate, increased gill mucus secretions, flaring of the gill arches, head shaking and restlessness before death. Such effects may be due to osmotic stress which affects the nervous system of the animal Palanichamy *et. al* (1985).

The present investigation demonstrated that despite the regulatory capability of the fish exposed to the toxicant, the oxygen consumption rate was indeed increased in the initial 24 h of exposure to lethal concentration of zinc [0.3561 mg/L] and after decrease in the oxygen consumption [0.1837mg/L] was noticed at the end of 96 h. Similar results have also been observed in different fish species for different chemical substances (Stamand *et. al.*, 1999; Chinni *et. al.*, 2002; Wu and Chen 2004; and Barbieri, 2007). The decrease in the oxygen consumption is probably the result of alterations of energy metabolism Oslen *et al.*, (2006). Some studies of the pathological effects caused by chronic exposure to chemical substances evidenced the gradual destruction of gills filaments, killing the fish by asphyxia (Barbieri *et. al.* 2002; Misra *et al.*, 1985; Zaccone *et. al.*, 1985 and Palanivelu *et. al.*, 2005). The oxygen consumption endpoint also provides an index for sublethal stress and for bio monitoring the potentially toxic effects of chemicals. Downing (1953) studied the effect of oxygen concentration on the toxicity of potassium cyanide to rainbow trout and revealed that, as the oxygen concentration increases the toxicity of potassium cyanide decreased. The decrease in the oxygen consumption in *C. gachua* exposed to zinc cyanide indicates the onset of acute hypoxia under stress. Futher, the fact that the drop in metabolic rate of the fish as a protective measure to ensure a low intake of toxic substance that cannot be ruled out. Reduced oxygen consumption at higher concentrations of cyanide could also arise as result of respiratory inhibiting factors that come into play.

The primary site of action of cyanide is presumed to be the central nervous system Isom and Way (1974) and Solomonson (1981). Cyanide acts through the inhibition of cytochrome C-oxidase in the respiratory electron transport chain of the mitochondria, impairing both oxidative phosphorylation Holland (1983) and Dreisenbach and Robertson (1987). Hence, a number of other enzymatic processes are inhibited which exacerbate the toxicity and cyanides is also potent stimulators of events contribute to the acute toxic syndrome. Gills are vital respiratory organs and cellular damage induced by the metal might impair the respiratory function of the fish by reducing the respiratory surface area. The observed increase in the OBF and TBF in the initial 24 h of zinc cyanide and decline there after has been reported by Qaisur (2011). The initial increase in the OBF as a primary response to sudden stress was also reported by Rajasekaran *et. al* (2009). In the present investigation the initial increase may be attributed to the sudden shock caused by the toxicant. This elicits the potency and sensitivity in the fish *C. gachua* in the test chemical. The ecological importance is that the damage to non target species in the environment and such attribute of the organisms could be effectively used as toxicity, biosensor of chemical stress.

Table 6.2: The Opercular Beat of *Channa gachua* in 96 Hours at Different Zinc Cyanide Concentrations and Time Interval

Exposue Time (Hr)	Control	96 h LC50 (343µg/L)
12	89.1±2.1	115±3.5
24	68.85±0.6	113±3.5
36	89.34±0.8	91.86±2.7
48	89.00±0.4	79.5±3.8
60	89.70±0.0	70.13±0.8
72	89.79±1.5	53.67±1.8
84	89.58±0.2	40±2.5
96	89.15±1.9	24.75±0.0

Table 6.3: The Tail Beat Frequency of *Channa gachua* at Different Zinc Cyanide Conc. and Time Interval

Exposue Time (Hr)	Control	96 h LC50 (343µg/L)
12	8.2±0.8	16.4±0.5
24	8.2±0.1	15±3.5
36	8.7±0.6	14±2.7
48	8.6±0.2	11±3.8
60	8.3±0.5	8.5±2.1
72	8.5±0.3	5.1±2.8
84	8.1±0.9	4.3±0.6
96	8.0±0.2	1.9±3.5

Table 6.4: Oxygen Consumption of *Channa gachua* at Different conc. of Zinc Cyanide and Time Intervals

	Exposue Time (Hr)				
Oxygen Consumption	Control	24	48	72	96
O2/ml/kg/hr	0.4812	0.3561	0.3102	0.2836	0.1837
SD±	0.0001	0.0003	0.0003	0.0004	0.0003
% change	–	-25.99	-35.53	-41.06	-61.82

REFERENCES

APHA AWWA and WPCF 1971: Standard Method for the Examination of Water and Waste Water. 14th Edition American Public Health Association Wasington, INC pp. 1193

Brett, J. R. 1964: The Respiratory Metabolism and Swimming Perforance of Young *Sockeye salmon*. J. Fish. Res. Bd. Can. 21: 1183-1226.

Bradbury, S.P. and Coast J.R. 1989: Toxicokinetics and Toxicodynamics of Pyrethroid Insecticides in Fish. Environ. Toxicol. Chem. 8: 373-380.

Chinni, S. Khan, R. N. and Yallapragada, P.R. 2002: Acute Toxicity of Lead on Tolerance Oxygen Consumption, Ammonia-N excretion and Metal Accumulation in *Penaeus indicus* post larvae. Ecotoxicol. Environ. Saf. 51(1): 79-84.

David, M. Ramesh, H. Deshpande, S.P. Chebbi, S.G. and Krishna Murthy, G. 2007: Respiratory Distress and Behavioural Changes Induced by Sodium Cyanide in the Fresh Water Teleost, *Cyprinus carpio* (Linn.). J. Basic. Clin. Physiol. Pharmacol. 18 (2): 1-11.

Dejour's, P. 1975: "Principles of Comparative Respiratory Physiology." Amsterdum. North Holland Publishing Company pp. 253.

Doudoroff, P. Anderson, B.G. Burdick, G.E. 1951: Bioassay Methods for the Evaluation of Acute Toxicity of Industrial Wastes to Fish. Sewage Ind. Waste, 23: 1380-1397.

Downing, K.M. 1953: The Influence of Dissolved Oxygen Concentration on the Toxicity of Potassium Cyanide to Rainbow Trout J. Biochem. pp: 61-64.

Dreisenbach, R.H. and Robertson, 1987: Handbook of Poisoning: Prevention, Diagnosis and Treatment. 12th Edition; Appleton and Lange, Norwalk, CT.

Finney, D.J. 1971: Probit Analysis, 3rd Edition, Cambridge University Press, London, pp. 333.

Gossellin, R,H. Hodge, R. Smith and M.Gleason, 1976: Clinical Toxicology of Products, 4th ed. Williams and Wilkins Press, Baltimore, pp. 12-24.

Holland, D.J. 1983: Cyanide Poisoning: An Uncommon Encounter. J. Emerg. Nurs. 9 (3): 138.

Mathangi, D.C. and Namasivayam, A. 2000: Effects of Chronic Sublethal Cyanide Administration on Brain Neurotransmitter and Behaviour in Rats: J. Occup. Health. 42: 88-90.

Mishra, V. Lal, H. Chawla, G. and Vishwanathan, P, N. 1985: Pathomorphological Changes in Gills of Fish Fingerlings (*Cirrhina mrigala*) by Linear Alkyl benzene Sulphonate. Ecotoxicol. Environ. Saf. 10: 302-308.

Murthy, A.S. 1987: Sublethal Effects of Pesticides on Fish: Toxicity of Pesticide to Fish. 2: 55-100.

Olsen, R.E. Sundell, K. Mayhew, T.M. and Ring, E. 2006: Acute Stress Alters Intestinal Function of Rainbow Trout, *Onchorhyncus mykiss*. Aquacultute. 250 (1-2): 480-495.

Palanichamy. S, Arunachalam, S. and Balasubraniam M.P. 1985: Toxic and Sublethal Effect of Ammonium Chloride on Food Utilization and Growth in Air Breathing Fish *Channa striatus*. Proc. Warm Wat. Aquaculture, Hawaii, pp. 465-480.

Palanivelu, V. Vijayavel, K. Balasubramanium, M.P. 2005: Impact of Fertilizer (urea) on Oxygen Consumption and Feeding Energetics in the Fresh Water Fish *Oreochromis mossambicus*. Environ. Toxicol. Pharmacol. 19: 351-355.

Qaisur Rahman, 2011: Studies on Some Factors Affecting Aerial and Aquatic Respiration in an Air Breathing Fish *Channa gachua* (Ham.) Ph.D. Thesis Vinoba Bhave University, Hazaribag, Jharkhand.

Welch, P.S. 1948: Limnological Methods McGraw Hill book Co. Inc. New York, London pp. 206-213.

Whitfield, A.K. and Elliot, M. 2002: Fishes as Indicators of Environmental and Ecological Changes within Estuaries: A Review of Progress and Some Suggestion for the Future. J. Fish. Biol. 61: 220-250.

World Health Organisation, 1996: Health Criteria and Other Supporting Informations for Cyanide, 2: 226-330.

Wu, J.P. and Chen, H.C. 2004: Effects of Cadmium and Zinc on Oxygen Consumption, Ammonium Excretion and Osmoregulation of White Shrimp (*Litopenaeus vannamei*). Chemosphere. 57: 1591-1598.

Zaccone, G. Locassio, P. Fasulo, S, and Licata, A. 1985: The Effects of Anionic Detergents on Complex Carbohydrates and Enzymes Activities in the Epidermis of the Cat Fish *Heteropneustes fossilis* (Bloch). J. Histochem. 17: 453-466.

Zuyev, G.V, and Bolyayen V.V. 1970: An Experimental Study of the Swimming of Fish in Groups as Exemplified by the Horse Mackerel *Trachurus mediterraneusponticus* Allev. J. Icthyol. 10: 545.

Ambient Air Quality Status in Selected Sample District from Nine Agro Climatic Zones of Uttar Pradesh, India

N.P. Singh[1]; **Archana Tyagi**[2] and **Hariom Tyagi**[3]

1. Principal, Meerut College, C.C.S.University, Meerut, U.P. (India).
2. Research Scholars, UGC Research Project, Geography Department, Meerut College Meerut (UP), India.
3. Environmental Research Coordinator, ESRO, Delhi, India.

INTRODUCTION

Population growth places additional pressure on the natural environment through the consumption of the natural resources and the generation of wastes and other input capable of the degrading the quality of soil, water and air. This causes loss of native flora and fauna and, as more recently noted, influence global climate change.

In last three decades, the rapid growth of industrialization and urbanization has created negative impact on environment. The industrial, municipal and agriculture waste containing pesticides, insecticides, fertilizer residues, organic pollutant and heavy metals in their effluent have been polluted surface and ground water. In the modern industrial era, rapidly growing of industrialization and urbanization has posted adverse impact on the environment and its all components. Air, water and soil everything of surface may changed its quality due to the increasing pollution (Bharti, 2012a).

The environmental imbalance gives rise to various environmental problems. Some of the environmental problems are pollution, soil erosion leading to floods, salt deserts and sea recedes, desertification, landslides, change of river directions, extinction of species, and vulnerable ecosystem in place of more complex and stable ecosystems, depletion of natural resources, waste accumulation, deforestation, thinning of ozone layer and global warming. The environmental problems are visualized in terms of pollution, growth in population, development, industrialization, unplanned urbanization etc. Rapid migration and increase in population in the urban areas has also lead to traffic congestion, water shortages, solid waste, and air, water and noise pollution are common noticeable problems in almost all the urban areas since last few years. Air is mainly a mixture of various gases such as oxygen, corbon dioxide, and nitrogen. These are present in a particular ratio . Whenever there is any imbalance in the ratio of these gases, air pollution is caused.

Pollution has serious implications for economic growth and welfare because of its impact on health, resource depletion, and natural calamities linked to climate change. There are two major groups of policy instruments for achieving pollution reduction: regulatory and market based economic instrument.Securing the environment is critical for India's future generations and not just a matter of international commitment. A degraded environment reduces the quality of life for all citizens, but the impact is particularly pronounced on the poor and vulnerable groups, as it is they who suffer the most from degraded access to clean water, air and sanitation, as well as from climate shocks. It is for this reason that, despite the fact that India's per capita greenhouse gas emissions are much below the world average and far lower than the average of developed countries, we have pursued policies which complement efforts towards mitigation of climate change.

The main forms of pollution are atmospheric pollution, land degradation and soil pollution, water pollution, and noise pollution. The main sources of atmospheric pollution are: (a) combustion of fuels to produce energy for heating and power generation in the household and industrial sectors; (b) exhaust emissions from the transport vehicles that use petrol, diesel oil, etc., and (c) waste gases, dust and heat from many industrial sites including chemical manufacturers and electrical power generating stations. Three main pollutants of ambient air quality are Sulphur Dioxide (SO_2), Nitrogen Dioxide (NO_2) and Particulate Matter. Carbon dioxide (CO_2) and methane (CH_4) contribute towards the greenhouse gas emission inventory in India.

Progress in agriculture due to use of fertilizers and pesticides has also contributed towards air pollution. Indiscriminate cutting of trees and clearing of forests has led to increase in the amount of carbon dioxide in atmosphere. Global warming is a consequence of green house effect caused by increased level of carbon dioxide (CO_2). Ozone (O_3) depletion has resulted in UV radiation striking our earth.

This chapter considers major environmental theme as "Air" and their current status using available data to highlight responses or actions under way to address them. According the chapter we discuss the air environment in the term of the source of air pollution, status and assessment of air quality, area of the critical air quality and the impact on human health.

According to the climate Uttar Pradesh are divided in to nine agro climatic zone and from that agro climatic zone we have selected nine sample district for the environmental study, districta as Lacknow, Allhabad, Agra, Ajamgarh, Bareilly, Bahraich, Farrukhabad, Jhansi, Rampur, Ghaziabad, The factors responsible for the short- listing this district are eco-resources, geology, geographical location, political and industrial zones and also the availability of the data for environmental parameters. These nine district of Uttar Pradesh are representative of the general environmental status of stat. Detail of Selected Sample District from Nine agro-climatic Zone given in below Table 7.1 and Figure 7.1.

Table 7.1: Area of Nine Agro Climatic Zone and Selected Sample District

Sl. No.	Zone	Area (Sq Km)	District	Area (Sq km) 2011	% of Sample District of Climatic Zone
1.	Babar and Tarai	1847319	Rampur	2366	0.13
2.	Western plain zone	1637424	Ghaziabad	1175	0.07
3.	Mid westren plain zone	1697125	Bareilly	4120	0.24
4.	South westren semi arid zone	2234222	Agra	4041	0.17
5.	Central plain zone	5647307	Farrukhabad	2182	0.03
6.	Bundelkhand zone	2961006	Jhansi	5028	0.17
7.	North eastren plain zone	2955485	Baharaich	4926	0.16
8.	Eastren plain zone	3808718	Azamgarh	4053	0.11
9.	Vindhyan zone	1381840	Allahabad	5481	0.40

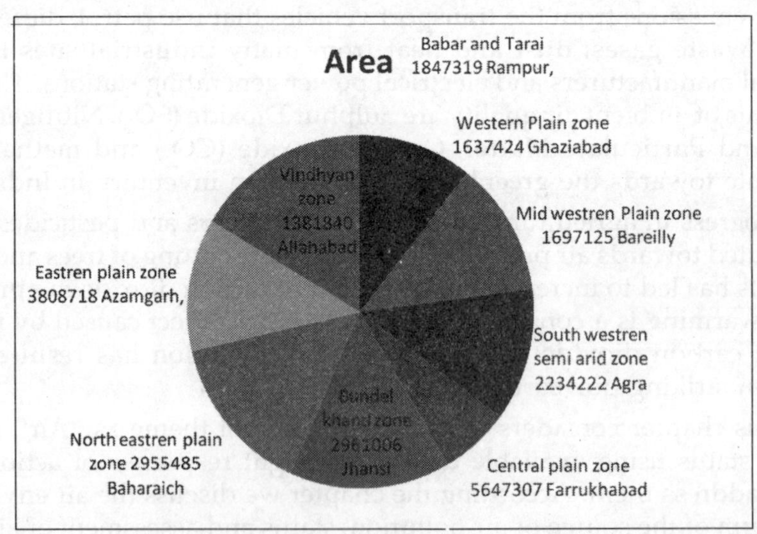

Fig. 7.1: Area of Nine Agro Climatic Zone and Selected District

AIR ENVIRONMENT

Air pollution encompasses the diverse array of natural and anthropogenic emission, including gaseous constituents, volatile chemicals, aerosols, and their atmospheric reaction products. Ambient air acts as an atmospheric sink where all emission are released. Many such emissions are in such small quantities that they get immediately dissipated and absorbed but continuous release of these pollutants build up in the air and pose hazard to human health.

CLIMATE OF UTTAR PRADESH

The climate in the state is both hot and cold .The climate is cool or cold from November to early March although the days are pleasant and often warm. After the middle of March, it gets to be hot and in May, it could rise to 45°C or even more .June is both hot and humid until the south-west monsoon breaks in all its fury. Thus, the temperature varies from 3°C or even 46°C.The humidity varies from 45 per cent - 50 per cent. The wind speed varies from 3.7-9.6 km/hr.

SOURCE OF AIR POLLUTION

1. **Point Sources:** Chemical plants, refineries, power plants, paper mills, cement plants, etc.
2. **Area Sources:** Dry cleaners, petrol stations, electroplaters etc.
3. **Line Sources:** Automobiles, railways, airways, Vehicles, etc.
4. **Natural sources:** Dust storms, volcanoes, forest fires, etc.

POLLUTION EMISSION INVENTORY

Secondary Data on source emission (point, area and line), collected from various Sources are analyzed for identification of critical parameters and hot spots. List of Major type of Industries of Nine Agro climatic Zone are contributing to air pollution are shown in Table 7.2.

Table 7.2: Major Type of Industries in Uttar Pradesh

Sl.No.	Districts	Type of Industries
1.	Lucknow	Distillery, Brewery, Iron & Steel including, Foundries, Rolling & Pickling, Casting, Eloctronics Silicates, Pesticides, chemicals, Cement, Electronics, Timber.
2.	Allhabad	Food Products, Tobacco and Tobacco Products, Silk Textile Products, Wood Products. Leather Product, Rubber Petrochemical Products, Non Metallic & Mineral, Basic Metal & Allow Industries, Metal Products & Parts Machinery & Machine Tools.
3.	Agra	Foundry, Glass Industries, Silicates, Refinery, Rubber Industries, Leather Industries, Distillery.
4.	Ghaziabad	Heavy & Medium Industries, Small Scale Industries, Handicraft, Rural Industries. Power plant, Foundry, Narora Atomic center, Distillery.

(Contd...)

Sl.No.	Districts	Type of Industries
5.	Bereilly	Sugar, Chemical, Power, small agroindustry.
6.	Behriach	Sugar, Chemical, Power, small agroindustry.
7.	Jhansi	Thermal Power Plant, Heavy Electrical, Fertilizers, Mostly Stone based industries, Handicraft, etc.
8.	Farrukhabad	Agro based Industries.
9.	Rampur	Agro based Industries.
10.	Lakhimpurkheri	Agro based Industries.
11.	Ajamgarh	Agro based Industries.

NATIONAL AMBIENT AIR QUALITY STANDARDS (NAAQS), 2009

Central pollution control board set a standard concentration for ambient air quality as given table 7.3.

Table 7.3: National Ambient Air Quality Standard

Pollutant	Concentration in Ambient Air Industrial, Residential, Rural and Other Area	Ecological Sensitive Area
Sulphur Dioxide (μg/m³)	80	80
Nitroger Dioxide (μg/m³)	80	80
RSPM (μg/m³)	100	100
Carbon monoxide(mg/m³)	2	2

Source: NAAQM guideline

AMBIENT AIR QUALITY INDEX

The Air Quality Index (AQI) levels are related to the measured concentrations of ambient respirable suspended particulate matter (RSPM), sulfur dioxide (SO_2), carbon monoxide (CO), ozone (O_3) and nitrogen dioxide (NO_2) over a 24-hour period based on the potential health effects of air pollutants.

An AQI level at or below 100 means that the pollutant levels are in the satisfactory range over 24 hour period and pose no acute or immediate health effects. However, air pollution consistently at "High" levels (AQI of 26 to 50) in a year may mean that the annual "Air Quality Objectives" for protecting long-term health effects could be violated.

"Very High" levels (AQI in excess of 201) means that levels of one or more pollutant(s) is/are in the unhealthy range.

Table 7.4: Air Quality Index and Health Implication

AQI	Air Quality Level	Health Implications
0-50	Excellent	No health implications.
51-100	Good	Few hypersensitive individuals should reduce outdoor exercise.
101-150	Lightly Polluted	Slight irritations may occur, individuals with breathing or heart problems should reduce outdoor exercise.
151-200	Moderately Polluted	Slight irritations may occur, individuals with breathing or heart problems should reduce outdoor exercise.
201-300	Heavily Polluted	Healthy people will be noticeably affected. People with breathing or heart problems will experience reduced endurance in activities. These individuals and elders should remain indoors and restrict activities.
300+	Severely Polluted	Healthy people will experience reduced endurance in activities. There may be strong irritations and symptoms and may trigger other illnesses. Elders and the sick should remain indoors and avoid exercise. Healthy individuals should avoid out door activities.

Source: AQI and Health Implications (HJ 663-2012)

STATUS OF AMBIENT AIR POLLUTION/QUALITY IN *SELECTED* DISTRICT OF NINE AGRO CLIMATIC ZONE OF UTTAR PRADESH

Ambient air quality is considered as background concentration of atmosphere . Monitoring of Ambient air quality is carried out to establish the impacts of various activities leading to generation of emission which has a bearing on ambient air quality.

All substance in ambient air exist as either particulate matter , gases or vapors.

The aerometric secondary data pertaining to Uttar Pradesh is collected from all possible sources like UPPCP, CPCB.etc.

The ambient air quality status in the studied region is assessed, based on secondary data collected. The Parameter selected for AAQM include RSPM, So2 and NOx ,CO as these are the major criteria pollutants representing emission from fuel usage in all commercial/industrial and domestic activities . The quality is assessed in cities – Lucknow, Allahabad, Kanpur, Agra, Jhansi, Bharich, Bareilly, Fharrukhabad, Lakhimpur Kheri, Rampur Ajamgarh,The values of RSPM, SO_2 and NOx have been compared with standards of CPCB. Data of selected sample districts collected from CPCB and SPCB Lucknow and discussion and data interpretation are given.

RSPM Level in Selected Sample District

The concentration levels of RSMP in the selected nine districts were observed to exceed, except for Ajamgarh district, the National Ambient Air Quality Standard (NAAQS) during the study period of 2010 to 2012.

Furthermore, the significant increase in concentration levels is identified, from 2010 to 2012, in the commercial areas of Gazi, Agra, Janshi, Ajamgarh, and Allahabad districts; residential areas of Rampur, Agra, Bareilly, and Janshi districts; industrial areas of Ghaziabad, Bareilly, Janshi, and Ajamgarh districts. Data of RSPM are showing to that the quality of Ambient air in respect to RSPM is not well except to Azamgarh District. The NAQS of RSPM is 100 μg/m³. The All data of RSPM level in Selected District are presented in graphical and tabulated form given below.

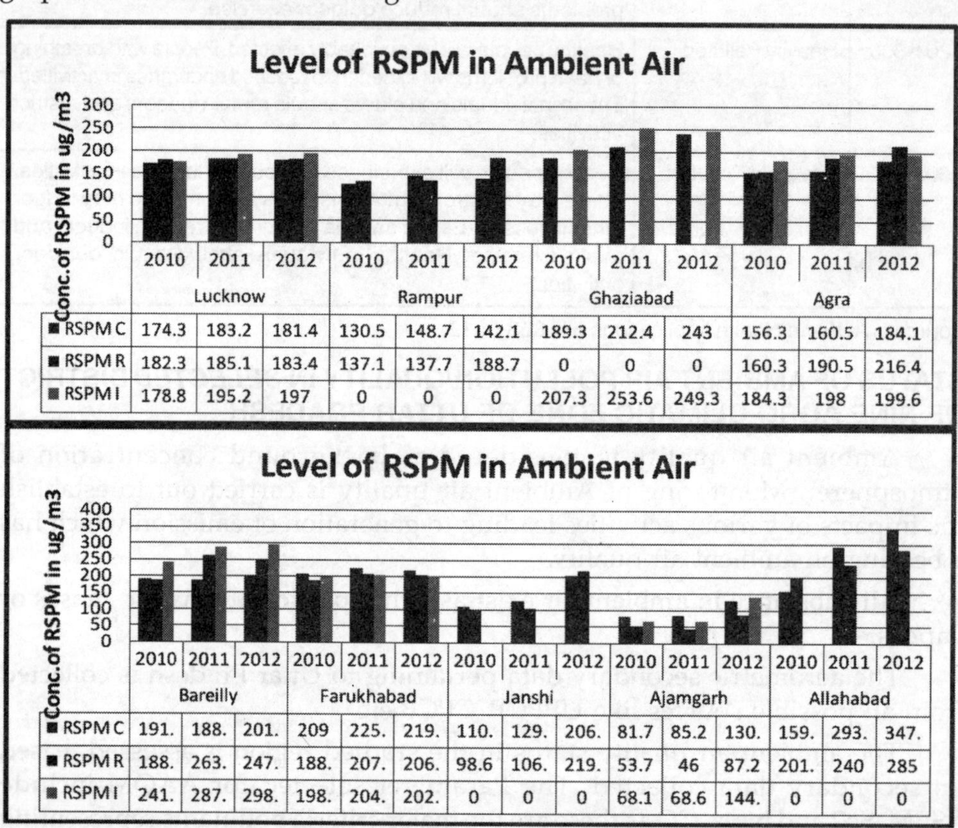

	Lucknow 2010	Lucknow 2011	Lucknow 2012	Rampur 2010	Rampur 2011	Rampur 2012	Ghaziabad 2010	Ghaziabad 2011	Ghaziabad 2012	Agra 2010	Agra 2011	Agra 2012
RSPM C	174.3	183.2	181.4	130.5	148.7	142.1	189.3	212.4	243	156.3	160.5	184.1
RSPM R	182.3	185.1	183.4	137.1	137.7	188.7	0	0	0	160.3	190.5	216.4
RSPM I	178.8	195.2	197	0	0	0	207.3	253.6	249.3	184.3	198	199.6

	Bareilly 2010	Bareilly 2011	Bareilly 2012	Farukhabad 2010	Farukhabad 2011	Farukhabad 2012	Janshi 2010	Janshi 2011	Janshi 2012	Ajamgarh 2010	Ajamgarh 2011	Ajamgarh 2012	Allahabad 2010	Allahabad 2011	Allahabad 2012
RSPM C	191.	188.	201.	209	225.	219.	110.	129.	206.	81.7	85.2	130.	159.	293.	347.
RSPM R	188.	263.	247.	188.	207.	206.	98.6	106.	219.	53.7	46	87.2	201.	240	285
RSPM I	241.	287.	298.	198.	204.	202.	0	0	0	68.1	68.6	144.	0	0	0

Source: State Pollution Control Board Lucknow

Note: Cdenotes to Commercial Area, Rdenotes to Residential Area, Idenotes to Industrial Area

Sulphur Dioxide Level in Selected sample District

The Sulphur Dioxide concentration in the ambient air of the selected District meet below standard limit of NAQS (80 μg/m³) in all represented zone during 2010 to 2012. The highest level of Sulphur Dioxide isobserved in Ghaziabad district but below standard limit. The All data of SO2 level in Selected District are presented in graphical and tabulated form given in next page.

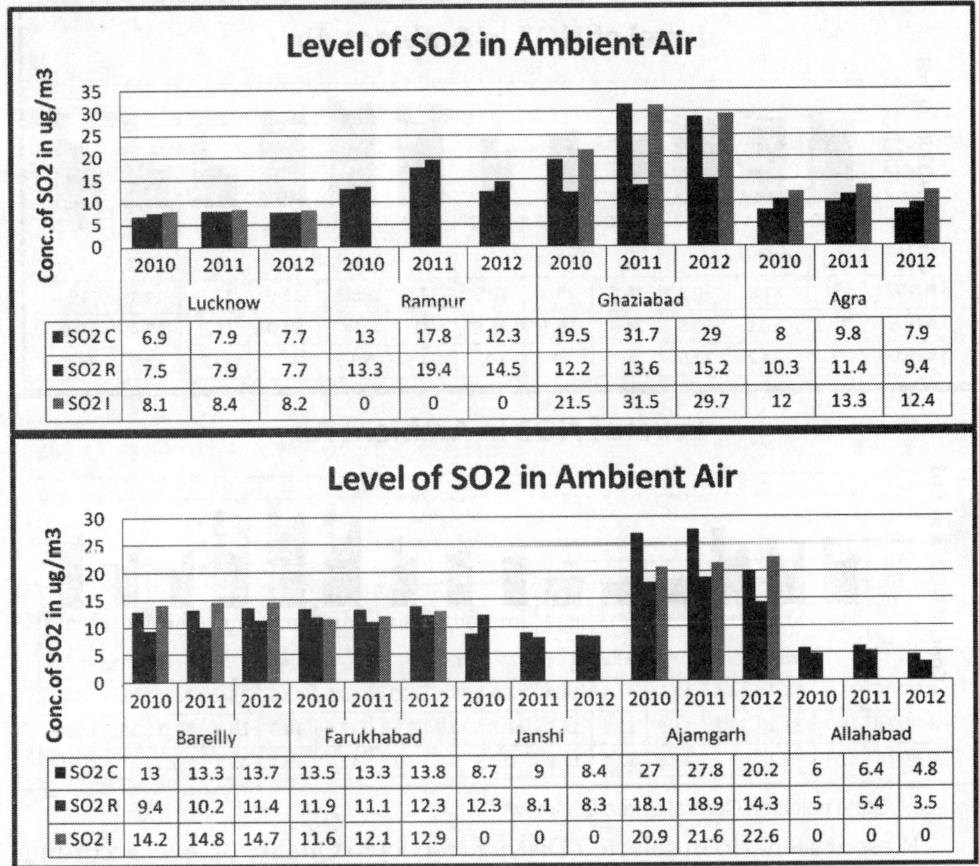

Source: State Pollution Control Board Lucknow

Oxides of Nitrogen Level in Selected sample District

The Oxides of Nitrogen concentration in the ambient air of the selected District meet below standard limit of NAQS (80 µg/m^3) in all represented zone during 2010 to 2012. The highest level of Oxides of Nitrogen isobserved in Ghaziabad District but below standard limit. The All data of SO2 level in Selected District are presented in graphical and tabulated form given in next page.

AREAS OF CRITICAL AIR QUALITY

In views of the analysis of the above data of sampling districts of Uttar Pradesh. It has been observed that value of RSPM is greater than the prescribed (standard) limits. Ghaziabad, Agra, Allahabad, Bareilly can be categories as alarming cities at the views of RSPM consideration.

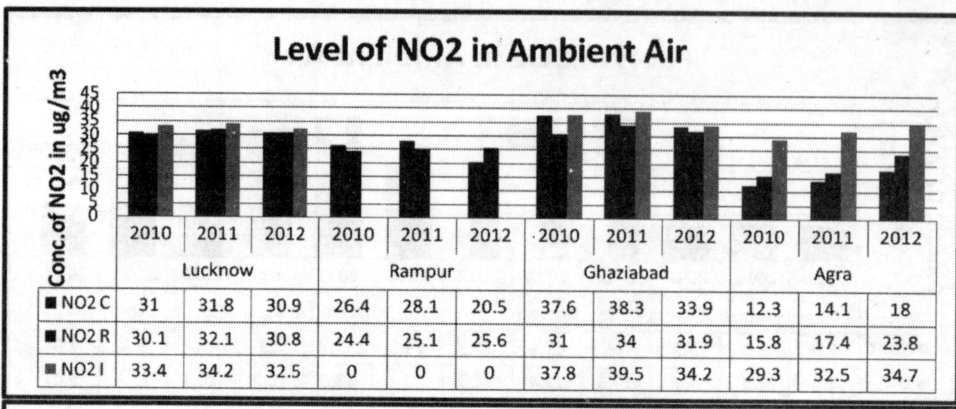

	Lucknow 2010	Lucknow 2011	Lucknow 2012	Rampur 2010	Rampur 2011	Rampur 2012	Ghaziabad 2010	Ghaziabad 2011	Ghaziabad 2012	Agra 2010	Agra 2011	Agra 2012
NO2 C	31	31.8	30.9	26.4	28.1	20.5	37.6	38.3	33.9	12.3	14.1	18
NO2 R	30.1	32.1	30.8	24.4	25.1	25.6	31	34	31.9	15.8	17.4	23.8
NO2 I	33.4	34.2	32.5	0	0	0	37.8	39.5	34.2	29.3	32.5	34.7

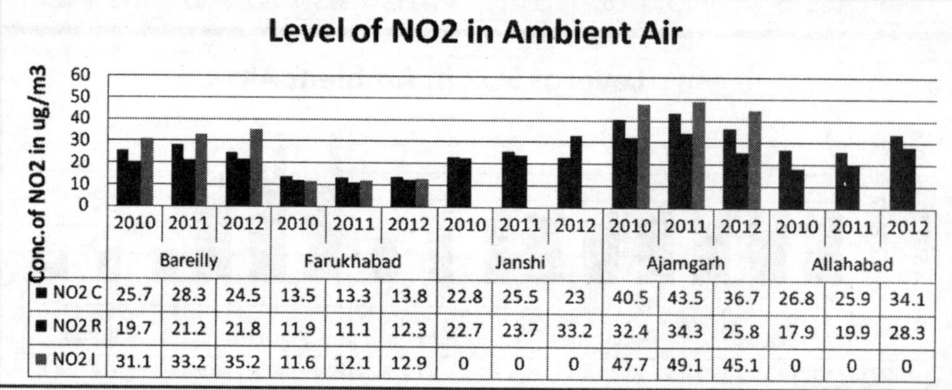

	Bareilly 2010	Bareilly 2011	Bareilly 2012	Farukhabad 2010	Farukhabad 2011	Farukhabad 2012	Janshi 2010	Janshi 2011	Janshi 2012	Ajamgarh 2010	Ajamgarh 2011	Ajamgarh 2012	Allahabad 2010	Allahabad 2011	Allahabad 2012
NO2 C	25.7	28.3	24.5	13.5	13.3	13.8	22.8	25.5	23	40.5	43.5	36.7	26.8	25.9	34.1
NO2 R	19.7	21.2	21.8	11.9	11.1	12.3	22.7	23.7	33.2	32.4	34.3	25.8	17.9	19.9	28.3
NO2 I	31.1	33.2	35.2	11.6	12.1	12.9	0	0	0	47.7	49.1	45.1	0	0	0

Source: State pollution Control Board Lucknow

Present scenario in selected District respect to Quality of level according AQI, all zone of District Ghaziabad are coming under Lightly Polluted category (Level varies 107.4 Residential area. To 120.4 Industrial Area during 2012), Bareilly and Allahabad also be coming under Lightly Polluted category. The reasons may be attributed as follows:

- Industrial operations for the steel,iron,cement,etc;
- Combustion and incineration of non fissile fuels;
- Agriculture, flash from coal;
- Vehicular emission;
- Domestic fuel (Wood, coal) consumption.

IMPACTS ON HUMAN HEALTH

The adverse impact due to high level of RSPM in the consumption with SO_2 and NO_x envisaged as:

- Considerable increase in illness;
- Acute worsening of chronic bronchitis;
- Increased absence of industrial of worker; and
- Children likely to experience increased incidence of respiratory dieses.

Table 7.5: Air Quality Index and Pollution Level of Selected Nine Sample District

Sample District	Year	Range of AQI of Sample District			Air Quality Level		
		2010	2011	2012	2010	2011	2012
Lucknow	Commercial	81.612	85.743	84.623	Good	Good	Good
	Residential	84.521	86.523	85.351	Good	Good	Good
	Industrial	84.734	91.425	91.425	Good	Good	Good
Allhabad	Commercial	74.07692	125.3846	148.5769	Good	Lightly Polluted	Lightly Polluted
	Residential	86.19231	102.0385	121.8462	Good	Lightly Polluted	Lightly Polluted
	Industrial	NA	NA	NA	NA	NA	NA
Agra	Commercial	67.92308	70.92308	80.76923	Good	Good	Good
	Residential	71.69231	84.34615	96	Good	Good	Good
	Industrial	86.76923	93.76923	94.88462	Good	Good	Good
Ghaziabad	Commercial	94.76923	108.6154	117.6538	Good	Lightly Polluted	Lightly Polluted
	Residential	94.6923	95.2307	107.453	Good	Good	Lightly Polluted
	Industrial	102.5385	124.8462	120.4615	Lightly Polluted	Lightly Polluted	Lightly Polluted
Bereilly	Commercial	88.42308	88.5	92.34615	Good	Good	Good
	Residential	83.76923	113.4231	108.1154	Good	Lightly Polluted	Lightly Polluted
	Industrial	110.4231	129.1923	133.8846	Lightly Polluted	Lightly Polluted	Lightly Polluted
Ajamgarh	Commercial	57.38462	60.19231	72.03846	Good	Good	Good
	Residential	40.07692	38.15385	48.96154	Good	Good	Good
	Industrial	52.57692	53.57692	81.5	Good	Good	Good

(Contd…)

Sample District	Year	Range of AQI of Sample District			Air Quality Level		
		2010	2011	2012	2010	2011	2012
Jhansi	Commercial	54.53846	63.15385	91.46154	Good	Good	Good
	Residential	51.38462	53.15385	100.5385	Good	Good	Good
	Industrial	NA	NA	NA	NA	NA	NA
Farrukhabad	Commercial	90.76923	97.11538	95.19231	Good	Good	Good
	Residential	81.57692	88.5	88.84615	Good	Good	Good
	Industrial	85.42308	88.07692	87.73077	Good	Good	Good
Rampur	Commercial	65.34615	74.84615	67.26923	Good	Good	Good
	Residential	67.23077	70.07692	88	Good	Good	Good
	Industrial	NA	NA	NA	NA	NA	NA

This AQI analysis indicates that there is a significant increase in emission causing much alram, imposing more stringent control requirements on source of air pollution than ever before. Hence, it is necessary to characterize air pollution emission sources and the best technology available to control them. Air pollution control strategy provides the guidelines needed to comply with the most recent air pollution standards and regulations for preservation of safe and better environment for the future generation. It aims at maximizing the control of gases and particulate emissions.

REFERENCES

1. Affect of Environmental Pollution; e: Business Record (7/11/2005).
2. Annual Reports of Central Pollution Control Board.
3. Bharti, Pawan Kumar (2012): Environmental Standard and Human Health, Discovery Publishing House Pvt. Ltd., Delhi.
4. CPCB (2009) National Ambient Air Quality Standard, Ministry of Environment and Forest.
5. Chauhan, A and Joshi, P.C. (2007): Analysis of Ambient Air Status of Haridwar City Using Air Quality Index.
6. Environmental Pollution and Impact on Public Health; Report of UNEP.
7. State Pollution Control Board, Uttar Pradesh
8. S.P. Kaushik, Archana Tyagi (2013): Air Pollution and its Impact on Human Health: Environmental Health and Problems; Discovery Publishing House Pvt. Ltd., Delhi, pp. 78-86.
9. WHO Guideline for Air Quality and Health.

Clinicopathological and Biochemical Studies on Tilipia Zilli Exposed to Climate Change and Cadmium Chloride (0.25 p.p.m.)

Mona Saad Zaki[1]; Ahmed Hassan Osman[2]; Olfat Mohamed. Fawzi[3] Suzan Omar Mostafa[3]; Nagwa Said Ata[4] and Medhat Khafagy[5]

1. Department of Aquaculture, Vet. Division, National Research Centre, Giza, Egypt.
2. Department of Pathology, Faculty of Vet. Med, Cairo University, Egypt.
3. Department of Biochemistry, National Research Centre, Giza, Egypt.
4. Department of Microbiology, Vet. Division National Research Centre, Giza, Egypt.
5. National Cancer Institute, Cairo University, Cairo, Egypt.

ABSTRACT

Heavy metals are recognized as cumulative toxic substances causing serious health hazards to man depending on their concentration.Fourty fish (Tilipia Zilli) were collected from Abbassa Sharkia government and fed commercial fish diet. Thirty fish were exposed to cadmium chloride) 0.25p.p.m.) And 30° temp. For 21 days. Ten fish were kept without treatment (control). Haematological analysis of the exposed group demonstrated a marked elevation in serum glutamic oxaloacetic transaminase, serum glutamic pyruvic transaminase, serum glucose, urea, creatinine, sodium, potassium and phosphorus, while serum calcium, haemoglobin and PCV were reduced. Histopathological examination of the fish exposed to cadmium chloride revealed necrobiotic changes of hepatocytes and epithelial lining of renal tubules spleen showed depletion of melanomacrophage centre. Necrosis of the gill filaments was also noticed. It could be concluded that cadmium chloride at 0.25 p.p.m induced deleterious effects in fish such as damage of liver, Kidney, spleen and gills, which were reflected on the biochemical and hematological parameters. Heavy metals induced cumulative effect; therefore equivalent lesions of fish may occur in humans. Moreover, immune suppression could play an important role in predisposing for further infections conditions. [Report and Opinion 2009; 1(2): 80-89]. (ISSN: 1553-9873).

Keywords: Pollution – cadmium, fish, immunity.

INTRODUCTION

Heavy metals are persistent contaminants in the environment that come to the forefront of dangerous substances such as cadmium, lead, mercury, copper and zinc causing serious health hazard in humans and animals [1-10]. The agricultural and industrial wastes partially treated or without treatment are being discharged into surface water [11-16]. Such metals are absorbed from polluted water through gills, skin and digestive tract of fish by bio-concentration and bio-magnification. Chronic cadmium toxicity or "itai-itai" disease was recorded [17-20].

Cadmium toxicity was interfered with calcium/phosphorus ratio [21, 22] Suppression of cell mediated and humoral response of mammals exposed to sublethal dose of cadmium has been reported [23-26].

Histophathological examination of fish exposed to cadmium showed edema of secondary gill lamellae, degeneration of hepatocytes and epitheliallining of renal tubules. Degeneration and necrosis in the gill lamellae of fish xposed to cadmium were noticed [13-19].

Heavy metals are recognized as cumulative toxic substances causing serious health hazards to man depending on their concentration.

MATERIALS AND METHODS

Experimental Design

Total of fourty fish 100-200 gm body weight of each was acclimatized a tized to laboratory conditions for two weeks before use. They were divided into control group (10 fish) and experimental group (30 fish) that was exposed to cadmium chloride at a concentration of 0.25 p.p.m. and 30° temp. for 21 days.

Blood samples were collected from the caudal vein after 7 and 21 days of exposure. Serum for biochemical analysis and heparinized blood for hematological investigations were obtained from each sample.

Biochemical Analysis

Test kits of Bio Merieux (France) were used for evaluation of serum glutamic pyruvic transminase and glutamic oxaloacetic transaminase [20]. Serum glucose was assessed according to Trinder [23]. Serum urea and creatinine were determined using kits of Bio Merieux (France). The concentration of cadmium, sodium, potassium and calcium were detected by using atomic spectrophotometry according to Forstner[13].

Hematological Examination

Blood hemoglobin (Rb) was assessed by Drabkin [12]. Hematocrit value was carried out by using microhaematocrit capillary tubes, centrifuged at 1200 r.p.m. for 5 min.

Bacteriological Examination

Bacterial isolation was done from skin, liver and kidney of fish on blood tryptose agar, MacConcky agar and tryptic soy agar plates. The plates were incubated aerobically and anaerobically. The bacterial isolates were identified morphologically and biochemically, according to Nomiyama [18].

The serum IgM was measured according to Fuda et. al. [15]. Antisera for fish were prepared by immunizing rabbits as previously described by Fuda et.al [15]. The procedure for labeling antibody fragment with enzyme was performed.

Elisa assay procedure: Assay was carried out in 96-well polystyrene ELISA microtiter plates (Titertex, Horsham, P A). The microtiter plates were coated with rabbit antigrey mullet IgM and were fractionated by DE-52 at a concentration of 40 µg/ml in 0.01 MPBS. A volume of 150l was dispensed into each well and incubated for 4 hrs at 4°C.

Blocking was achieved after one washing with 200µl of 0.01 MPBS + 0.1% 20 µl per well and two washings with 200 µl of PBS +1% PBS. 0.01% thiomerosol was added to each well and incubated for 2 hrs. at room temperature.

Incubation of samples and standards after washing was carried out as described above. 100 µl of sample and standard were placed into the appropriate wells in the microtiter plates and incubated at room temperature.

Incubation with peroxidase labeled antibody after washing was done as described above, each well received 150 µl of peroxidase labeled antibody 1:1600 in PBSBSA, followed by incubation for 12 hrs. at room temperature.

Histopathological Examination

Specimens from gills, liver, Kidney and spleen were collected from both control and exposed groups at the end of experiment. The samples were fixed in 10% neutral buffered formalin. Five-micron thick paraffin sections were prepared and stained with H&E for microscopic examination [27]

Statistical analysis: The obtained data were subjected to the student T test.

RESULTS

Serum biochemical analysis: Fish exposed to cadmium chloride (0.25 p.p.m) showed a significant icrease of SGPT and SGOT activity with pronounced elevation of urea and creatinine by 1st, 2nd, 3rd week of exposure. High level of sodium and potassium in serum of exposure fish was noticed (Table 8.1). Hyperglycaemia and hypocalcemia were noticed along the experimental period with-marked elevation of serum cadmium (Table 8.2).

Haematological profile: Reduction of Hb concentration and P.C.V value were observed (Table 8.2).

Table 8.1: Effect of Cadmium Chloride .25p.p.m. on Kidney and Liver Function of Tilipia Zilli

Exposure Time	SGOT U/L	SGPT U/L	Urea mg/dl	Creatinine mg/dl	Sodium Meg	Potassium Meg
1st week (control)	90.0 ± 0.17	20.7 ± 1.7-5	3.29 ± 0.27	0.76 ± 0.72	124 ± 0.57	4.19 ± 0.07
1st week of exposure	91.00 ± 2.40	25.5 ± 0.73	3.90 ± 0.34	0.81 ± 0.01	131 ± 0.76	4.60 ± 0.02
2ndst week (control)	90.00 ± 0.10	22.1 ± 1.48	3.30 ± 0.28	0.75 ± 30	120.3 ± 4.8*	4.33 ± 0.58
2ndst week of exposure	125 ± 0.45*	29 ± 2.1*	3.91 ± 0.13**	0.90 ± 0.19**	138 ± 0.70**	5.9 ± 0.08
3rd week (control)	90 ± 2.2	20.00 ± 0.05	3.20 ± 0.27	0.72 ± 0.27	126 ± 4.2	4.1 ± 0.09
3rd week of exposure	136 ± 2.46*	35 ± 1.56*	4.6 ± 24*	0.99 ± 0.18**	148 ± 7.6	6.25 ± 0.13

* Segnificant $P < 0.05$ ** Highly significant $P < 0.01$

Table 8.2: Some Hematological and Biochemical Changes in Tilipia Zilli Exposed to Cadmium Chloride

Exposure Time	P.C.V %	Hemoglobin gm/dl	Glucose mg%	Cadmium p.p.m	Calcium mg/dl	Phosphonis mg/dl
1st week (control)	21.00 ± 0.06	8.7 ± 0.3	62 ± 1.20	0.05 ± 0.01	5.6 ± 0.32	4.2 ± 0.07
1st week of exposure	17.9 ± 0.05	8.1 ± 0.01	68 ± 0.46	0.08 ± 0.016	4.00 ± 0.87	6.1 ± 0.21
2ndst week (control)	22 ± 0.29	8.1 ± 0.36	60 ± 0.05	0.054 ± 0.068	5.4 ± 0.91	4.1 ± 0.66
2nd week of exposure	17 ± 1.97	7.00 ± 0.98**	70 ± 1.93**	0.12 ± 1.03*	4.2 ± 0.73*	6.4 ± 0.12*
3rd week (control)	20.0 ± 1.32	8.1 ± 0.07	62.2 ± 0.70	0.04 ± 0.01*	4.4 ± 0.73	3.9 ± 0.1
3rd week of exposure	16.9 ± 0.8	6.91 ± 0.23*	84 ± 0.02*	0.16 ± 082*	3.5 ± 0.88*	6.1 ± 0.6*

* Segnificant $P < 0.01$ ** Highly significant $P < 0.05$

Bacteriological examination: Pure culture of *Streptococcus spp., Staphylococcus spp. Agrobacterium spp., Flavobacterium spp. and Lactobacillus spp.* were isolated from the internal and external organs of exposed fish (Table 8.3).

Table 8.3: Bacteriological Recovered in Tilipia Zilli Exposed to Cadmium Chioride (0.25 p.p.m)

Bacterial Strain	External Surface	Internal Organs	Internal Organs Liver	Gills
Agrobacterium spp.	$4.1x10^7$	$3.8x10^6$	$3x10^4$	$5x10^7$
Flavobacterlum spp.	$7x10^7$	$6.2x 10^6$	$6X10^3$	$7.3X10^8$
Staphylococcus spp.	$6x10^5$	$5x10^4$	$6.2x10^3$	$4.2x10^6$
Streeptococcus SPP.	$5x10^7$	$9x10^5$	$7x10^6$	$3x10^7$
Lactobacillus spp.	$3.3x10^3$	$4.4x10^6$	$2x10^3$	$2x10^6$

Determination of fish IgM: There was a significant decrease in total protein and IgM level from the first week of exposure until the end of last week (Table 8.4).

Table 8.4: Influence of Cadmium Chloride 0.25 p.p.m on 1gM and Protein Level

Exposure Period	1gM/old	Total Protein/neg/dl
Control	0.98 ± 0.13	7.84 ± 0.23
1st week of exposure	0.80 ± 0.23**	7.00 ± 0.69*
2st week of exposure	0.74 ± 0.84*	6.42 ± 0.29*
3rd week of exposure	0.68 ± 0.44 *	6.2 ± 0.48*

* Segnificant P< 0.01 ** Highly significant P < 0.05 ± Standard errors

Pathological Findings

Macroscopical lesions of exposed fish revealed congestion in all internal organs after 21 days. Liver appeared friable and dark red. Peticheal haemorrhages around the operculum, and abdominal cavity were observed. Congestion and edema of gill lamellae were seen (Fig. 8.1).

Histopathological examination revealed necrobiotic changes in hepatocytes and disorganisation of hepatic cord (Fig. 8.2). Kidney showed shrinkage of glomerular tufts and degeneration of proximal tubular epithelium (Fig. 8.3). The anterior Kidney showed depletion of melanomacrophage center (Fig. 8.4). Sloughing of epithelial lining of secondary gill lamellae with lymphocytes, oesinophils, polymoph infiltration were observed (Fig. 8.5). Necrosis of both primary and secondary gill lamellae was sometimes seen (Fig. 8.6). Hyperplasia of primary and secondary lamellar epithelium associated with shortening and fusion of gill lamellae with obliteration of interlamellar space were noticed (Fig. 8.7). Rupture of pillar cells and capillaries associated with lamellar telangiectasis were also observed (Fig. 8.8).

Fig. 8.1: Congestion of All Internal Organs of Exposed Fish

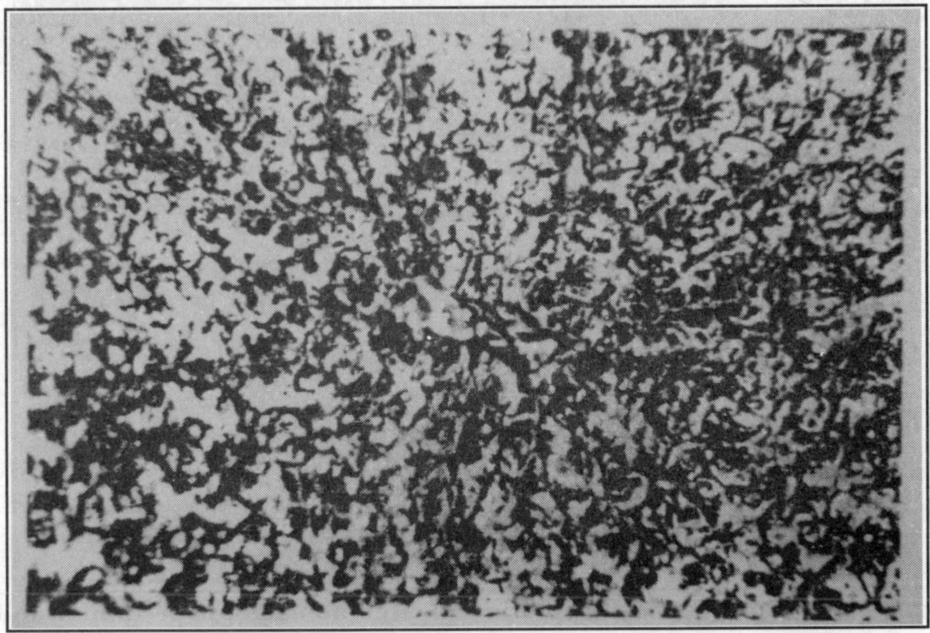

Fig. 8.2: Liver Showing Necrobiotic Changes of Hepatocytes (H & E X 400)

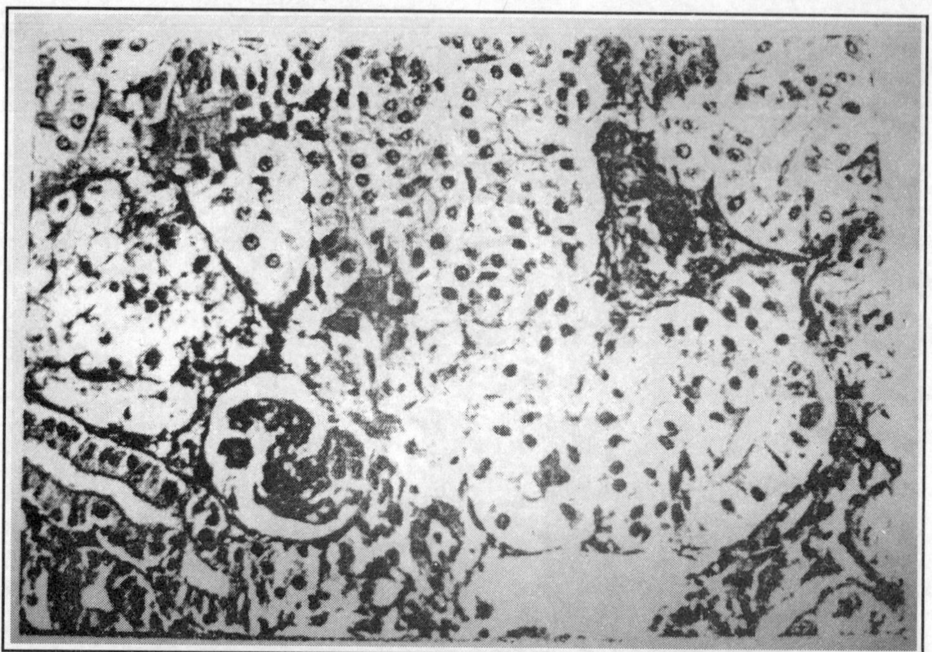

Fig. 8.3: Kidney Showing Shrinkage of Glomerular Tufts and Degeneration of Tubular Epithelium (H & E X 400)

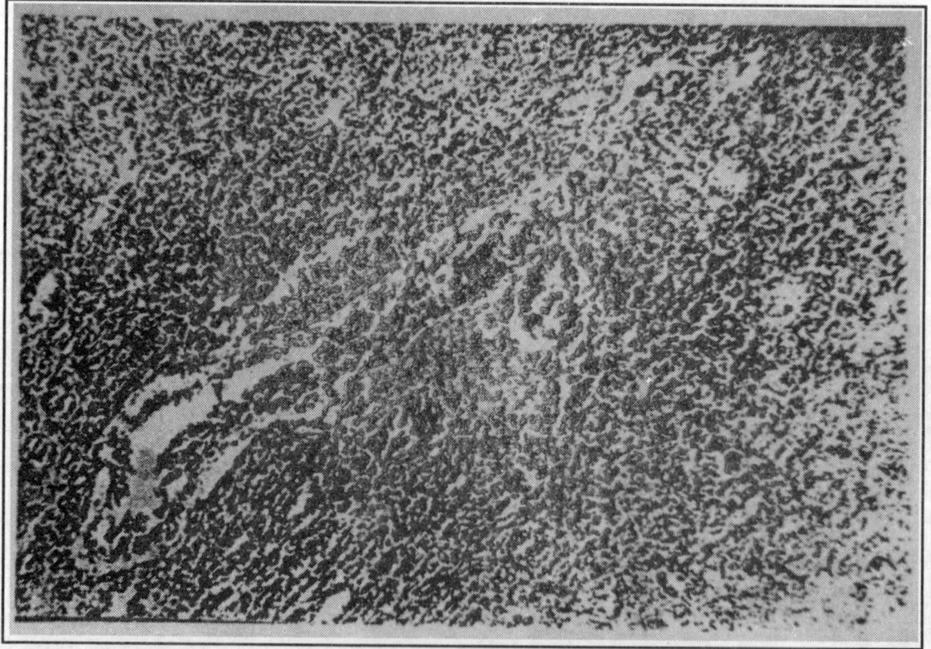

Fig. 8.4: Spleen Showing Depletion of Melanomacrophage Center and Haemopoietic Elements (H & E X 100)

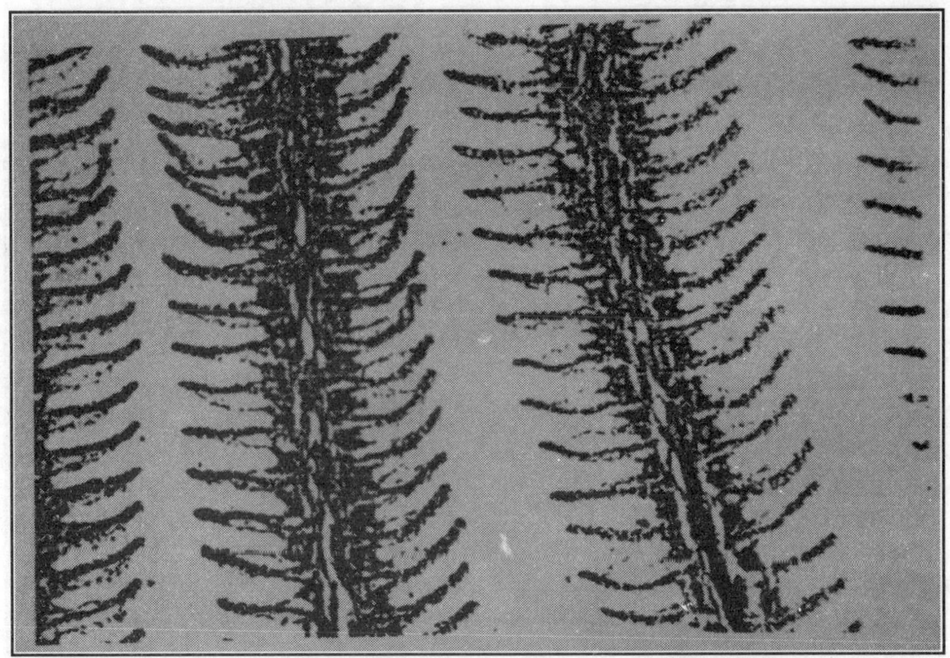

Fig. 8.5: Sloughing of Epithelial Lining of Secondary Gill Lamellae (H & E X 100)

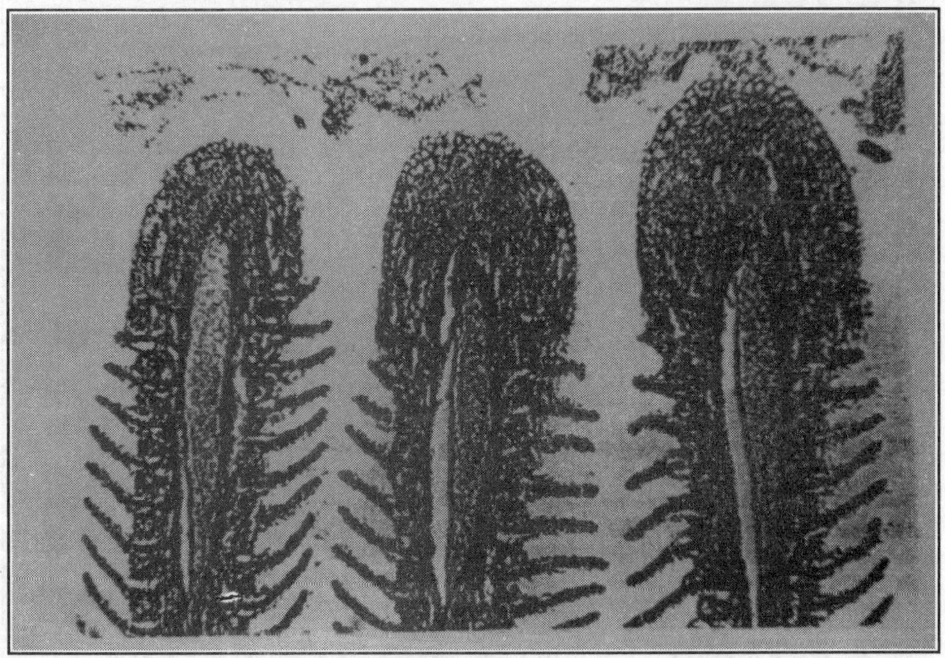

Fig. 8.6: Hyperplasia and Fusion of Secondary Gill Lamellae (H & E X 200)

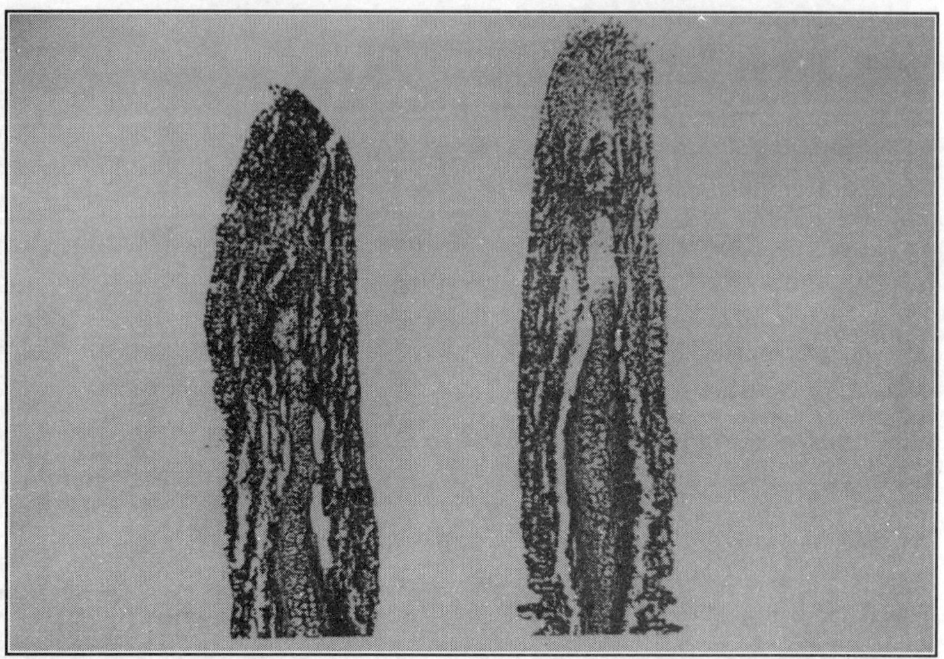

Fig. 8.7: Necrosis of Both Primary and Secondary Gill Lamellae (H & E X 200)

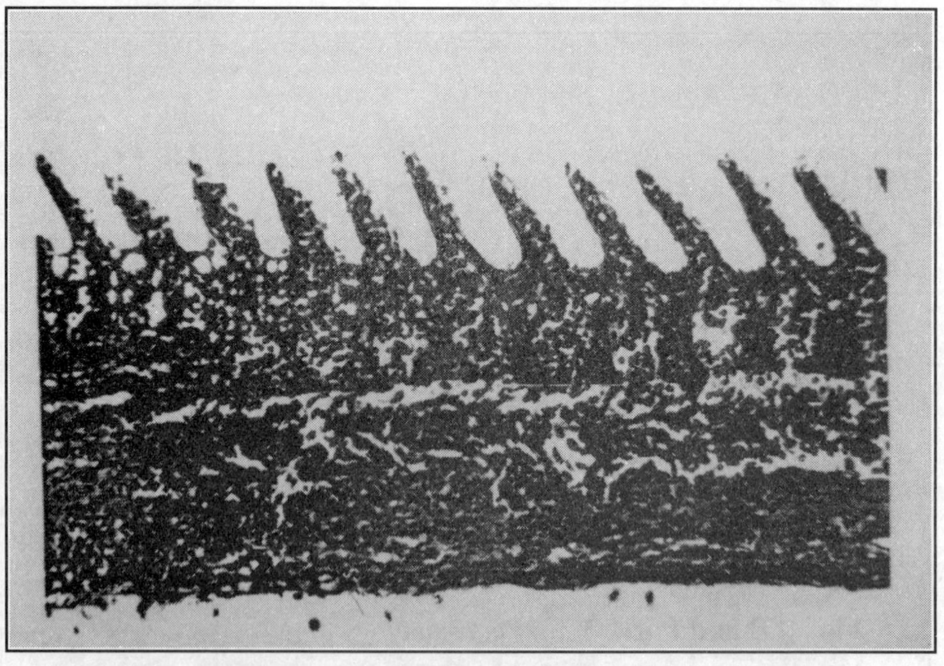

Fig. 8.8: Gill Lamellae Showing Telangiectasis (H & E X 400)

DISCUSSION

Aforementioned data of exposed fish to cadmium chloride (0.25 p.p.m) for 3 weeks revealed an elevation of serum GPT, GOT, urea and creatinine.

These findings are in agreement with previous results. Elevation of urea and creatinine beside liver enzymes in cadmium-exposed fish may be attributed to liver and kidney injury. Reduction of calcium level in serum may have resulted from its increased excertion in urine through inhibition of calcium ATPase enzyme. On the other hand, increase of the phosphorus level in serum of exposed fish was noticed. Cadmium chloride toxicity leads to disturbance in blood electrolytes followed by skeletal changes [23, 25]. Hyperglycemia was observed in the present work which coincides with that obtained in Rainbow traut and salmogaidneri [25]. The blood glucose level was affected by the rate of carbohydrate metabolism under hypoxia and stress conditions. Hyperglycemia is attribute to stress stimuli followed by rapid secretion of both glucocorticoids and α-techolarnines from the adrenal tissue [2]. Regarding to hematological profile exposed fish, hemoglobin and P.C.V. values were decreased. These results are in agreement with previous findings [17, 18]. The erythropenia resulted from reduction of Hb concentration and P.C.V. value in Kwait Mullet due to disturbance of osmoregulatory mechanism accompanied with destruction of gill membrane and failure of gas exchange [19]. Cadmium interfered with sulpha-hydride groups of essentials enzymes [4, 25]. Heavy metals are recognized as cumulative substances leading to serious health hazards to man and animals [6-9].

In the present study, a significant decrease of IgM and total protein during the experimental period were observed. Reduction of IgM level indicated that the cadmium chloride toxicity leads to suppression of immune system of exposed fish which become susceptible to any infective agents [15, 20]. There is a significant decrease in IgM level in fish exposed to cadmium chloride if compared with control which may have resulted from high cortisol secretion that was indicated by hyperglycemia in exposed fish.

Macroscopical examination of fish exposed to cadmium chloride for 21 days revealed a congestion of all internal organs and friable bloody liver. These findings are in agreement with those mentioned by other authors [1-9].

Degeneration and necrosis of hepatocytes may be attributed to the cumulative effect of cadmium and to the increase of its concentration in the hepatic tissue during experimental period. These results agreed with Frolin et al. [14], who stated that liver has an important detoxical role of exogenous waste products as well as externally derived toxins such as heavy metals.

Necrobiotic changes of epithelial lining of renal tubules were observed especially the proximal convoluted tubules that were reflected on electrolytes reabsorption such as calcium, phosphorus, potassium and sodium. These findings come parallel to those previously reported.

It could be concluded that cadmium chloride at 0.25 p.p.m induced deleterious effect in fish such as damage of liver, kidney, spleen and gills, which were reflected on the biochemical and hematological parameters. Heavy metals induced cumulative effect; therefore equivalent lesions of fish may occur in humans. Moreover, immune suppression could play an important role in predisposing for further infections conditions.

Gills showed sloughing of epithelial lining and necrosis of some lamellae. Hyperplasia, shortening and fusion of the secondary gill lamellae that may lead to a great disturbance of gas exchange and ionic regulation were noticed [28]. Lamellar telangictasis resulted from rupture of pillar cells and capillaries under effect of chronic irritation of cadmium chloride and leads to an accumulation of erythrocytes in the distal portion of the secondary lamellae [29]. The subepithelial space of the secondary gill lamellae was infiltrated with inflammatory cells. This finding is in agreement with that previously mentioned [29, 30]. Mucinous metaplasia of lamellar epithelial lining is considered as adaptive mechanism against heavy metal toxicity. These alterations are in agreement with those previously mentioned [31].

It could be concluded that cadmium chloride at 0.25 p.p.m induced deleterious effects in fish such as damage of liver, Kidney, spleen and gills, which were reflected on the biochemical and hematological parameters. Heavy metals induced cumulative effect; therefore equivalent lesions of fish may occurr in humans. Moreover, immune suppression could play an important role in predisposing for further infections conditions.

REFERENCES

1. Abbas, H.H., K.H. Zaghloul, and M.A. Mousa, 2002. Effect of Some Heavy Metal Pollutants on Some Biochemical and Histopathological Changes in Blue Tilapia, *Oreochromis aureus*. Egypt. J. Agric. Res., 80(3): 1395-1411.
2. Abbas, W.T. 2006. Fish as an Indicator for Pollutants in Aquatic Environment. Ph.D. Thesis, Zoology Department, Faculty of Science, Cairo University, Egypt, 144 pp.
3. Abdel-Baky, T.E. 2001. Heavy Metals Concentrations in the Catfish, *Clarias gariepinus* (Burchell, 1822) from River Nile, El-Salam Canal and Lake Manzala and Their Impacts on Cortisol and Thyroid Hormones. Egypt. J. Aquat. Biol. & Fish., 5(1): 79-98.
4. Abernthy A.R. and P.M., Cutnbie 1999. Bull Environ. Contoam. Toxicol. 17: 595 (1999).
5. Abou El-Gheit, E.N., M.S., Zaki, A.A., Abo El-Ezz, H.A. El-Cherei, 2001. Vertebral Column Curvature Syndrome in Common Carp *Cyprinus Carpio* L. Fish. J. Egypt. Vet. Med. Ass., 61(5): 57-69.
6. Abou El-Naga, E.H.; K. M. El-Moselhy, and M. A. Hamed, 2005. Toxicity of Cadmium and Copper and Their Effect on Some Biochemical Parameters of Marine Fish *Mugil Seheli*. Egypt. J. Aquat, Res., 31(2): 60-71.
7. Ahmed, Y.F.; M.M., Mohamed, I.Z., El-Nemer, K.I. El-Desoky, and S.S. Ibrahim, 1998. Some Pathological Studies on the Effect of Cadmium and Mercuric Chlorides on the Gonads of Catfish (*Clarias lazera*). Egypt. J. Comp. Pathol. Clin. Pathol., 11: 72-81.

8. Authman, M.M.N. 2008. *Oreochromis niloticus* as a Biomonitor of Heavy Metal Pollution with Emphasis on Potential Risk and Relation to some Biological Aspects. Global Veterenaria, 2(3): 104 -109.
9. Authman, M.M.N., E.M. Bayoumy, and A.M. Kenawy, 2008. Heavy Metal Concentrations and Liver Histopathology of *Oreochromis niloticus* in Relation to Aquatic Pollution. Global Veterenaria, 2(3): 110-116.
10. Bahnasawy, M.H. 2001. Levels of Heavy Metals in Catfish, *Clarias gariepinus* from Different Habitats and Their Effects on Some Biochemical Parameters. Egypt. J. Aquat. Biol. & Fish., 5(1): 99-125.
11. Burger, J., M. Gochfeld, C., Jeitner, S.Burke, and T. Stamm, 2007. Metal Levels in Flathead Sole (*Hippoglossoides elassodon*) and Great Sculpin (*Myoxocephalus polyacanthocephalus*) from Adak Island, Alaska: Potential Risk to Predators and Fishermen. Environmental Research, 103: 62-69.
12. Drabkin, D., 1964. Bio Chem., 164, 703.
13. Forstner N. and G.T.W., Wittmann 2007. Metal Pollution in the Aquatic Environment. Springer-Verlag, Belin.
14. Frolin, L, C. Haux, L., Karkson-Norgren, P. Runn, and A. Larsson 1986. Aquatic Toxicol. 8:51.
15. Fuda, H., K., Sayano, F. Yamaji, and Haraj, 1991. Comp Brioche, Physiol, 99 A 637-643.
16. Gad, S.C. and C.S., Weil, 1986. Statistics for Toxicologists. In Hayes. A. W. 2nd.
17. Matsubara, A., S. Mihara, and R., Kusuda, 1985. Bull Japan Sac, Sic. Fish. 51m 921.
18. Nomiyama, K., 1988. "Bacteriological Test Book ". Vol. 2 pp. 15-23. Pergamon.
19. O'Neill, J.G., 1981. Bull. Env. Contam. Toxico!., 27: 42-48.
20. Reitman, S.,and S. A., Frankel, 1957. Am. J. Clin. Pathol. 28, 56.
21. Stephen, W.I. 2004. Zinc, Cadmium, Mercury and Lead. Stephen, W.I. Ed.; Blackwell Scientific Publications.
22. Stostiof, M.K. 1993. "Fish Medicine" W.B. Saunders Company, Philadelphia, Lonion, Toronto, Montreal, Sydney, Tokyo (1993).
23. Trinder, P., 1960. Ann. CUn Brioche. 6, 24.
24. Vinodhini, R., and M. Narayanan, 2008. Bioaccumulation of Heavy Metals in Organs of Fresh Water Fish *Cyprinus carpio* (Common Carp). Int. J. Environ. Sci. Tech., 5 (2):179-182.
25. Vosyliene, M.Z. and A. Jankaite, 2006. Effect of Heavy Metal Model Mixture on Rainbow Trout Biological Parameters. Ekologija., 4: 12-17.
26. Zaki, M.S., and A.H. Osman, 2003. Clinicopathological and Pathological Studies on Tilapia Nilotica Exposed to Cadmium Chloride (0.25 ppm) Bull. NRC, Egypt., 28 (1): 87-100.
27. Carleton H., "Carleton's; Histopathological Technique" 4th Ed. London, Oxford University, Press, New York, Toronto. (1979).
28. Balah, A.M., El-Bouhy, Z.M. and Easa, M.E.I.S., Histopathlogical Studies in the Gills of Tilipia Nilotica "Oreochromis Niloticus" Under the Effect of Some Heavy Metals. Zagazig Vet. J., Vol. 21, No. 3 pp. 351-364. (1993).
29. Randi, A.S., Monserrat J. M., Rodrigue E.M. and Romano L.A., J. of Fish Diseases 19, 311 (1996).
30. Pascoe, D., Evans, S.A. and Woodworth, J., Arch. Env. Contam. Toxicol., 15:481. (1986).
31. Stostiof, M.K. "Fish Medicine". W.B Saunders Company, Philadelphia, London, Toronto, Montreal, Sydney, Tokyo (1993).

[illegible] 1990. [illegible] as a Cause [illegible] of Heavy Metal Pollution with Emphasis on Tolerance [illegible] Biological Approaches [illegible] [illegible] 22(3): 1049-60.

9. Authman [illegible], [illegible] and A. M. Kenawy. 2008. Heavy Metal Concentrations and Liver Histopathology of Oreochromis niloticus in Relation to Aquatic Pollution. Global Veterinaria 2(3): 110-116.

10. Bannaswamy [illegible] 2001. Levels of Heavy Metals in Catfish [illegible] Different Habitats and Their Effects on Some Biochemical Parameters. [illegible] Aquat. Biol. & Fish. 5(1): 95-125.

11. Burger, J., M. Gochfeld, C. Jeitner, S. Burke and T. Stamm. 2007. Metal Levels in Flathead Sole (Hippoglossoides elassodon) and Great Sculpin (Myoxocephalus polyacanthocephalus) from Adak Island, Alaska: Potential Risk to Receptors and Fishermen. Environmental Research 103: 62-69.

12. Dyer [illegible] Dev. [illegible] Chem. [illegible]

13. [illegible] N. and [illegible] 2007. Metal Pollution in the Aquatic Environment, Springer Verlag, Berlin.

14. [illegible] 1994 [illegible] Karlsson-Norrgren [illegible] and [illegible] Larsson. [illegible] Aquatic Toxicol. [illegible]

15. [illegible] 1994. Comp. Biochem. Physiol. 30 A: [illegible]

16. [illegible] and [illegible] 1986. [illegible] Toxicologists [illegible]

17. [illegible] 1985. [illegible]

18. [illegible] S. 1985. [illegible] Vol. 2 pp. [illegible] Research.

19. [illegible] 1981. Bull. Env. Contam. Toxicol. 27: 42-48.

20. [illegible] 1977. [illegible] 23: 95.

21. [illegible] 2011. Zar's Graphing, Measuring and [illegible] Blackwell Scientific Publications.

22. [illegible] 1984. [illegible] Saunders Company, Philadelphia, London, Toronto, Montreal, Sydney, Tokyo, 1984.

23. [illegible] 1999. Ann. Clin. Biochem. [illegible]

24. [illegible] 2008. Bioaccumulation of Heavy Metals in Organs of Fresh Water Fish Cyprinus carpio (Common Carp). Environ. Sci. Tech. [illegible]

25. [illegible] M. and [illegible] 2006. Effect of Heavy Metal [illegible] Mixture on Biochemical Parameters. [illegible]

26. [illegible] and A. [illegible] 2009. Clinicopathological and Pathological Studies in [illegible] Exposed to Cadmium Chloride (0.25 ppm). [illegible] 4(0): 87-106.

27. Carleton [illegible] Carleton's Histopathological Technique. 4th Ed. London, Oxford University Press, New York, Toronto (1976).

28. [illegible] Histopathological Studies in the Gills of Tilapia nilotica (Oreochromis niloticus) Under the Effect of Some Heavy Metals [illegible] Vol. 21, No. 1, pp. [illegible] (1993).

29. [illegible] Notes [illegible] Diseases 19: 41 (1996).

30. [illegible] and Woodworth, J. Arch. Env. Contam. Toxicol. 17: 157 (1988).

31. [illegible] W.B. Saunders Company, Philadelphia, London, Toronto, Montreal, Sydney, Tokyo (1984).

Index